Frame
of MIND

LITTLE CREEK PRESS®
AND BOOK DESIGN
Mineral Point, Wisconsin

Little Creek Press®
A Division of Kristin Mitchell Design, Inc.
5341 Sunny Ridge Road
Mineral Point, Wisconsin 53565

Book Design and Project Coordination:
Little Creek Press®

First Edition
May 2020

Printed in the United States of America

For more information or to order books:
visit stevendekanich.com • www.littlecreekpress.com
or email: hello@stevendekanich.com

Library of Congress Control Number: 2020904748

ISBN-13: 978-1-942586-78-4

Some names and identifying details have been
changed to protect the privacy of individuals.

Cover image: Lightstock, ©Kevin Carden

Dedication

For all people who are faced with illness or an
insurmountable problem—there is hope!

For Brett,

Best wishes to a new friend !

Steve

Reviews for *Frame of Mind*

The correct "frame of mind" is key to thriving (not just surviving) in life. Joey is a wonderful example of what the human spirit can do when a person focuses not solely on their circumstances but on what they can achieve despite what life may throw at them. Resilience, perseverance, and true faith are the key to growth and thriving in life and Joey teaches us that in every chapter and turn of his life. He ran and continues to run the race worthy of his calling.

The thriving human spirit doesn't say "Why me?" It says, "Why not me, what does God want me to learn from this and how can I use my circumstances as a testimony to His goodness?" Job well done Joey!

—Daniel M. Ibach, MD

Frame of Mind is not only a story of courage, but it demonstrates the power of the human mind to overcome seemingly impossible obstacles and reach for one's dreams. Dekanich relays his amazing life experiences, good and bad, into a captivating tale that will make you realize your own dreams are obtainable, and the roadblocks of life are passable with the right attitude and support.

—Ellen Boatner, Communications Specialist

Mom and I shared the experience. For many years she encouraged dad to share his story in hopes that it would inspire those who face similar battles. Finally in fulfilling his promise to her, this story of persistence and true faith will hopefully resonate with others and aid their journey.

—Annette M. Dekanich, RN, BSN, OCN, MBA

STEVEN J. DEKANICH

In his semi-autobiographical novel, *Frame of Mind*, Steven Dekanich has created a character, Joey Slunisky, who contends with many of the issues Dekanich has dealt with during his life: multiple life-threatening cancers beginning as a teenager, operation and rehabilitation again and again through the years and dreams that seem impossible given the impediments life throws up. Like Dekanich, Joey learns valuable lessons about the part his attitude plays in surmounting the obstacles and achieving his goals. Along the way, Joey is helped by the positive influence of his doctors, his college professors, his family and friends, and finally the woman with whom he falls in love. Joey's story speaks hope and courage to readers facing their own challenges.

—Connie Jordan Green, Author and Workshop Leader

Author Steven J. Dekanich has written a book filled with heart, warmth, humor and memorable characters. This is the story of Joey Slunisky, a young man who is diagnosed with cancer just as he is about to start college. Joey goes through the ordeal of surgery and recovery, seemingly overcoming this setback in his life, only to be diagnosed with cancer time and time again. Joey reacts to these continuous disruptions in his life as we all would—with shock, anger, disbelief and, in some cases, despair. However, thanks to the intervention of kindly Dr. Saabs, Joey is able to overcome both the physical and mental anguish that these continuous diagnoses bring into his life. This is a book about hope in the face of adversity, the life-affirming energy that comes from pursuing one's dream, and a reminder that our ultimate success comes from the love of family and friends—but most importantly from our own positive frame of mind.

—Diane Franklin, Principal, Franklin McMullen Communications

Table of Contents

STEVEN J. DEKANICH

Acknowledgments

First, the ideas for this book were inspired by personal experience, reading a vast number of positive mental attitude books and listening to inspirational speakers.

Second, were the ideas, support and encouragement from my family:

MY LATE WIFE LINDA: Your love was unconditional. You always saw me as I could be and not as I was and believed in me when I didn't believe in myself. Even when cancer was stealing your life your first thoughts were always for Annette and me. I miss and love you. May God bless your soul in a very special way.

MY DAUGHTER ANNETTE: You are not just a daughter; you're a best friend. From the first time I held you to now, my love for you grows deeper each day. I love you so much! You are a very impressive young lady and I'm proud to be called your dad.

FOR MY WIFE ALOYSIA (ALI): When my life was rushing towards a very black abyss, you saved me and gave me a reason to go on. You were the catalyst that inspired me to finish the book. The hours you spent editing and reducing the word count, the ideas you had for the title and the cover made *Frame of Mind* come alive. Without your support *Frame of Mind* would still only be a file on my computer. You're living proof that angels breathe and I thank you for making my dream come true. We're two apple halves who found each other and I'm so grateful that God brought you into my life. I love you.

FOR MY MOTHER MARGARET: You were an incredibly strong woman and raised Carolyn and me by yourself. You showed me the importance of accountability, hard work and compassion. I'm thankful you were my mother and I miss and love you.

FOR MY SISTER CAROLYN: You helped raise me, which was no easy task. You are the most giving person I've ever met and you love unconditionally. Thank you for keeping mom's Christmas meal tradition alive and thank you for everything that you did and are doing for me, I love you.

FOR MY BROTHER-IN-LAW BOB: You were a father figure and big brother all rolled up into one package for me. You introduced me to my first microscope, helped me with chemistry and helped guide me through this crazy life. I still enjoy our conversations and I'm grateful for you.

FOR MY BEST FRIEND GEORGE: Just before I saw you in freshman chemistry, I was contemplating quitting school. During the early years in college, you helped get me through some rough times and now, more than 50-years later, we're still friends! I'm thankful for you.

Introduction

Everyone has problems. When we are blindsided by a life-altering event, it seems as though an uncaring dagger has pierced through the picture of our world and the canvas upon which it is painted is slashed open to flap helplessly in the wind. Our first reaction is to cower and hope the problem will go away. However, the longer we wait, the more the canvas rips until it seems impossible to mend. What do we do?

How we repair the gash and handle our problems—whether it's illness, death, financial setbacks, social conflicts, work, school, you name it—determines the future of our very existence. It comes down to whether our problems control us or we control them. Our frame of mind, positive or negative, will determine how we paint the picture between the borders of that frame and determine if we live the full lives that God intended or go to the grave with our dreams still in us.

Life experiences have shredded the canvas of my frame of mind many times. These experiences have included nineteen recurrences of cancer, the loss of my first wife from cancer, a company closing down around me shortly after I left a promising engineering career with another company, open heart surgery, an abscess that covered the left lobe of my liver, a diverticular bleed that resulted in losing eighteen inches of my colon, a bowel obstruction, a total knee replacement, torn retinas, a heart pacemaker implant and, just recently, a diagnosis of multiple myeloma. My list of challenges goes on and on. I've walked the walk and, with God's help, repainted my canvas using paints that I've had in my own possession or borrowed from someone who was stronger than me at a particular moment in time. Because of my life's experiences, I can empathize with many of the things that you may be going through. It is my hope that this book will provide entertainment and inspiration to help you get through your problem and paint a positive picture between the borders of your frame of mind.

You are the reason this book was written. Relax, sit back, and enjoy *Frame of Mind!* ✦

Chapter 1

Why?

Acrid odors of antiseptic, alcohol, and liniment crept under the door and filled the room with the smell of pain, sickness, and death. Pacing back and forth, Joey felt the walls wrapping around him tighter than a straightjacket. Sighing deeply, he looked around the room but couldn't focus on anything. He gently touched the soft bandages that covered the biopsy areas on his neck and shoulder, wondering about his diagnosis. Unconsciously feeling the muscles in his right arm as he flexed it, Joey walked past the vacant second bed and leaned against the wide windowsill.

His mind mercifully took him to a football game in the fall of 1968. The thwack of massive shoulder pads striking the defensive linemen echoed in his helmet. Suddenly a behemoth running back crashed through the line and headed straight at him. Adrenaline rushing through his body, Joey's eyes widened as he relived the play. A thudding knock brought him back to reality. Here he was, just a year later, at the general hospital in Sharon, Pennsylvania. As the heavy door opened, Joey turned to face it. The expression on Dr. Sabbs' face said everything.

STEVEN J. DEKANICH

Sabbs' smile was a lie. He hated this moment and all moments like it. Looking at Joey, he saw a vibrant young man with his whole life ahead of him. How could he tell an eighteen-year-old that, in a few days, life as he knows it will never be the same? It seemed like an eternity to Joey before Dr. Sabbs spoke. "Joey, let's sit down over here."

"Sir, I think I'd rather stand if you don't mind."

Sabbs crimped his lips and nodded. "Okay, Joey …. The results have come back positive. You have cancer."

Joey's lips tightened as he looked at Sabbs. Taking a deep breath and slowly letting it out, he asked, "What can I expect?"

Sabbs was somewhat relieved. He had not anticipated such a calm reaction. He locked eyes with Joey and answered, "What you have is adenocarcinoma. There is a malignant tumor in your thyroid and parathyroid area, and it has spread into your left shoulder muscle."

"What … what does that mean?"

"It means you need surgery."

Eyes widening, Joey asked, "What is this going to do to me physically?"

"Until we operate, I won't know for certain to what extent the cancer has spread. I'm not going to sugarcoat anything. A good part of your recovery is going to depend on you and the attitude you have after the operation."

Sabbs walked over to Joey, reached out, and squeezed his shoulder. Looking him in the eyes, Sabbs said, "Joey, the worst-case scenario could leave you without a voice or the use of your left arm."

Joey's knees started to buckle. "Oh, my God, no! My family doctor told me I had swollen glands!"

Sabbs grabbed Joey to keep him from collapsing. He eased Joey down to an overstuffed chair. His forehead furrowed, he chose his words carefully. "Joey, we're doing what we need to do. I can assure you that we're going to use all of the knowledge the medical profession has to offer to help you beat this thing. We're also going to need your help and cooperation. Joey, you can't control some things that happen to you. However, you can control how you respond. In your case, you can do one of two things. You can feel sorry for yourself, or you can accept that you have cancer and decide that you'll do whatever it takes to beat it."

The whites of his eyes streaked with red, Joey slowly rose from the chair. With his head down and his brain not thinking, he walked to the window. Small particles of dust danced tauntingly before him in a sunbeam, and memories flooded his mind. The glory times in football—reckless abandon and total disregard for life or limb helped him to overcome his size and excel as a defensive back. The rope climbs in gym class—no one could catch him going up or coming down. He moved his hand through the dust particles, scattering them like forgotten dreams. His thoughts turned somber. *This is all behind me now. I wonder what the future holds for me? Will I be disfigured and look like a freak? Will I have the coordination that I once had? My God, what's going to happen to me?*

Tears rolled down his cheeks as he stepped into the sunbeam and looked out the window. Children were playing and laughing on the sidewalk below. They looked so healthy and happy, without a care in the world.

Joey thought back to a childhood that was wrought with sickness and injury. At the age of seven, he had a bleeding stomach ulcer. Scarlet fever ravaged his body with a 104.5-degree fever when he was eleven. The fever resulted in a cracked eardrum and a temporary hearing impairment. At age twelve, he sustained several cracked ribs and a dislocated hip in an automobile accident. At fourteen, a benign tumor blocked his sinus passages and had to be removed.

These afflictions caused so much pain and suffering that many times he prayed his next breath would be his last. Each time, God had not granted his wish, and he overcame the illness or injury. These thoughts actually lifted his spirits. Since it happened so many times before, why shouldn't he recover again?

The warmth of the sunbeam penetrated to his marrow and calmed him. He turned away from the window. "Dr. Sabbs, you told me the worst possible things that could happen to me after the operation. You also said that how much I recover depends on me. How can that be?"

The lines on his forehead softening, Sabbs walked over to Joey. "You've played a lot of sports, right?"

Puzzled, Joey nodded.

"If you were playing a team evenly matched with your team, what do you think was the determining factor for winning? It was attitude and your frame of mind. Look at the Olympic competitors. They're the ultimate in athletic achievement. However, even if they've trained for ten years to get to the Olympics but lose their concentration or will to win for just a split second, they lose. The same thing is going to hold true for you."

"Yeah, right! Look, I can understand if you're evenly matched with an opponent, but am I evenly matched with what's growing inside my body? Look at my neck! It's twice the size it should be! How can I keep my attitude when I've seen cancer kill so many other people? Some of my greatest sports heroes got cancer and … they didn't make it. Why should it be any different with me?"

The deep furrows returned to Sabbs' forehead. He took off his glasses and stared at the floor for several seconds. Without moving his head, he shifted his gaze to Joey's eyes. "I don't know if it will be any different with you," he said in a soft voice. "Only God knows that. But I do know this. If your destiny calls for it to be different and you survive and live a long life, what you do starting from this point will determine the quality of life you'll live."

Sabbs' words kept Joey from trying to verbally fence with him. He just stood there nodding his head.

Putting his glasses on, Sabbs said, "Joey, I've been in this business a long time, and I've seen a lot of things. In a couple of days, you will be going through some rough times, and they may seem bigger than you. I want you to remember that you're not in this alone. You're in an excellent medical facility. Here again, you must keep your mind on your goal, which is to recover and rebound. It's not going to be easy, but it can be done." Making sure he maintained eye contact with Joey, Sabbs continued, "Joey, I can help you, but I'll need your cooperation. Will you work with me?"

"I guess I don't have much choice."

Sabbs didn't say anything.

Clenching his fists, Joey walked away from Sabbs. He wanted to punch the wall, but it was brick. *Damn! Why is this happening to me?* Bowing his head, Joey squeezed his fists until his knuckles turned oyster white. His whole body tensed, and his short bursts of breath could be heard throughout the room. The nape of his neck resting on his shoulders, Joey tightly closed his eyes, put the palms of his fists against his temples, and pushed.

With his fists still against his temples, Joey began to bring his head upright when his left wrist came in contact with his neck bandages. Relaxing his clenched fists, Joey put his right hand on the bandages. They were soft and actually felt comfortable, but underneath the cotton facade was a monster. If this monster was not stopped, it would consume and destroy him.

Burying his face into cupped hands, Joey cradled his head. He slowly raised his head and let his hands drag and distort his facial skin until they came to his neck. His hands rested on the bandages for a few seconds. Turning to Dr. Sabbs, he said, "Yes, I'll work with you."

"Good. Let's sit down, and we'll talk about what needs to be done to help you."

The sun was setting when Dr. Sabbs left the room. Joey walked to the window and was awestruck by the kaleidoscope of colors against a crystalline sky. Each cloud formation greedily captured the sun's rays and burst into vibrant reds, hot pinks, and deep blues. All too soon, the brilliantly colored monarchs of the sky gave up their moment of glory and reluctantly transformed into slate gray ghosts.

"Humph," muttered Joey, "It happens to clouds too."

Joey stood in silence for a long time. Sighing deeply, he turned and walked away from the window. He plopped into the overstuffed chair, raised his feet directly from the floor even with the seat of the chair, locked his knees and pointed his toes. He tightly gripped the chair arms and effortlessly pressed himself out of the chair and held a perfect "L" seat for thirty seconds. He wondered if he'd be able to do this after the operation?

Joey lowered himself into the chair and sat thinking about what Dr. Sabbs said. All in all, after the talk, he felt better. Although it didn't change his situation, at least now he knew what he was up against. It was a tangible thing to be dealt with and handled.

Lost in thought, Joey didn't hear the door slowly open.

"Joey," said a shaky voice.

Joey looked up and saw the tear-streaked face of his older sister. Her quivering lips allowed the faint impression of a smile. Not only was the cancer ravaging Joey's body, but it was also taking its toll on his loved ones. Joey stood up and walked to his sister. "I guess Mom told you."

Squeezing her eyelids shut and then slowly opening them, Cheryl Lynn nodded. Swallowing hard, she sniffed and asked, "How are you feeling?"

Looking at his sister from the corner of his eyes, Joey grinned. "Ya know, this is a real pain in the neck."

Just then, Mrs. Slunisky walked into the room followed by a nurse carrying Joey's supper.

"Great!" said Joey. "I'm starving! Oh, hi, Mom."

As he sat down to eat, his mother asked, "What did the doctor say?"

Eyeing his meal, Joey began to salivate as he answered, "He said he talked with you and discussed the operation."

As she watched her son inhale the food, Mrs. Slunisky thought, "How can he eat at a time like this?" She waited for him to swallow before asking, "Did he say anything else?"

Joey put his fork down and said, "He told me the operation is scheduled for 7:00 a.m. Thursday."

"The day after tomorrow?" asked Cheryl Lynn.

"Afraid so," said Joey. Easing the food tray table out of the way, he stood up from the bed and said with a quivering voice, "Mom, Dr. Sabbs told me that the operation should last about eight to ten hours. The incision will extend from the back of my left ear down my neck and across my shoulders. He doesn't know at this time how much will be removed. He also told me the worst case could leave me without a voice or the use of my left arm."

Trying to swallow a lump that wouldn't go down, Cheryl Lynn thought, "Dear God, what did Joey do to deserve this?"

Seeing the tears streaming down Cheryl Lynn's face, Joey walked over to her and put his hand on her shoulder. She embraced him

STEVEN J. DEKANICH

with a force that almost knocked the wind out of him. "I know I shouldn't be doing this in front of you," she said, "but I ... can't help it."

Tears welled in Joey's eyes as he tried to comfort his sobbing sister. Her eyes also stained in red, Mrs. Slunisky looked at her son and daughter and dreaded the days to come.

After several minutes, Joey moved Cheryl Lynn to arms' length and said, "Do you know you're getting snot all over my shoulder?"

Wiping her nose and chuckling, she focused her eyes on Joey's bandages. "I don't want anything to happen to you."

"I'll be all right. With people like you and Mom pulling and praying for me, I can't lose."

Suddenly the door swung open, and in swaggered two of Joey's closest friends. "Hey, man, how the hell are you?" asked Rudy, his teeth and lips forming into a perfect Cheshire cat grin.

Philo chimed in, "Some guys will do anything to be waited on by pretty student nurses."

Quickly wiping his eyes, Joey said, "Ya know, there are a couple who are real knockouts."

During the course of the evening, friends and relatives continued to come to visit until they filled the room and stood out in the hall. Returning from a staff meeting, Mrs. Schwartz, the charge nurse, said, "I'm sorry. Only two visitors allowed at a time. The rest of you can wait in the lobby and take your turn to visit or come back tomorrow."

Rudy, who was sitting on the floor, slowly stood up, stretched his massive six-foot, five-inch body, and lumbered over to Mrs. Schwartz. Biting the cuticle of his right index finger, he looked at her nametag and said, "Ah, Mrs. Schwartz, we're not making that much noise. Why do we have to leave?"

Mrs. Schwartz's big-boned five-foot-five-inch frame did not give an inch. She glared up into Rudy's eyes and answered, "Because it's hospital rules, that's why."

"Can you please make an exception tonight?" asked Cheryl Lynn.

Feeling every eye in the room on her, she said, "I guess if all of you went to the waiting room at the end of the hall, it would be all right. But if you get too loud, I'll kick everyone out. Understand?"

The rest of the evening was spent in the waiting room talking and joking. At 8:30 p.m., Mrs. Schwartz appeared in the doorway and said, "Sorry, folks, visiting hours are over."

Stifling his Cheshire grin, Rudy exclaimed, "Come on, Mrs. Schwartz—"

Putting her hands on her hips, Mrs. Schwartz raised her eyebrows and looked at Rudy from the corner of her eyes. "Don't you give me any back talk, young man. Joey has a busy day tomorrow and needs his rest."

Rudy threw his hands up shoulder height and widened his eyes. "Yes, ma'am! We're leaving right now! Joey, we'll see you tomorrow."

Several people got up to leave. Watching them put their coats on, Joey said, "Thanks for coming. You've made things a lot easier for me."

Mrs. Slunisky, Cheryl Lynn, and Joey's Aunt Helen were the last to leave. Joey followed them into the hallway. Looking up into her son's eyes, Mrs. Slunisky said, "I guess they'll be running tests tomorrow."

"It sounds that way," replied Joey as he watched Mrs. Schwartz evict several visitors from another room.

"Can I bring you anything tomorrow?" asked Cheryl Lynn.

"How about a pepperoni pizza with double cheese from Bello's?"

Pointing her finger at her little brother, she said, "You got it!"

"Great! I'm looking forward to it already!"

STEVEN J. DEKANICH

A delighted grin coming to her face, Aunt Helen asked, "You mean you're going to eat a hospital meal and pizza?"

"Sure. I'm still a growing boy!"

Joey escorted them to the elevator. As he pushed the button, he looked at the floor and said, "Thanks for being here for me."

Tears welling in her eyes, Mrs. Slunisky hugged her son and said, "We'll always be here for you."

Everyone's eyes were glimmering by the time the elevator doors opened. As his family got on the elevator, Joey swallowed hard and said, "I'll see you tomorrow." Forcing a smile, he added, "I'm really looking forward to the pizza."

As the elevator headed to the ground floor, Mrs. Slunisky stared at the wall. In a low voice, she said, "When I talked with Dr. Sabbs today, he said if this had been caught several months ago, it would have been a simple operation in his office." Her voice grew louder, and she clenched her fists. "Dr. Braun treated Joey for swollen glands for almost six months! If he didn't know what was wrong, why didn't he say so? Damn him!"

"Mom, Dr. Braun has been our doctor over twenty years," Cheryl Lynn replied. "You know he's pulled Joey and me through some terrible sicknesses. He's only human. I don't think he would intentionally do something to hurt us. Be thankful Aunt Helen was seeing Dr. Sabbs and told him about Joey's neck."

The elevator came to a bouncing halt, and the doors opened. In silence, the three ladies walked past the abandoned reception desk and out of the hospital through the automatic doors onto the dimly lit sidewalk. "It's starting to get cold," said Aunt Helen, pulling her scarf around her neck.

Her shoulders noticeably sagging, Mrs. Slunisky said, "Winter is coming early this year in more ways than one. Oh, God, why?"

Biting her bottom lip and fighting back her own tears, Aunt Helen said, "Joey's a strong boy. We've got to pray and believe he's going to be all right."

As they reached their cars, Aunt Helen gave her sister and niece a hug. "Good night," she said. "I'll see you tomorrow."

Cheryl Lynn unlocked the passenger side of her car for her mother before walking around to the driver's side. After driving several miles, Cheryl Lynn broke the oppressive silence. "What do you think is going to happen?"

Mrs. Slunisky rubbed the back of her neck, closed her eyes and leaned against the headrest. After a moment, she opened her eyes and stared at the roof of the car. "I don't know. I pray to God that he'll be all right, but I just don't know. Why didn't Dr. Braun say he didn't know what was wrong with Joey? WHY?" ✦

STEVEN J. DEKANICH

Chapter 2

I'm going to be all right, mom.

The sound of bottles clinking and feet shuffling across the floor woke Joey. A gentle hand tapped him on his shoulder, and a pleasant voice whispered, "Mr. Slunisky, I need to get some blood from you."

Blinking his eyes, Joey saw a young lab technician holding a flashlight and a tray full of test tubes. Yawning, he asked, "What time is it?"

Turning on the indirect lighting in the room, the technician smiled and said, "It's about five-thirty."

Joey groggily sat up and rolled up his sleeve. "Why do you people have to take blood so early in the morning?"

Clamping the tourniquet around his arm, she said, "I guess because you were the first person on my list. Oh, my! You have good veins! This should be quick."

Watching the technician plug in the first of five test tubes, Joey saw the deep red stream shoot into the tube and fill it within a few seconds. After the fifth test tube was full, the technician released the tourniquet, pulled the needle from Joey's vein, and applied a cotton ball. "Please bend your arm and hold it."

His eyes finally starting to focus, Joey watched her write his name on each test tube and place the tubes in the first five slots on her tray. She turned and gently pulled Joey's arm down and removed the cotton ball. Putting the cotton ball back in place, she said, "It looks like the bleeding stopped, but I'll put a piece of tape over it anyway. The technician turned off the lights and said, "You can go back to sleep now. Have a good day."

It seemed like he had just closed his eyes when he heard the door open again. More blood work?

A gentle but firm hand moved his shoulder back and forth. "Mr. Slunisky, it's time to wake up. You have several tests scheduled, and you need to get up and get washed."

Joey opened his eyes and focused on the most enchanting brown eyes that he had ever seen. Sitting straight up, he said, "Ah, please, ah, you can call me Joey."

Her cheeks blushing ever so slightly, she said, "Okay, Joey. You can call me Kathy. Here is your facecloth and towel. The shower is right down the hallway on your left."

"Does this mean I'm not getting any breakfast this morning?"

Walking to the door, Kathy smiled. "That's right. As soon as all of your tests are completed, I'll get you something to eat."

"I'll hold you to that."

Kathy winked at him and spun around the door. Her long silky black hair suspended in the air was the last thing Joey saw.

Falling back into bed, Joey stared at the ceiling and whispered, "Wow!"

STEVEN J. DEKANICH

During the course of the day, Joey lost track of the number of tests he had. It was past 3:00 p.m. when he returned to his room. Joey's stomach complained vigorously for its lack of attention. He heard a knock on the door and watched it slowly open. His pulse increased, and he quickly stood up from the bed. Joey's smile sagged when Mrs. Schwartz came in carrying a food tray.

A rare smile coming to her face, Mrs. Schwartz asked, "How did your tests go?"

Joey sighed deeply and sat on the edge of the bed. "I can't believe all the stuff they did to me."

Mrs. Schwartz set the tray down on the tray table, easing it in front of Joey. "Yes, they do have quite a testing regimen, but that's good. You want to make sure they know everything about you before surgery."

Taking off the serving lid, Joey stared blankly at the conglomeration of food in front of him. "Thanks," he said, handing the lid to Mrs. Schwartz.

"Kathy thought you would be hungry after your tests, so she ordered this for you."

A perk of life came back to his face. "So, why didn't she bring it?"

"She's off-duty."

"Oh. She's so pretty, isn't she?"

"That she is," said Mrs. Schwartz, turning to walk out of the room. "That she is."

"Mrs. Schwartz," said Joey.

She stopped at the doorway. "Yes?"

"Will I still get supper tonight?"

"You sure will."

At 6:30 p.m., Joey's mother, sister, and brother-in-law walked into the room. Joey's eyes focused on the large flat white box with green edges and big red letters spelling BELLO'S. Anthony set the box down and opened the lid. The celestial aroma graced everyone in the room. His mouth watering like Pavlov's dog, Joey said, "That smells great! Let's have some!"

Cheryl Lynn took a steaming piece of pizza from the box. She quickly caught a hanging gooey mass of cheese, piled it on top, and handed the piece to Joey.

"What did they do today?" asked Anthony.

Joey longingly looked at the pizza in his hand and almost took a bite, but decided against it. "I've had everything done to me from being stuck with needles, probed with fingers, and going into a miniature tunnel with lights in it. As a matter of fact—"

"I see all of the tests haven't affected your appetite." Those words came from Aunt Helen, who was standing in the doorway.

Holding the pizza up as a toast to his aunt, Joey said, "You're right."

"How are you feeling?" she asked.

Voraciously attacking the piece, Joey chewed a few times, and angling his mouth to keep the pizza from falling out, he said, "For starting the day off at five-thirty this morning, I feel good."

"You don't look any worse for the wear," said Rudy as he and Philo entered the room. "Got any pizza left?"

"Yeah, as a matter of fact, I saved a piece for you and Philo."

The edges of his mouth sagging a bit and his forehead wrinkled, Philo asked Joey, "You feeling all right?"

Joey shrugged his shoulders. "I feel great now, but tomorrow may be a different story."

An ominous silence blanketed the room. It seemed like everyone blinked at the same time and stared at the floor. Wetting his lips

STEVEN J. DEKANICH

with his tongue, Rudy blurted, "Did you know Mrs. Schwartz wasn't going to let me on this floor? She said she doesn't understand how a nice boy like Joey could have a friend like me. Imagine that."

Joey crossed his arms and squinted his eyes. "Yeah, imagine that."

At that moment, a huge, heavily muscled, black orderly came to the doorway. "I'm here to prep you for your surgery tomorrow," said the massive black man.

"Mind if we stay?" asked Rudy.

Expressionless, the orderly pushed the supply cart into the room. Looking at Joey, he picked up the razor and said, "They can stay if you want, but I get kind of nervous when people watch me work."

Wide-eyed, Joey said to no one in particular, "I'll see you in the waiting room."

Mrs. Slunisky was the last to walk out and shut the door. Pulling out the pan from the supply cart, the orderly looked at Joey and said, "I know you from somewhere."

"Your name's Callahan, isn't it?"

"Yeah."

"You should know me. You ran over me ten times in last year's Hornets/Tigers football game."

His eyebrows rising and a smile of recognition coming to his face, Callahan pointed his finger at Joey. "That's it! That's where I saw you before! Man, that was some game."

"For you maybe. My body hurt for a week afterward."

As he expertly spread the creamy lather over Joey's face, neck, and shoulders, Callahan asked, "Do you want to know something?"

"What? That you beat us by four touchdowns?"

Easing the razor up Joey's neck, Callahan stopped and said, "No, man. You and I both know your team was outclassed. But you never gave up until the final whistle blew, and I respect that in a person. If your whole team played with your heart, you would have probably beaten us." Callahan rinsed the razor off in the pan. "They tell me you're scheduled for some pretty serious surgery in the morning."

His eyes dropping to the floor, Joey nodded in acknowledgment.

Laying the razor down, Callahan grabbed Joey's shoulder. "Look at me, man! I want to tell you something."

Joey raised his eyes to meet Callahan's.

"You keep your heart and don't give up because, man, if anybody can beat this thing, you can. Don't give up. You got that?" Callahan's grip tightened on Joey's shoulder until it hurt.

"I got it."

"Good! You better, or I'll come back and whip your butt."

Grinning, Joey clasped Callahan's hand. "We wouldn't want that to happen now, would we?"

Callahan carried the pan into the bathroom and poured the shaving water down the drain. He strolled back to the cart, opened the side compartment, and tossed the pan inside. Towering over Joey, he softened and said, "Good luck tomorrow, man."

Hopping up from the bed, Joey said, "Thanks. Let me get my robe on, and I'll walk with you down the hall. My family is probably wondering what happened to me."

"Yeah. I'll bet they're thinking you got your throat slit early."

Joey cringed at the thought. As they approached the waiting room, the buzz of conversation met them halfway down the hall. Joey said, "It really sounds like they missed me, doesn't it?"

Callahan smiled and continued on.

Rudy jumped up when Joey walked through the doorway. "Let me check it out. Hey, I couldn't have done better myself."

A smirk coming to his face, Joey cocked his head. "Oh, really?"

It was 8:45 p.m. when Mrs. Schwartz walked into the waiting room. Rudy started to get out of his chair, and she gently placed her hand on his shoulder and eased him back into his chair. "We're going to be good tonight, aren't we?"

Dropping his head, Rudy replied, "Yes, ma'am."

The smile not totally disappearing from her face, she looked at the rest of the group. "Folks, I hate to tell you this, but visiting hours were over fifteen minutes ago. Joey is going to have a long day tomorrow and needs his rest."

The joyful air of the room shattered like a window being struck by a baseball. Jagged red bolts began to streak across the whites of everyone's eyes. Many of Joey's visitors refused to look at him, and others quickly glanced away when he made eye contact. Clearing his throat, Joey said, "I want to thank all of you for your support and prayers. It means a lot. A guy couldn't ask for a better group of friends and relatives. And I …" Joey bit his bottom lip. "Thanks."

Rudy walked over to Joey and gave him a bear hug that lifted him off his feet. As he set Joey down, his quivering lips made speech difficult. Rudy paused before each word as if Joey's life would end the moment he finished. "I'm praying for you, man. Everything's … oh, hell." Spinning around on his heels, he ran out of the room.

Solemn-faced, Philo said, "He's really worried about you, and so am I. I wish I knew what to say right now, but I don't."

Joey hugged Philo. "You've already said enough. A person couldn't ask for better friends than you and Rudy." Stepping back from Philo, Joey smiled. "Tell Rudy that Mrs. Schwartz was probably right, but I'm still glad to have him as a friend. I'll see you later!"

Joey's eyes met his mother's, and as he embraced her, he thought, "What am I putting you through?"

Joey accompanied his mother, sister, brother-in-law, and Aunt Helen to the elevator. On the way, Mrs. Slunisky said, "We'll be here at five-thirty."

"But I'm not scheduled for surgery until seven."

Looking over the top of his glasses, Anthony said, "We know that, but we want to be here with you before you go to surgery."

Shaking his head, Joey said, "Okay, I'll see you in the morning." He hugged them all again before they got on the elevator. Joey watched the numbers over the elevator doors until he saw their elevator had arrived on the ground floor. A chill went through his body, and he shifted his eyes to the floor. He sighed deeply, turned, and walked back to his room.

As he passed the nurses' station, Mrs. Schwartz asked, "Can I get you a snack? Remember, you can't have anything after midnight."

"Yes, please. How about some potato chips and a cola?"

"Coming right up."

Joey raised the back of his bed, tore open the bag of potato chips, popped the can of cola, and placed them on the server next to him. Turning on his TV, he watched *Those Magnificent Men in Their Flying Machines*.

About ten o'clock, Mrs. Schwartz walked into his room. "Young man, you've got a busy day tomorrow. Turn the TV off and get some sleep. Dr. Sabbs said it would be all right for you to have a sleeping pill if you wanted it."

"No, that's okay." Joey shut off the TV and lowered the back of his bed. "I should be able to fall asleep."

"All right," said Mrs. Schwartz, turning off the lights. "I wish you the best tomorrow. I'll be praying for you Joey."

"Thanks," said Joey, effortlessly pulling the covers over his shoulders.

To relax, Joey stretched himself several times from toe to head. He turned over on his stomach and began to drift off. Suddenly, he felt something wet on his chest. Turning on the light, he saw a shiny crimson stain covering his chest and the bed sheet. Running

STEVEN J. DEKANICH

his hand over his chest, he was shocked that everything felt wet and sticky. Then he touched the base of his neck and could feel the warm fluid oozing from under the bandage and between his fingers.

"Just great," he thought. "I must have pulled the stitches apart from my biopsy when I was stretching." Sitting up, Joey took off his pajama top. He looked down and saw a steady crimson stream flowing down his chest and staining the waistband on his pajama bottoms. Grabbing some tissues, he tried to wipe the blood off but only succeeded in smearing it. Getting out of bed, Joey crumpled a wad of tissues in the middle of his chest to keep the blood from dripping on the floor. He walked out of his room and quickly headed toward the nurses' station.

Mrs. Schwartz was tending to a patient when she heard a scream. Running out into the hallway, she exclaimed, "What's wrong?"

A wide-eyed student nurse, with her hand over her mouth, was staring at Joey.

Holding the blood-soaked tissues against his chest, Joey shrugged his shoulders and asked, "Got a bandage?"

Sighing deeply, Mrs. Schwartz said, "Come on. Let's see what you did and get you cleaned up and back into bed."

At 4:30 a.m., Joey was awakened by an unfamiliar voice. "Mr. Slunisky, it's time to get up. I'm here to take your bandages off, and then I want you to take a shower. After that I have disinfectant that I want you to apply to your stitches, your shoulder, and neck area. When you've done that, put on this gown and return to your bed. You are not to wear any undergarments. Do you understand?"

"Yes, ma'am."

Joey picked up the disinfectant, facecloth, towel, and his gown and walked to the shower. Joey silently showered and wondered what the end of this day would bring. He turned up the hot water and let the hot stream beat on the back of his neck and shoulders.

After showering and toweling himself dry, Joey looked in the mirror and stared at the stitches on the side of his neck and across the front of his throat. They looked like miniature train tracks. Taking a deep breath through his nose, he let the air escape between his lips. He stared at the stitches a few more seconds and then applied the disinfectant. He picked up the hospital gown, looked at the humiliating garment, and thought, "The guy must have been perverted who invented this thing." He put his arms through each sleeve, pulled the gown to his chest, and tied the tie around his neck. Searching for the waist ties, Joey mumbled to himself, "This is just great. There's only one string." Joey reached back with his right hand and cinched the back of the gown, He picked up his pajamas with his left hand and cautiously stepped out into the hallway. No one in sight! Joey dashed down the hallway, ducked into his room, threw his pajamas on the chair, and dove under the covers. He wasn't in bed for five minutes before his door opened and in walked his mother, sister, brother-in-law, and Aunt Helen.

"Good morning," said a solemn-faced Mrs. Slunisky.

"Did you get any sleep last night?" asked Cheryl Lynn.

Joey smiled and said, "You'll never believe what happened last night."

"What's that?"

"I popped a couple of stitches and started to bleed everywhere."

A nurse carrying a foot-long hypodermic syringe stopped Joey's words. Joey's voice cracked as he said, "That's a big needle."

Nodding her head, she smiled. "Yes, and it's all for you. This shot is to relax you."

"Yeah, right! The thought of that thing sticking in me is making me pretty tense."

Taking the cap off the needle, the nurse said, "You need to roll over on your side."

"Roll over on my side?"

"That's right. This shot doesn't go into your arm."

"Oh, man," grumbled Joey as he reluctantly rolled over.

Pulling the sheet and his gown back, the nurse expertly drove the needle home and injected the contents. Extracting the needle and covering Joey back up, she said, "There! That wasn't so bad now, was it?"

"If you say so," said Joey rubbing his hip.

"It should take about five minutes for the shot to take effect. If you need to go to the bathroom, ring for help."

Joey watched as the nurse walked out the door. "Oh, crud," he thought. "She had to say that. Now I have to go to the bathroom. I better go now before the shot kicks in."

Grabbing the back of his gown, he started to get up.

Frowning, Mrs. Slunisky asked, "Where do you think you're going?"

"I'm going to the bathroom."

"But the nurse said not to get out of bed without help," said Cheryl Lynn.

"Look, I could have been there and back if we weren't talking." Sighing deeply, Joey continued, "I'm sorry. Please turn your heads for a moment."

Joey was coming out of the bathroom when the charge nurse walked into the room. "What do you think you're doing?"

"I'm all right."

Firmly taking a hold of his arm, she said, "Sure you are. A lot of intoxicated people feel the same way just before they get into an accident. I'm going to help you back into bed, and I want you to stay there! Understand?"

His head beginning to swim, Joey smiled and slurred, "Sure I do."

Looking at Anthony, the nurse said, "Make sure he stays there."

Anthony nodded an acknowledgment.

Looking up at the ceiling, Joey said, "Ya know, this shot hasn't done anything to me." He closed his eyes and drifted off to sleep.

At five after six, Joey's visitors could hear the rattling sounds of a gurney coming down the hall. Their breathing became shallow, and their eyes widened when they heard the gurney stop outside Joey's door. They cringed as the door opened and in walked two large men dressed in white scrubs.

Checking his bracelet, one of the orderlies said, "Mr. Slunisky, we're here to take you down to the operating room. Do you understand?"

Joey indistinctly muttered, "Of course I understand. Like I said before, that shot didn't have any effect on me."

Raising the bed to the height of the gurney, the orderly smiled and said, "Okay, since the shot didn't affect you, we need you to scoot over from your bed onto the cart."

Joey felt strong hands expertly help him from his bed to the gurney. "You guys are better than that nurse with the horse needle."

Watching the orderlies cover her son and strap him down, Mrs. Slunisky was overwrought with grief. Her breathing became shallow as tears streamed down her face. Squeezing her only son's hand, she said, "God be with you."

Mrs. Slunisky's words opened the gates of tears for Joey's relatives, and whimpering filled the room.

His mind clearing, Joey looked up at his mother and said, "I'm going to be all right, Mom."

Through blurry eyes, Mrs. Slunisky cupped Joey's hand with hers, pulled it to her damp cheek, and responded, "I know you are, son."

STEVEN J. DEKANICH

As the others walked over to the cart, Joey thought, "I never realized how much you mean to me." Fabricating a smile, he said, "I just want to say that all of you mean more to me than anything, and I thank God that he has blessed me with such a caring family."

With one orderly at the foot and the other at the head of the gurney, they began to guide Joey into the hallway. Mrs. Slunisky and Cheryl Lynn walked on the left side of the gurney, and Anthony and Aunt Helen walked on the right. Reaching the elevator, Mrs. Slunisky said, "Wait!" Her body trembling, she leaned over and hugged her son. Standing upright, Mrs. Slunisky could only manage to bite her bottom lip. No words would come out.

The elevator doors opened. The orderlies were guiding the gurney into the elevator when Joey looked at his sister and said, "How about a pizza tonight?"

Unable to speak, Cheryl Lynn nodded her head.

The elevator doors slowly closed, and Joey was gone. ✦

Chapter 3

He's alive!

The elevator came to a stop, and the orderlies waited for the doors to open. The front orderly guided the gurney out of the elevator, and in silence, the two men rolled Joey down the hall to the operating room. Joey was being lulled to sleep by the rhythmic clicking of one of the wheels when Dr. Braun walked out of one of the side rooms. Joey and Dr. Braun saw and recognized each other at the same time, but neither said anything.

The orderlies pushed the gurney down the corridor until they were slowed down by two large swinging metal doors. The gurney separated the doors, and Joey strained to pick his head up. He could see another hallway with people dressed in green scrubs and masks covering their mouths and noses. They were scurrying here and there like ants whose hill had just been stepped on. Joey's gurney was pushed in line behind several other gurneys. One of the orderlies squeezed Joey on the shoulder and said, "Good luck," and Joey was left unattended.

A nurse lifted his right arm and checked his ID bracelet. "Good morning, Mr. Slunisky. It will be a few minutes before you go in."

Once again, Joey was left alone. He closed his eyes as his head began to swim. Suddenly, he felt the gurney move. A rush of adrenalin roared through his veins. He opened his eyes wide and thought, "This is it!" His stomach fluttered, and he felt queasier than he'd ever felt on a new thrill ride. Despite the relaxing shot, Joey's heart pounded in his throat as he inched closer to the room that would change his life forever.

An uncontrolled shiver swept through his body as he was guided into the operating room. Although he wanted to scrunch under the covers, his curiosity made him lift his head. Masked strangers in green scrubs spoke in muffled voices and busily checked pieces of equipment. His eyes focused on the stainless steel operating table when he heard an unfamiliar voice. "Mr. Slunisky, we're going to slide you onto the table."

"It feels like a meat locker in here," Joey said as the nurse began to undo the straps around him.

"Yes, it does. Now just relax and let us move you."

Joey felt three pairs of hands quickly whisk him on top of the operating table. As he was moved from the gurney to the table, Joey's gown came opened. The sudden intimate contact with the icy cold tabletop momentarily stiffened his body, and the air rushing into his lungs refused to leave. Finally, he yelled, "This thing is cold!"

Everyone in the operating room momentarily stopped what they were doing and looked at Joey. Chuckling as she tucked some blankets under Joey, one of the nurses said, "Let's get you wrapped up until everything is ready." She wrapped him up like a cocoon but left his right arm out from under the blanket.

Another nurse taped his palm to a flat board and said, "I'm going to hook up the IV. You'll feel a little prick, but the pain won't last."

The needle was going into his vein when he heard, "Good morning, Joey."

"At last, a familiar voice!" Joey thought as he replied, "Good morning, Dr. Sabbs."

"Mrs. Schwartz left a note about you pulling a couple of your stitches open last night and scaring one of our students half to death by bleeding all over yourself."

A faint smile coming to his lips, Joey said, "I didn't mean to scare her. I'm sorry."

"Actually, I thought it was kind of amusing. Oh, good morning, Dr. Yeng."

"Good morning, Dr. Sabbs. Is our patient ready to go to sleep this morning?"

Joey looked over the top of his forehead and made eye contact with Dr. Yeng.

"Ah, yes, he looks more than ready." Injecting a syringe of thiopental sodium into the IV line, Dr. Yeng continued, "You go to sleep now."

Milliseconds after the injection, a cold rush came over his body, and Joey wildly looked around the room.

Putting his hand on Joey's shoulder, Dr. Yeng said, "Don't fight it. Just relax."

An invisible force made his head spin and seemed to levitate his body. Suddenly, everything went black.

The elevator doors closed, and Cheryl Lynn began to sob uncontrollably. Anthony put his arm around her shoulders and guided her to the waiting room. Joey's mother and aunt followed in silence. Dazed, each found a seat and didn't say a word.

STEVEN J. DEKANICH

A few minutes later, Dr. Braun came into the room. Mrs. Slunisky saw him first. Her knuckles turned white, and her fingernails dug into the palms of her hands as she got out of her chair. Fury filled her gray-blue eyes, and she said, "How could you? Because of you, my son may never have a voice or use his arm."

Dr. Braun bowed his head until his chin touched his chest. Sighing deeply, he stared at the floor. "I've read Joey's chart," he said. "Mrs. Slunisky, I am so sorry."

Cheryl Lynn's shrill voice could be heard throughout the whole floor. "A lot of good that does my brother!"

Painfully searching for the right words, Dr. Braun continued in a low voice, "Mrs. Slunisky, I saw no indications that Joey had cancer. I would never have done anything to intentionally hurt him."

Her eyes softening slightly, Mrs. Slunisky said, "Dr. Braun, you've been our doctor for years and have helped us through many illnesses. I appreciate you coming up here, but at this moment, I cannot discuss this matter with you."

Crimping his lips together, Braun continued to look at the floor. He turned and walked to the doorway. Before leaving the room, he stopped and said again, "I'm sorry."

After Dr. Braun left, the room was silent. As minutes turned into hours, the fear of not knowing attacked the vulnerable hearts of Joey's family. Foreboding illusions sprang up in each person's mind, and imaginations began to run wild. They were living in their own self-made nightmares.

Mrs. Slunisky thought back to her meeting with Dr. Sabbs when she heard him say, "I'm sorry, Mrs. Slunisky. Your son has cancer."

Devastating words. The words turned into gall and soured the pit of her stomach. Although she could see Dr. Sabbs' lips move, her brain refused to hear anything. She wanted to flee, escape from this moment. Instead, she dug her fingernails into the thick leather arms of the chair until her nails started to separate from the flesh. The throbbing hands held her captive, and her rapid breathing caused all of the words to run together. "This can't be happening!"

Dr. Sabbs gently took her left hand and waited for Mrs. Slunisky's darting eyes to meet his. "All of the tests have come back positive. Believe me, Mrs. Slunisky, I wish I was wrong, but I'm not. We must act quickly."

"But, Dr. Sabbs, Joey is starting college next week and—"

Sabbs tightened his grip. "Mrs. Slunisky, I assure you that I can help Joey, but we must act quickly or he may die."

The words struck her heart like a hot branding iron, and fear made a twisted knot of her insides. Struggling for each word, she asked, "What needs to be done?"

"The operation that your son is about to have is going to be very traumatic and could leave him without a voice or the use of his left arm."

"This can't be happening!" she shrieked as she yanked her arm away.

Surprised by her quickness and strength, Dr. Sabbs paused. Taking a deep breath and exhaling, he said, "It is happening, Mrs. Slunisky. You can seek another opinion, but I would stake my career on what the results would be."

Anxiously rummaging through her purse for a tissue, she ignored Sabbs' comment.

"We must do something. The longer we wait, the worse it will get."

Staring off into oblivion, her hand stopped, but she did not speak. She closed her eyes, and unchecked tears left shining streaks running down her thin cheeks. Finally, she straightened her sagging shoulders and relaxed the grip on her purse. She reopened her eyes and looked at the man who held her son's life in his hands. In a shaky voice, she asked, "Is there anything that I can do to help?"

Handing her a tissue, Dr. Sabbs said, "Yes, there are many factors that will enter into Joey's recovery."

"What do you mean?"

"After the operation, if he does lose the use of his arm or voice, I want you to care for him, but make sure he still does things for himself. If everything is done for a handicapped person, soon that person believes he isn't capable of doing anything. A person who could have contributed to society regresses within himself and becomes a true invalid."

Mrs. Slunisky's eyes widened at the implication. "Are you saying that my son is going to be an invalid?"

Shaking his head, Sabbs said, "No. I'm trying to keep that from happening. Positive emotions will play a very important part in Joey's recovery."

"What can I do to help?"

"I want you to impress upon Joey that this is not the end of the world and that he can still be an active and productive person. While he is in the hospital and after he is discharged, his mind needs to be occupied with other things. It will be very important that Joey has as many visitors as possible without tiring him. Once we operate and see exactly what we have, I'll be able to tell you more specifically what else I want you to do."

The weight of her son's dilemma was more than her heart could bear. But Sabbs' confidence and reassurance gave her a counterbalance of hope to cling to. Through teary eyes, she said, "I'll do whatever you say."

Walking her to the door, Sabbs said, "There is one other thing that I want you to do."

"What's that?"

"Pray."

Trying to take Dr. Sabbs' advice, Mrs. Slunisky tried to pray, but she shuddered as she imagined her son's neck being ripped open. *Oh God, what if he isn't as good as they say? Did I do the right thing?*

Cheryl Lynn closed her eyes and remembered events from her and Joey's years of growing up. One memory in particular took command of her thoughts. "Come on, Sis. I'll bet I can beat you this time," Joey had said.

"You think so, huh?" Cheryl Lynn replied as she sat down at the kitchen table.

Putting his elbow on the tabletop and keeping his forearm perpendicular to the surface, Joey smiled and said, "Yep."

Cheryl Lynn put her elbow on the table and locked hands with Joey. "Okay, let's see how much stronger you got since yesterday."

"Ready? Go!" Joey desperately applied pressure to Cheryl Lynn's hand and began to move it down to the left. When her hand was an inch from the tabletop, Cheryl Lynn began to slowly move Joey's hand back up. "Uh, come on, dang it!" *Thump!* His hand hit the table. "You wait until I'm a teenager!"

"Now he can put my arm down with one finger," Cheryl Lynn thought. A cold chill ran down her spine as she said to herself, "Oh, my God. Will he be able to use his arm after this?"

The bond between Joey and Anthony was closer than a natural father-son or big brother-little brother relationship. Anthony recalled spending hours with Joey, hunting, fishing, and doing homework problems. The thought of losing Joey left a great void inside him. This void became a vortex that drained all of the energy from his body. He could see Joey falling into a black abyss, and he couldn't do anything to help him.

Aunt Helen thought about Joey and their hiking, fishing, and camping trips together. She said under her breath, "Dear God, Joey's like a son to me. How could You let this happen to someone so filled with life? Please have mercy on him."

Several hours passed before Mrs. Slunisky said, "I have to get up and walk around. Just sitting here is killing me."

"Let's check the nurses' station for news," suggested Cheryl Lynn.

Together, the foursome walked to the nurses' station. Fearful expectation made Mrs. Slunisky's words shaky. "Any news about Joey?"

Scowling, Ms. Rasp looked up from her paperwork. "You'll need to be more specific. What's the patient's full name?"

"Joey Slunisky. He is being operated on for throat cancer."

Rummaging under her scattered papers, Ms. Rasp found Joey's chart. Glancing at the chart, she mumbled to herself, "When are these young punks going to learn not to smoke?"

Mrs. Slunisky's snow-white hair intensified the reddening of her face. Her eyes locked with Ms. Rasp's, and she said, "I'll have you know, my son does not smoke. The cancer that he has is a result of X-ray treatments that he had as a child for an enlarged thymus, and his condition was aggravated by a football injury."

A grunting noise came from her throat as a contemptuous smile formed on her face. "I'm sorry. We haven't received any information on your son. We'll let you know as soon as we hear something."

Seven agonizing hours passed, and still no word. Visibly distraught, Mrs. Slunisky walked back to the nurses' station. "Has anything been reported on Joey Slunisky?"

Ms. Rasp ignored the question and continued to do her paperwork. Sensing that Mrs. Slunisky was not going to leave, she raised her eyes. Through deeply furrowed eyebrows, she stared at Mrs. Slunisky for several seconds before saying, "No, I haven't heard anything yet. I told you before. I'll inform you as soon as I hear something."

"Isn't there any way to find out how the operation is going? He has been in there so long."

"Look, I'm very busy. I have to finish these reports before three o'clock. If I get the time, I'll check on your son when I'm done." Abrupt as her words, she looked back down at her work and completely ignored Mrs. Slunisky.

Coming in early to relieve the day-shift charge nurse, Mrs. Schwartz witnessed the episode. Seeing her, Mrs. Slunisky pleaded, "It's been over seven hours since Joey has gone to surgery, and we haven't heard anything. Is there anything you can do to find out what is going on?"

Setting her purse down, Mrs. Schwartz glared at Ms. Rasp and said, "I'll call right now and find out the status."

Mrs. Slunisky anxiously waited for Mrs. Schwartz to get off the phone. "How is he?"

"Joey is still in the operating room. Everything is proceeding normally, but he will be in there for several more hours. I'll call again in another hour to check on the status and will let you know."

"Thank you."

Mrs. Schwartz stood behind the nurses' station and watched Joey's mother walk back to the waiting room. She waited a few seconds and then in a low voice said, "Ms. Rasp, I want to see you in my office. Now!"

Throwing her pen down and bouncing it across the desk, Ms. Rasp jerked herself out of the chair and followed Mrs. Schwartz into the office. Mrs. Schwartz closed the door, turned, and demanded, "Why did you treat Mrs. Slunisky like that?"

"Treat her like what?"

"You made it very clear that you wouldn't take the time to find out the status of her son until you finished your paperwork. Young lady, I could see not taking the time if you were working with a patient. But all you were doing was busy work! That lady is going through living hell not knowing what is happening to her son, and you couldn't care less!"

Crossing her arms, Ms. Rasp said, "I have some things I need to do right after work, and all my paperwork has to be done before I can leave. If I had the time, I would have called to find out. Besides, she could have talked to one of the other nurses if she really wanted to find out what was happening."

Her eyes widening and blood pulsing in her temples, Mrs. Schwartz replied, "Your job is to care for and help people. Not just the patients, but the family members of the patients too. When you transferred to this floor, we were told you had an attitude problem. Your record shows that you are discourteous with the patients and their visitors. What I just observed substantiates that. A negative attitude like yours is not only a black mark against this hospital, it could mean the difference between recovery or death of a patient."

Ms. Rasp unfolded her arms. "I never thought about it like that," she said. "Look, I've had a lot of personal problems recently, and I guess I was bringing them here."

"The hospital is no place for your personal problems. If you need counseling, we can make arrangements for that. Until then, be the best support system for patients and visitors. I will not tolerate any more outbursts like the one I have just witnessed. Do I make myself clear?"

True to her word, Mrs. Schwartz called the operating room every hour. She was told that a considerable amount of neck and shoulder muscle had to be removed and that Joey had hemorrhaged and lost several pints of blood. Mrs. Schwartz buffered the report and passed the general information onto Mrs. Slunisky.

After ten agonizing hours of waiting, a smiling Mrs. Schwartz walked into the waiting room. "Joey is in the recovery room and doing well. Dr. Sabbs will be here shortly to discuss the operation with you."

Tears of relief filling her eyes, Mrs. Slunisky said, "Oh, dear God, it's finally over. How is Joey?"

"I'm sorry, but I don't know more than that. Dr. Sabbs will go over the details with you."

"Thank you for being so kind and keeping us informed."

Cheryl Lynn asked, "Will he still have a voice? Can he use his arm?"

Before Mrs. Schwartz could answer, Mrs. Slunisky exclaimed, "He's alive! Even if he can't use his arm or speak, he is still with us. To hear Mrs. Schwartz say that Joey is doing well, I know in my heart that he's going to be all right." ✦

Chapter 4

I can't lift my arm!

Ten minutes after Mrs. Schwartz announced that Joey was in recovery, Dr. Sabbs entered the waiting room. Although his smile was broad, the black shadows under his eyes augmented a gaunt, exhausted face. Focusing on Mrs. Slunisky, he said, "Before I go into detail, I want you to know that Joey is in the recovery room and doing fine. It was a long battle with complications, but I believe we got all of the cancer."

Tears welled in Mrs. Slunisky's eyes as she cupped her hands over her mouth and said, "Oh, thank God."

Cheryl Lynn asked, "What had to be done?"

"This was a very complex surgery. We had to remove most of his thyroid and parathyroid glands. The cancer spread into sections of the thyrohyoid, omohyoid, sternohyoid, scalenes, trapezius, deltoid, and platysma muscles. Massive sections of these muscles had to be removed, which will make it very difficult for Joey to use his left arm and keep his head up. Removing part of the thyroid gland may affect his body metabolism. Removing the parathyroid glands could make it difficult to regulate the calcium balance in his body. If his body cannot regulate and maintain his calcium level, he could experience severe cases of tetany … or muscle cramps. It will be several days until we can determine to what extent Joey will be physically handicapped."

Physically handicapped! The words impaled their hearts and left their eyes gawking. Although they had heard the words before, the reality was not driven home until now.

His weary eyes scanning each face, Sabbs intuitively knew that each person would want to do everything for Joey. Clearing his throat, he said, "How much Joey recovers not only is going to depend on how he handles this, it's going to depend on how you handle it. He's going to need your support but not your sympathy. Joey is now going to be faced with a physical handicap. Please don't allow him to develop a mental handicap."

Frowning, Aunt Helen asked, "What do you mean?"

Running his hand through his close-cropped hair, Sabbs looked at Aunt Helen and said, "Let me use a real life example. Several years ago, I had to amputate the right arm of a middle-aged gentleman. All that he had left was a stub. This man was a farmer, and his wife was a homemaker. He had two children at home and two in college. His family loved and cared for him, but they let him do things for himself. This farmer knew his responsibilities and decided that he would do whatever was necessary to continue to care for his family. Consequently, he did not feel sorry for himself because of his affliction. As a matter of fact, he did not call himself handicapped— he said he had a minor nuisance."

"Whatever became of him?" asked Aunt Helen.

"We fitted him with an artificial arm, and after several months of therapy and training, he was able to use the arm in his chores around the farm. He said it didn't look very pretty, but he was able to drive his tractors, bale hay, plant and harvest his crops, and many other things. As a matter of fact, he played Captain Hook in his son's school play of *Peter Pan*. This man did not allow himself the excuse of a mental handicap.

"Now, let me tell you about another man who was five years younger than the farmer. This man was a millwright in a local steel mill. He was never sick a day in his life, and he had an active life with his family and the community. One day, he was working with some heavy machinery in the mill, and his arm was pinned and crushed between two large gears. As with the farmer, I had to amputate this man's arm above his elbow so he was left with only a stub.

"While he was in the hospital, he recovered as quickly as the farmer. We fitted him with an artificial arm, and he went to therapy and training to use the arm. However, when he went home, his family began to do everything for him because they didn't want him to strain himself. Actually, because it took him longer to do things, they were impatient and didn't want to wait. These were things that he could have done if he had been given the chance.

"Because his family did everything for him, I literally saw the spark of life drain from the man. Over a period of time, he never wanted to push himself to learn how to use the artificial arm to its fullest potential or develop his left arm. There were times during therapy or visiting my office when he would break down and cry and say that he wasn't of use to anyone anymore. In a matter of a few years, I saw the man become wheelchair-bound. He had to have someone shave him, feed him … do everything for him. As you can imagine, this became a tremendous burden not only on him but also his family."

Mesmerized by the story, Aunt Helen asked, "Whatever happened to him?"

"They buried him last year."

"Oh, my."

"Now do you understand why I said please don't let Joey develop a mental handicap?"

It almost looked rehearsed when they all nodded and said "yes" simultaneously.

"Please don't take this the wrong way. Joey is going to need your support and help, especially at the beginning. But if you see something that you feel he can do for himself, give him the opportunity to do it. Even if it takes him five times as long, let him do it. He will be better in the long run."

For the next few seconds, no one said a word as they tried to assimilate Sabbs' advice.

Sabbs broke the silence by saying, "I apologize if I have come on too strongly about this. If it were anyone else, I probably wouldn't have talked like this. But let me tell you something. Joey has a fighting spirit that needs to be let out. The worst thing you can do for a person like Joey is to do too much for him." Sabbs looked at his watch. "I have some other tasks to tend to. Mrs. Schwartz will periodically check on Joey. Joey is a fighter, and I think he'll be all right regardless of the outcome."

With a faint smile coming to his face, Dr. Sabbs nodded adieu and walked out of the waiting room.

Approximately ten hours after Joey was taken into the recovery room, the anesthesia began to wear off. As he lay there, Joey heard muffled sounds that seemed as if they were coming from another world. Eventually, the sounds melded into a voice. Like the first rays of light on a misty morning, the voice penetrated through the cloud that surrounded his brain. "Joey? Can you hear me? Joey, it's time to wake up."

STEVEN J. DEKANICH

Although he wanted to stay in the deep comfortable slumber where everything seemed just right, the sharp distinct voice would not allow it. Reluctantly, he opened his eyes and began to focus. He saw a smiling nurse in a white uniform standing next to his bed looking at him.

Touching his arm, the nurse said, "Hello, Joey. The operation is over. You're in the recovery room. You're going to be all right."

Rubbing his tongue over the roof of his mouth, Joey said in a slurred voice, "Can I have a drink of water?"

"Not yet. We don't want you to get sick on us."

"Man, am I thirsty," he said as he drifted off to sleep. Joey floated in and out of consciousness for the next hour. When he became reasonably coherent and could keep his eyes open for longer periods of time, one of the nurses said, "I think he can go up to his room now."

The nurses began moving Joey's bed around and disconnecting and reconnecting tubes. Looking down, Joey could make out a large white bandage around his neck. The bandage felt as if it was cinched against his chin because it was very difficult to move his head. Five tubes protruded from the bandage or "horse collar," as Joey later called it. The tubes were placed in various locations inside the incision and connected to a suction pump. Joey's right hand was strapped to a board with an intravenous needle sticking in a vein on the top of his hand.

Two orderlies secured a strap over Joey's chest and another over his legs and began to slowly transport him back to his room. Joey's right hand softly gripped the board, and the tape over the intravenous needle pulled at his skin. *Something isn't right. What is it?* A frightening thought with crystal clarity raced through his muddled brain: *I don't feel anything on my left arm. I can't lift my arm!* ✦

Chapter 5

An eerie resonance filled the room.

Joey's semiconscious state kept him more in touch with the obscure than with reality. His family was waiting for him in the hallway as the orderlies wheeled him off the elevator. Joey's eyes refused to focus, and all their faces got jumbled together and made his head spin. The sticky phlegm on the roof of his mouth snared his tongue like an inhumane mousetrap. Desperately trying to free his tongue, he could only manage to emit a weak and raspy sound from his lips. "Hi, how are you doing?"

The barely audible words stopped Mrs. Slunisky dead in her tracks. She cupped her hands over her mouth and cheeks, and the tears streaming from her eyes made small puddles where her fingertips pushed against her cheekbones. It was hard to understand the words over her cupped hands: "He still has his voice! Thank God in heaven, he still has his voice."

"What did you say?" asked Cheryl Lynn.

Removing her hands from her face, she answered, "Joey can talk!"

Looking down the hall, Mrs. Slunisky and Cheryl Lynn saw Anthony open the door for the two orderlies as they hurried to get to the room. While the orderlies lifted him from the gurney to his bed, Joey's eyes focused on a nurse he had never seen before. In a slurred whisper, he asked, "Can Mrs. Schwartz come in here?"

Checking the tubes coming from his bandage, the nurse said, "I'm sorry, Joey. She went off-duty several hours ago."

His eyes rolled back in his head, and his eyelids slowly closed as he said, "What time is it?"

The nurse looked at her watch. "It's past three o'clock in the morning."

In words that were barely distinguishable, he said, "Wow, it's still early. This went a lot quicker than I thought it would."

Seeing that Joey had drifted off again, the nurse turned to his family. "He's going to say a lot of things in the next few hours and probably won't remember any of it when he wakes up."

The massive bandage around Joey's neck looked like an outdated deep-sea diving apparatus without the helmet. The thickness of the bandage was almost as wide as Joey's shoulders. It was molded to the top of his shoulders and cinched tightly under his chin. Like tentacles from a grotesque sea creature, the five tubes protruding from the bandage quivered and swayed with each breath that Joey took. All of the tubes were plugged on the end, and a pale yellow fluid oozed slowly into each tube. One by one, the nurse took each tube and held it so the end was above Joey's neck. She then pulled out the plug and inserted each tube into a port on a suction pump. When she finished, the nurse turned on the pump. The *toosh, woosh, toosh, woosh* sound emitting from the pump sounded like a frightened scuba diver.

His eyes never leaving her hands, Anthony asked the nurse, "What is the purpose of this thing?"

Making an adjustment to slow down the pumping action, the nurse said, "This is a peristaltic pump. It actually has a similar pumping action as a human's digestive tract. Its purpose is to make sure that all of the infectious fluids that are building up in Joey's neck are removed to minimize the possibility of infection around the rest of his body."

"How long will he be hooked up to the pump?"

"It's hard to say. Dr. Sabbs will let us know when we can take Joey off the unit." Satisfied with the pumping rate, the nurse continued, "He'll probably sleep for most of the night. We'll be back to check on him, but in the meantime, if you need us for anything, just push this button."

When the nurse left the room, the others walked over to Joey's bed. The fatigue and anxiety of the last twenty hours magnified the impact of the sight. The young man, once so vibrant and full of life, lay totally disheveled and unconscious before them. His hair was matted in sweat. The lids of his eyes, covered with petroleum jelly, were closed and swollen. Yellow blotches of prep material stained the sides of his face and underneath the exposed areas of his chin. The yellow fluid oozing down the tubes coming from the horse collar bandage made grotesque leaps each time the pump cycled. His right hand was strapped to a flat board and had an IV needle stuck inside the vein on the top part of his hand.

Standing dumbfounded, each person thought, "What have they done to you?"

Glancing at the faces of the others in the room, Mrs. Slunisky said, "We've been here for over twenty hours. Why don't the rest of you go home and try to get some sleep. I'll stay here with Joey."

Cheryl Lynn responded indignantly, "I want to stay."

Anthony nodded his head. "I think your mother is right. We've been here a long time, and we're all tired. Why don't we get some rest? Then we can come back and spell your mom."

Fighting back a yawn, Aunt Helen said, "Cheryl Lynn, I think Joey's going to be in good hands with the nurses and your mother. We should be able to get a few hours of sleep without having to worry that much about him. Why don't we do that and come back in the next couple of hours?"

Pressing her lips tightly together, Cheryl Lynn glared at Anthony. "Well … okay. We can sleep for a few hours, but I'm coming back as soon as I wake up."

When the others left, an eerie resonance filled the room. All that Mrs. Slunisky could hear was the labored breathing of her son and the rhythmic pulsing of the pump. Occasionally, Joey would awaken for brief periods, and she was able to get him to take a few sips of water. While Joey slept, Mrs. Slunisky sat back in the overstuffed chair. Instantly, she fell into a deep sleep laced with nightmares. Yelling out, Joey writhed in pain. She would try to run to him, but her feet would not move. The intensity of her struggle to get to him awakened her.

Rubbing her arms to drive off the horror of the dream and the night chill in the room, she watched her son sleep. "Why did this have to happen to you? What did I do so wrong to make God punish you like this?" she said out loud.

"Nothing that you have done wrong has caused Joey's affliction."

Sabbs' voice echoed through the room and startled Mrs. Slunisky. "Dr. Sabbs! What are you doing here?"

"I have an early surgery this morning and wanted to check on Joey before I went down." Checking Joey's pulse, Sabbs asked, "Has Joey been awake at all since he came back to the room?"

"Yes, he's been awake several times for a few minutes. I was able to get him to drink a few sips of water each time."

"That's good, that is very good." With a deep breath, Sabbs said, "Mrs. Slunisky … the comment you were making as I came into the room about what did you do to inflict this upon Joey … there is nothing you did that has caused Joey's cancer. Please bear in mind that you have been up for a considerable length of time and you are under a tremendous stress. The feelings that you are feeling are really quite normal for a person in your circumstance. I know it's an easy thing to say, but try to refrain from this type of destructive thought process. It could lower your resistance, and you could make yourself ill, and neither you nor Joey can tolerate that."

Turning to look at Joey, Mrs. Slunisky said, "Just look at him. Why did this have to happen? Was it something that I did or didn't do that caused this?"

"Mrs. Slunisky, outside of the effects of drugs, alcohol, smoking, or sexually transmitted diseases on infants, the illnesses and afflictions that we get are not the result of another person being good or bad. I'd like to think that our God is a loving and forgiving God and He's not out to get us because of what another person has done with their life. I want to reiterate that Joey needs you more now than he ever has in his life. At this moment in your life and in Joey's life, you cannot afford to have a pity party. Joey needs you focused and not self-demeaning."

"You have a remarkable way of coming directly to the point, don't you?"

"I find that is the easiest way to operate." A faint smile came to his face. "No pun intended." His face sobering, he added, "Joey's a fighter, and he's going to be all right." Sabbs rechecked Joey's bandage and left the room. Once again, Mrs. Slunisky was left alone in the dimly lit room to ponder her thoughts about her son.

STEVEN J. DEKANICH

It was almost 7:00 a.m. when Cheryl Lynn walked through the door. The bags under her eyes showed that she had not gotten much sleep. Taking off her coat, she asked, "How's Joey?"

Getting up from the overstuffed chair, Mrs. Slunisky said, "He woke up several times last night, but all in all he rested pretty well."

"How are you doing?"

"I'm exhausted, but I'll be all right. Where's Anthony?"

"He's parking the car. He should be here in a few minutes. Mom, I don't think it would be a good idea for you to drive. Why don't you let Anthony take you home to get some rest?"

Although her body cried for repose, she said, "That sounds like a good idea, but I'm not going until he wakes up again."

Knowing it was best not to argue, Cheryl Lynn said, "Suit yourself. What all happened last night?"

"Well, he woke up several times. Each time, he wanted a drink of water or his lips wetted. There was another thing that happened that really left an impression on me."

"What's that?"

An uncontrolled yawn distorted Mrs. Slunisky's face. "Oh, excuse me," she said. Blinking her eyes, she continued, "Dr. Sabbs came in here early this morning to check on Joey. That man is truly concerned and cares for Joey. His bedside manner is one of the best I have ever seen. He gives you a sense that things are in control and everything that can be done is being done. From day one, he has shown deep concern not only for Joey but for the whole family. He seems to know what a person feels like when they are going through this living hell. He has a knack for saying the right thing at the right time to calm a person and let them know everything that can be done is being done.

"What did he say?" Cheryl Lynn asked.

"Well, last night after everybody left, you might say that I was having … what did he call it? Oh, yes, a pity party because of what was happening."

"A pity party?"

"Yes. I was blaming myself for everything that has happened. Dr. Sabbs told me those kinds of thoughts were destructive and I couldn't afford to do that because Joey needed me to be strong for him. That's why he called it a pity party. I was basking in my own self-pity without even realizing it. At the time, I didn't believe it. But after he left, I thought about it and realized he was right."

Mrs. Slunisky and Cheryl Lynn walked over to stand by Joey's bedside. After a moment, Anthony came into the room. Taking off his coat, he asked, "How is he?"

"It's been a while since he's been awake, but I think he's doing all right," Mrs. Slunisky said. Turning her gaze away from Joey, she noticed Anthony's steamed-up glasses and red fingers. "You look like you've been in a freezer. Is it that cold out there?"

Rubbing his hands, Anthony nodded. "It went down to twenty degrees last night, but it's not much warmer than that now."

"Sounds like a great day to go rabbit hunting," said a weak raspy voice.

They all turned their eyes to Joey. "How do you feel, son?" Mrs. Slunisky asked.

"Like I've been hit by a truck. Everything hurts. How did the operation go?"

"It was a success," Cheryl Lynn said. "They think they got everything."

"Yeah, they got everything all right, including my arm."

"What do you mean?"

Closing his eyes, Joey said, "I can't lift my arm."

Joey's words hung in the air and engulfed them like hoarfrost. Visibly shaken, Mrs. Slunisky asked, "Can you feel anything in your arm?"

Opening his eyes and staring at the ceiling, Joey answered, "I can feel the texture of the blanket, but the arm refuses to move when I want it to."

"We'll call Dr. Sabbs and see what can be done."

"I pray to God something can …" Joey said, closing his eyes and drifting back to sleep.

An hour later, Sabbs entered the room. "How's our patient doing?"

Joey opened his eyes and stared blankly. "Not too well. I'm nauseous, I hurt, and I can't move my arm."

"You seem to have a pretty good voice, though."

"Yeah, but I still can't move my arm."

"Let's have a look." Dr. Sabbs spent several minutes examining Joey. Putting his stethoscope around his neck, he said, "Joey, the fact that you still have feeling in your left arm and hand is a good sign. It's going to be a waiting game now. We'll just have to see how things progress in the next few days."

Joey's breaths became short and distinct as he said through clenched teeth, "It just won't move … it just won't move!"

"You just came back from surgery. Give it some time." Looking at his watch and then squeezing Joey's left arm, Sabbs said, "Joey, I have to leave, but I'll be back to check on you later this evening." He nodded to the others and walked out of the room.

A few seconds later, Mrs. Slunisky hurried after him. Seeing him about to enter the elevator, she called out, "Dr. Sabbs!"

Sabbs turned and saw Mrs. Slunisky moving toward him. He stepped back and let the elevator doors close. "Yes, Mrs. Slunisky?"

Breathing heavier than normal, she said, "Dr. Sabbs, I know you're busy, but can I have a few minutes of your time?"

Dr. Sabbs looked at his watch. "I have a few minutes. How can I help you?"

"What can we truly expect with Joey's arm?"

"It's hard to say. This is going to be something that only time will tell. At this moment, I don't know if there will be enough muscle tissue left for Joey to build up and compensate for his loss. If there isn't, he will not be able to move his arm. If there is, he may or may not be able to move his arm."

"What do you mean?"

Sabbs leaned against the wall and folded his arms. "As I said before, Joey's attitude is going to play a major part in his recovery. If he has the wherewithal to move his arm and doesn't desire or need to move it, he won't. I've seen it happen many times."

"How do you get him to desire to move his arm?"

"You don't.... Mrs. Slunisky, this is something that must come from within Joey. You can only pray and support him, but you can't do it for him."

Distraught, Mrs. Slunisky clasped her hands and put them to her lips. Staring at the floor, she whispered, "Oh, God, I pray his arm moves again."

Squeezing her shoulder, Sabbs said, "So do I, Mrs. Slunisky, so do I." ✦

STEVEN J. DEKANICH

Chapter 6

Thank you dear lord for bringing my son back to me.

The constricting bandage around his neck and the frustration of not being able to move his left arm intensified Joey's pain. Electrified bolts shot down his neck and across his shoulders and crashed together in convulsive spasms at the base of his throat. The excruciating pain had to be counteracted by heavy sedation.

Heavy sedation and the threat of complications required that Joey have someone with him twenty-four hours a day. Although many wanted to help, Joey's mother, his sister, Aunt Helen, and his cousin Dot committed to stay with him. Anytime, night or day, Joey would drift on the border of consciousness, and when he opened his eyes, hazy images of one of these four people were always with him. Even in his drugged state, having them at his side gave Joey a feeling of inner peace, and as a result, they would always hold a special place in his heart.

After several days, Sabbs began to wean Joey off the pain medication. However, the trauma of not being able to move his arm sent Joey into a psychological downward spiral. Outside of occasionally wanting his lips wetted with water or lemon swab sticks, he refused to eat or drink. It was Monday evening, and Joey was having a particularly hard time.

Mrs. Schwartz furrowed her brow in concern as she took Joey's vital signs. Turning to Mrs. Slunisky, she asked, "Would you come with me to the nurses' station?"

Mrs. Slunisky nodded and followed Mrs. Schwartz out of the room.

When they reached the nurses' station, Mrs. Schwartz put Joey's chart on the desk and asked, "Have you ever seen Joey in this mental condition?"

Mrs. Slunisky unconsciously wrung her hands. "I've never seen him like this," she replied, her body visibly slumping. "It's … it's almost as if he's giving up on life. I just don't understand it."

Taking a look at Joey's chart, Mrs. Schwartz said, "I know one thing. His temperature has been steadily climbing for the last day and a half. He's beginning to dehydrate, and if he doesn't snap out of this, he'll be back on intravenous. Do you know anything that might spark the old Joey?"

"Believe me, if I did, I would have done it already." Seeing Rudy and Philo getting off the elevator, Mrs. Slunisky continued, "Maybe these two will make a difference."

"Hi, Mrs. Slunisky," said Rudy. "How's Joey?"

Crimping her lips together, Mrs. Slunisky sighed. "He's not doing very well. He won't drink, he won't eat, and he won't talk. Why don't you see if you can do something to cheer him up?"

"That shouldn't be too hard. We'll have him up and running around the room before we leave."

Walking toward Joey's room, Philo said, "This sure doesn't sound like Joey."

"No, it doesn't," agreed Rudy.

When they entered the room, Rudy and Philo were not prepared for what they saw. Their closest friend, who was always upbeat and smiling, lay in bed, expressionless. Joey stared blankly into space, causing Rudy to stammer, "Hey … hey, man, how are you feeling?"

No response, not even a twitch.

For the next several minutes, Rudy and Philo tried saying and doing things to cheer Joey up. But each comment or antic was never acknowledged. Finally, Rudy snapped, "What the hell's wrong with you, man!"

Staring at the ceiling, Joey shot back, "Do you want to know what's wrong with me? I'll tell you what's wrong with me! Half my neck and shoulder were cut out, I can't move my arm, and I feel like a damn freak! That's what's wrong with me! Now why don't you get the hell out of here and leave me alone!"

His teeth clenched, Rudy let out a low guttural growl. "Okay, man, we'll leave you alone. But let me tell you something before we go. I never expected to hear that crap come out of your mouth."

"You don't know—"

"Shut up, and let me finish! Sure, I don't know what you're going through 'cause I've never been sick. But since you've come down with this junk, I've been reading about other people who have had cancer. Some of them were a whole lot worse off than you. Today a lot of those people own their own businesses, and some went onto college and have successful careers. Do you know the difference between them and you?" Rudy walked over to Joey's bed and shot an index finger into his face. "They didn't feel sorry for themselves." Rudy glared at Joey for several seconds. "You're pathetic."

Mrs. Slunisky and Mrs. Schwartz were walking toward Joey's room when Rudy and Philo came out. "What happened?" asked Mrs. Slunisky.

Biting the inside of his cheek, Rudy looked into Mrs. Slunisky's eyes. "I guess I lost my cool. I'm sorry. I probably said some things I shouldn't have said.... You're right. I've never seen him like this either."

"Please don't take whatever Joey said personal. He's not himself."

"Mrs. Slunisky, you should know us better than that by now. We're not going to abandon him over a few stupid words. We'll be back tomorrow."

Mrs. Slunisky reached up and hugged them. "God bless you both. You're really special friends."

"I'll second that statement," said Mrs. Schwartz. "You know, Rudy, you're not so bad after all."

His eyes twinkling and the Cheshire grin returning to his face, Rudy replied, "Thanks, Mrs. Schwartz. You really made me feel better … I think. See you tomorrow."

Mrs. Slunisky walked into Joey's room and sat down. For twenty minutes, he didn't acknowledge her presence in the room. Finally, Joey asked, "Mom, my lips are dry. Can you wet them?"

Giving him a glass of water, Joey only took enough water to barely wet his lips. Keeping the glass close to his mouth, she said, "Why don't you try to drink some more?"

"No, I don't want anymore."

The scene repeated itself several times during the next few hours. Joey would ask to have his lips moistened, and Mrs. Slunisky would plead with him to drink more. It was almost ten o'clock when Joey said, "Mom, can you wet my lips?"

Holding the glass to his mouth, she said, "Please, Joey, try to drink more. Your body needs fluids."

"Don't tell me what my body needs! I don't want to drink anymore. Understand?"

Shifting her eyes from her son to the floor, Mrs. Slunisky bit her bottom lip. Sighing deeply, she said, "If you want your lips wetted, do it yourself!" She slammed the glass down on the tray table, turned, and walked out of the room.

Staring at the ceiling, Joey listened to the rhythmic *toosh woosh* sound of the pump. The longer he lay there, the guiltier he felt. "I'm a real jerk," he thought. "I've verbally slammed the closest people in my life. They were trying to help me, and I drove them away. I gotta get out of bed."

Each time Joey tried to raise himself up, his head would tilt backward and prevent him from sitting up. Holding the back of his head with his right hand, Joey pushed and supported the back of his head and sat up. Waiting for the dizziness to pass, Joey pulled each tube from the pump and holding them, he slid out of bed. Joey slowly walked out into the hallway. He saw his mother talking with Mrs. Schwartz at the nurses' station and made his way toward them.

Both ladies were speechless. A weak smile forming on his face, Joey said, "Mom, I'm sorry for how I acted. Can I have some ginger ale?"

"Now you're talking!" exclaimed Mrs. Schwartz, her voice reverberating up and down the hall.

As Mrs. Schwartz hurried to get the ginger ale, Joey looked at his mother. Seeing the relieved look on her face made him feel better.

After a moment, Mrs. Schwartz came back with the can of ginger ale. "We need to get you back to your room and hook you up," she said. "You're leaking all over the floor."

Looking at the tubes in his hand, Joey saw the pale yellow fluid oozing from the ends of the tubes and dripping on the floor. "Sorry about that."

"Honey, right now, I wouldn't mind if you leaked all over the hospital!" Handing the ginger ale to Mrs. Slunisky, Mrs. Schwartz put her arm around Joey. "Let's get you back to your room anyway."

Joey's changed attitude began to speed up the healing process. He didn't need the intravenous bottle, and within days, the pain began to subside. It was Friday afternoon, and Mrs. Slunisky, Cheryl Lynn, Aunt Helen, and Dot were visiting Joey. After the dark nights of surgery, pain, and medication, the sun shining through the window created an effervescence in the room.

Holding the back of his head, Joey sat up and said, "Ya know something? I feel really raunchy."

Her face turning ashen, Mrs. Slunisky said, "What's wrong? Does something hurt?"

"No, Mom. I meant I'd give anything to be able to take a shower."

"You can't do that in your condition," said Cheryl Lynn.

Rubbing her chin, Dot said, "I think I can help. I'll be right back."

A few minutes later, Dot came back into the room with a big smile on her face.

"Where did you go?" asked Cheryl Lynn.

"I talked with the nurse and told her about Joey's request. And I asked her if we could give him a bath if we keep his bandages dry."

Joey's face turned as red as a tomato. "You what?"

A minx smile coming to her face, Dot said, "Don't worry. We're just going to wash your hair, face, chest, and back. I think you'll feel a whole lot better after that."

Relieved at hearing the details and looking forward to the pampering, Joey said, "Okay, let's get started."

Mrs. Slunisky watched as Dot carefully washed Joey's hair. Her mind reflected back to the horror of the past few days. Resting her head back, she silently prayed, "Thank you, dear Lord, for bringing my son back to me." ✦

STEVEN J. DEKANICH

Chapter 7

Am I going to die?

Realizing his attitude influenced his mental state as well as that of his friends and relatives, Joey subconsciously put on a positive mask. Wearing this mask helped him cope with the fact that his left arm refused to work properly. His fingers would move erratically, but unaided, he could not lift his arm from his side. When he was alone, he would use his right hand to grab his left wrist and lift the arm above his head. When he opened his hand, his arm would flop down to his side like a rag doll's arm attached only by a few threads. Hundreds of times during the day and night, he would lift the arm and let it go, and hundreds of times, the arm fell loosely to his side.

It was Monday afternoon before lunch when Joey decided to try something different. *What if I hold the arm as high as my shoulder?* Grasping his wrist, Joey lifted the arm to shoulder height and let it go. Once again, it flopped lifelessly to his side. But something felt different. Joey grabbed his wrist and lifted the arm again. Instead of immediately dropping it, he tightened the muscles in his back. Pivoting at his waist, Joey leaned back and let go of his wrist. For one second, the arm stayed up.

"All right!" exclaimed Joey. "Wait until Dr. Sabbs sees this!"

A boxer smelling victory couldn't have attacked his opponent as quickly as Joey did. Again, he grabbed his left wrist and raised his arm to shoulder height. Looking like he was supporting a hundred-pound weight with his left hand, he leaned back as far as he could, tensed the muscles in his back and chest until sharp pains shot through his neck, and let the wrist go. He fought to keep it suspended. "Thousand one, thousand two, thousand three..." The arm began its slow descent. He leaned farther back but couldn't stop it from flopping to his side. Exhausted, Joey sat on the edge of the bed breathing as if he had run a hundred-yard dash.

Her long silky black hair was the first thing Joey saw. Exhaustion turning to exuberance, Joey exclaimed, "Kathy! Watch this!"

Jumping up, Joey accidentally popped a tube loose from the peristaltic pump. "Oh, crud," he said as the tube swung from the pump and emptied its contents on the floor.

Setting his food tray on the tray table, Kathy said, "That's okay. Let me get you hooked back up, and I'll wipe the floor."

Joey admired her as she quickly reconnected the tube to the pump. Grabbing several tissues, she bent down at the knees and wiped up the sticky yellow fluid. Tossing the tissues in the garbage, Kathy froze for a moment as her eyes met Joey's. Blushing, she said, "What did you want to show me?"

Speechless for several seconds, Joey eventually refocused on what he had been doing before Kathy came in. "Oh … yeah. Hold my left wrist."

Feeling her soft palm around his wrist, Joey was suddenly aware of his heart pounding. For a moment, he was unable to form words.

"I'm holding your wrist. What should I do now?"

Trying to concentrate, Joey closed his eyes. "Lift my arm up to shoulder height." Feeling his arm move, Joey opened his eyes and stared at his left hand. Tensing his muscles, Joey leaned back and said, "Let go of my wrist and step back."

Kathy opened her hand and stepped back.

Straining with all his might, the arm stayed up for one second … two seconds … three seconds … four seconds … but struggle as he would, the arm began its slow descent to his side. Red-faced and exhausted, he looked at Kathy. His heavy breathing muffling the words, he asked, "What do you think?"

"Joey, that's wonderful!" Kathy exclaimed. "How long have you been able to do that?"

"The last half hour. Isn't it great? Ya know, my mother told me that I had people praying for me everywhere, and I believe that's why I'm able to do this right now."

Cupping his right hand between her hands, Kathy gazed into Joey's eyes. "I'm glad you feel that way. The power of prayer is an awesome thing, and if you continue to believe that, you'll be amazed by what can happen."

"It's been the prayers and something else that has helped me."

"What's that?"

"It's been people like you, my family, my friends, and the rest of the hospital staff who pulled me through this. Everyone has made me feel I can overcome this, and it makes me want to try harder. When I held my arm up just now, that was the longest that I have been able to keep it up. I did it because you were here. Thank you."

A radiant smile spread across Kathy's face. Gently taking hold of her hand in his palm, Joey slowly pulled Kathy toward him.

"How's my favorite and only brother today?"

Startled, Kathy and Joey jerked their hands away from each other. Joey turned and saw his sister standing in the doorway, a mischievous smile on her face. His face, meanwhile, glowed like a beacon. "I'm doing great," he said.

"I can see that."

"I'll talk to you later," Kathy said. "Enjoy your lunch."

Cheryl Lynn waited for Kathy to leave the room and then said, "Wow, this is a first!

"What's that?"

"My brother gets food and doesn't have it half-wolfed down before the nurse leaves the room. What has distracted my little brother?"

Walking through the door, Mrs. Slunisky asked, "What? What distracted Joey?"

Joey cocked his head toward his sister. "It's not what you think … well, maybe … not totally what you think. Let me show you." Grabbing his left wrist, Joey lifted his arm up to shoulder height. Tensing the muscles in his back, he let the arm go and held it suspended for two seconds.

Her eyes wide, Mrs. Slunisky pressed her hands against her cheeks. "Oh, my God! You can move your arm! How does it feel?"

"When I hold it up, it hurts in my neck and the back of my shoulder—"

"You shouldn't put a strain on your neck."

"Mom, my neck's going to be all right. I figure once I get the muscles built up, the pain should go away. Isn't this great …"

The news of Joey holding up his arm spread like wildfire. On Monday night, a real celebration was planned in the waiting room. After getting it okayed with Mrs. Schwartz, Mrs. Slunisky called Joey's closest friends and told them what she had planned.

Joey sat on the edge of his bed and thought, "It's past seven o'clock, I wonder where everybody is."

STEVEN J. DEKANICH

Mrs. Schwartz appeared in the doorway, pushing a wheelchair. Poker-faced, she said, "Joey, I need to unhook you and take you downstairs for testing."

Frowning, Joey asked, "Why? What's wrong?"

"Young man, I don't have time for your questions."

Joey studied Mrs. Schwartz's face and decided that she was serious, so he didn't say another word.

Plugging the last tube, she said, "Now, I want you to get into the wheelchair."

Perplexed, Joey lowered himself into the wheelchair and wondered, "What's wrong with me?"

After fixing the footrests, Mrs. Schwartz quickly pushed Joey into the hallway.

His nose pointing upward, Joey deeply inhaled. "It smells like someone is making pizza."

Quickening her pace, Mrs. Schwartz snapped, "I don't smell anything."

Wondering what he did to provoke her, Joey sat back in the chair as it sped toward the elevator. Mrs. Schwartz began to slow down, and instead of continuing to the elevator, she abruptly stopped Joey's wheelchair at the waiting room door. Looking inside, Joey saw about twenty close friends and relatives.

"Surprise!" they yelled in unison.

"What the ..." The words freezing in his mouth, Joey turned his whole body to look back at Mrs. Schwartz. "I can't believe you were in on this too. You had me really freaked out. I didn't know what was happening."

Patting his shoulder, Mrs. Schwartz said, "Honey, after what you did to one of my students with that bleeding-all-over-yourself trick, this was the least I could do."

A roar of laughter shook the waiting room. Swaggering over to the wheelchair, Rudy knelt down and picked up the footrests. Standing up, he offered his hand to Joey and popped him out of the chair. "Buddy, we got plenty of pizza here, and no one would let me have a piece until you got here. Are you hungry?"

"I'm starving!" Joey said. "Let's eat!"

During the course of the evening, eight large Bello's pizzas were devoured, the conversation buzzed, and Joey showed everyone how he could keep his arm suspended. All too soon, Mrs. Schwartz appeared in the doorway. "Folks, I really hate to break this up, but visiting hours are over."

Sitting on the floor, Rudy was resting his arms on top of his drawn-up knees. His Cheshire grin not fading, he said, "Mrs. Schwartz, you always seem to have a knack for messing up a good party."

Putting her hands on her hips, Mrs. Schwartz cocked her head. "Oh, I meant for everyone to leave except you. You need to pick up the paper plates and cups and put them into the garbage."

His grin changing to a frown, Rudy said, "Ah … I promised my mother I'd pick up something for her from the store. If I don't leave now, it will be closed."

"And what was that?" asked Rudy's mother.

"His face looking like a squeezed beet, Rudy jumped up and said, "Mom! I forgot you were here.… Ah, Mrs. Schwartz, what did you want me to do?"

After an outburst of laughter by all, Joey walked over to Rudy, reached up, and put his arm around his shoulder. "That's okay, Rudy. We'll take care of it. But you could bring me a double-cheese pepperoni pizza tomorrow."

Looking at Joey from the corner of his eyes, Rudy said, "I would have gotten off cheaper if I'd have kept my mouth shut."

"Yeah, I know. But it's too late for that now."

STEVEN J. DEKANICH

"If it would be anyone else but you, I wouldn't do it. But since your gimp arm is starting to work, a Bello's pizza would probably help."

His arm tightening around Rudy's shoulders, Joey said, "I want to thank you for being what I needed you to be when I needed you to be it."

"I'm not sure I understand how I needed to be what you needed me to be when you needed me to be it. But I'm glad I was able to be what you needed."

Mrs. Schwartz crossed her arms. "What I need you to be right now is gone! Scoot!"

"Yes, ma'am!" said Rudy. Turning to walk out the door, Rudy stopped, looked back at Joey, and gave him a thumbs-up. "Philo and I will be here early tomorrow. We'll share the pizza and your dinner."

"Sounds good."

The last four people to leave were Mrs. Slunisky, Cheryl Lynn, Anthony, and Aunt Helen. "This party was great!" Joey told his mother. "Thank you!"

Easing his Stetson onto his head, Anthony said, "We're just glad to see you back with us and recovering better than anyone expected."

With tears of joy filling her eyes, Mrs. Slunisky said, "God has been good."

"Yes, He has, Mom. Come on. I'll walk you to the elevator."

After hooking Joey back up to the pump, Mrs. Schwartz observed, "This unit isn't drawing much fluid anymore. I'll check with Dr. Sabbs and see if we can get you off this thing in the morning."

"That sounds great!"

"I'm glad everything is working out for you."

Holding the back of his head, Joey eased himself back on the pillow. He waited for Mrs. Schwartz to pull up the bed rails, then looked at her and said, "Me too. Hey, thanks for tonight."

"My pleasure. Good night."

It was almost eleven o'clock when stabbing pains shot through Joey's hands and feet. Desperately trying to turn on the light, Joey couldn't get his right hand to work. From the dim glow of the nightlight, Joey was horrified when he looked at his right hand. The thumb was being pulled and pushed into the palm of his hand while his four fingers grotesquely wrapped themselves around it. Struggling to force his hand open, Joey attempted to straighten it out. His thumb and fingers were extended poker-straight, but his palm was still folded in half. When he tried relaxing his hand, the thumb immediately was drawn into his palm, and the fingers wrapped around it like a reptile trying to squeeze the life out of its prey. A charley horse couldn't come close to describing the excruciating pain Joey felt in his feet. The balls of his feet were being drawn to his heels, and the muscles in his calves knotted into hard lumps under his skin. A giant invisible claw began to wad Joey up into a ball and ruthlessly squeezed the breath out of his heaving lungs. His eyes wild with fear, Joey wondered, "Am I going to die?" Each time he tried to straighten up to ring for a nurse, the claw would wrench him back into a ball and punish him for trying to escape. Almost losing consciousness from the pain, Joey somehow managed to try again. Using every ounce of strength and determination left in his body, Joey forced his right arm from his side and began to straighten it out. Forcing his fingers open, he lunged for the nurses' call button. With no finger dexterity, luckily he was able to depress the call button. The person who responded sounded like a voice from heaven. "May I help you?"

STEVEN J. DEKANICH

Convulsive pain shooting through his whole body, Joey mumbled, "I need help."

"What was that?"

As the air rushed out of his lungs, the claw crumpled him back into a distorted ball of flesh and bone. Suddenly, the lights in the room came on, and Mrs. Schwartz and another nurse were at his side, ripping the bed covers away. Mrs. Schwartz was horrified to see Joey's twisted body. "Joey, what's wrong?"

Joey's vision was so blurry that he could barely focus on the two figures at his bedside. Breathing rapidly, he gasped, "I … I don't know. Oh, God, it hurts!"

Turning to the other nurse, Mrs. Schwartz said, "Carolyn, stay with him and make sure he doesn't hurt himself while I call Dr. Sabbs."

Within minutes, Mrs. Schwartz was back in the room with two syringes. Under Dr. Sabbs' orders, she was instructed to give Joey two injections, one to calm him and the other to replace the calcium that his body lost. About five minutes after the injections, the pain subsided. Wiping the sweat from his forehead with a facecloth, Mrs. Schwartz said, "You gave us quiet a scare, young man."

Joey's heavy breathing made his words difficult to understand. "What happened? I never felt anything like that before."

Easing the cloth from his forehead to his cheeks, Mrs. Schwartz said, "What you just experienced was a severe case of tetany."

Unsuccessfully trying to take a deep breath, Joey asked, "What's tetany?"

Turning the facecloth over, Mrs. Schwartz laid the cool side down on Joey's forehead. "Basically, it's due to a lack of calcium in your body. Now try to rest."

Mrs. Schwartz covered Joey and waited until he was sleeping soundly before she left his side.

Easing the door closed, Mrs. Schwartz walked toward the nurses' station. Mrs. Patterson, the night shift charge nurse, saw her coming and said, "Pulling some unscheduled overtime tonight?"

Looking at her watch for the first time since the incident, Mrs. Schwartz said, "Oh, my gosh! It's almost one o'clock in the morning! I didn't realize it was that late. When Joey was going through the tetany, my only concern was for him."

"I know," said Mrs. Patterson. "Carolyn Jones told me how quickly you responded to Joey's situation."

Pressing her lips together, Mrs. Schwartz shook her head. "You know, Madge, I hope I'm wrong, but right now it doesn't look good for Joey."

Joey slept through the night and never heard Kathy come into his room. Gently easing his shoulder back and forth, she said, "Joey, it's time to wake up. How do you feel?"

Slowly opening his eyes, he said, "Oh, man. It feels like I've been hit by a train. Everything hurts."

"With the muscle spasms you went through last night, it's understandable why you feel like you do."

"Kathy, what happened to me last night?"

"I'm really not qualified to say. Dr. Sabbs has you scheduled for some blood tests this morning."

"Come on, Kathy. What's wrong with me?"

Sighing deeply, she looked at Joey and said, "I could get in a lot of trouble for this. But it looks like—"

Holding the back of his neck, Joey sat up. "Wait! Don't tell me. You're the last person that I want to get into trouble. I'll wait for Dr. Sabbs."

STEVEN J. DEKANICH

A smile formed at the edges of Kathy's lips. She leaned over and kissed Joey on the cheek. "Thank you."

Looking deeply into her eyes, Joey felt no pain. "Kathy, I—"

The sound of test tubes clinking stopped Joey's words. Checking his order and his ID bracelet, the technician said, "Mr. Slunisky, I need to get some blood."

Kathy smiled at Joey. "I'll see you later."

Joey watched her walk out of the room before he said, "Okay."

The technician had just finished drawing the blood when Mrs. Slunisky and Cheryl Lynn walked into the room. Cheryl Lynn asked, "How do you feel?"

Not waiting for Joey to answer, Mrs. Slunisky said, "We heard what happened last night."

Joey shook his head and held his stomach. "Mom, I thought I had a high pain threshold, but I never experienced anything like last night. Have you talked with Dr. Sabbs?"

"I talked with him early this morning. He said he was ordering a series of tests for you and would get with us after he analyzed the results."

Dr. Sabbs came into Joey's room about three-thirty that afternoon and was met with anxious faces. He walked over to Joey and sat on the corner of his bed. "How are you feeling?" he asked.

"It feels like I just finished the first day of summer football camp. What happened to me last night?"

"Joey, what happened to you is called hypoparathyroidism. The calcium level in your blood fell below a normal level and caused severe muscle spasms known as tetany."

"Is it like tetanus?" asked Cheryl Lynn.

"From a muscle spasm standpoint, it is similar," said Sabbs, turning his head toward Cheryl Lynn. "However, tetanus is caused by certain bacteria. In Joey's case, it is caused by the parathyroid glands malfunctioning." Looking back at Joey, he continued, "During the last operation, I left two of the parathyroid glands intact. They appeared normal, and I had hoped they would be able to keep your body supplied with calcium. The test results show the glands are not functioning, and I hate to say this, Joey, but they must come out."

Frowning, Joey asked, "You mean I have to have surgery?"

Sabbs nodded. "Yes, Joey, that's correct. I'm sorry, but we have no other choice. You're scheduled for surgery first thing in the morning."

Stunned, Mrs. Slunisky's mouth fell open. Struggling, she was able to ask, "If the glands aren't working, what harm would it be if we left them where they are?"

"It's a guarantee that infection would set in and a good possibility the cancer would regenerate itself in that area. I know this is not easy to accept, and I'm sorry, but the operation must be done."

Staring at his blankets, Joey mumbled, "I thought I would be going home soon."

Squeezing Joey's shoulder, Sabbs said, "Let's get over this hurdle, and then we'll talk about you going home."

It was quiet for several seconds. Suddenly, Joey slammed his fist on the tray table sending his water glass and pitcher crashing to the floor. He glared at Sabbs and shouted, "I was beginning to feel good. I thought I was going home soon. It's just not fair!"

Standing up from the edge of the bed, a stone-faced Dr. Sabbs said, "That's right. It's not fair. But who said life is fair and will always be a bed of roses? That is not and never will be the case. Every living person suffers each day of his life. The difference is those who complain about it seem to create their own living hell in their minds. But the other kind of people, even though they may be hurting just as bad if not worse than the complainer, move on with their lives."

　　　　　　　STEVEN J. DEKANICH

The news of Joey's situation shocked everyone. Mrs. Slunisky's and Cheryl Lynn's phone seemed to ring constantly with the same questions being asked: "He seemed to be doing so well. What happened? Is there anything we can do?"

The response to the latter question was always the same: "Pray."

That evening, Joey had his usual gathering of visitors. Dr. Sabbs walked into the room. After nodding hello to Joey, he turned to the others. "I'm going to do the prep for Joey's surgery tomorrow. If everyone would please step out until we're finished, I would appreciate it."

When he and Joey were alone, Sabbs efficiently began the prep work. Unhooking the last tube from the pump, he said, "Joey, this operation won't be as severe as the last. You shouldn't have any problems recovering."

"And if I do?"

Physically, you're not going to be affected any more than you have been. No additional muscle tissue will be removed—only your two remaining parathyroid glands."

"Oh, great! So my body's going to freak out for the rest of my life because of the lack of calcium?"

"Joey, we have medication to keep you from … freaking out. Let me tell you something, young man, I don't know if you realize it, but you're a walking, talking miracle."

"What do you mean?"

"Remember when I told you about the possibilities of losing the movement in your arm and losing your voice? Because of people praying and pulling for you, and because of your own attitude, you beat the odds. Think of this next operation as … like the tackle you missed in last year's Greenville game."

"How did you know about that?"

"My nephew played in that game. He was the one who sidestepped you."

"How can I forget? I made a fool of myself in front of two thousand people."

"But you came back and intercepted a pass at a very critical time in that game."

"What are you leading up to?"

"Joey, what you're going through now is a temporary setback, like the missed tackle. You didn't dwell on that incident and came back to make a key play in the game. Decide in your mind that you're going to turn this setback into a comeback."

"Do you really think I can?"

"Joey, if I didn't believe it, I wouldn't be saying it."

Nothing more was said while Sabbs carefully cut away the heavy bandage around Joey's neck. Joey felt as if a thousand pounds were removed from his neck the moment Sabbs lifted the "horse collar" away from his shoulders. Using a strong-smelling antiseptic solution, Sabbs expertly cleaned Joey's neck and shoulders and carefully shaved the area to be operated on. Preparing to put on a fresh bandage, Sabbs said, "Everything looks good. You're healing quickly."

"Would you mind if I looked in a mirror?"

Reaching for the mirror in the compartment of Joey's tray table, Dr. Sabbs said, "Of course not."

The initial sight stunned Joey. The hole in his left shoulder was deep enough to fit two fists. Half of his neck was gone. The exposed carotid artery pulsed just below his skin, and his trachea was vividly outlined by the skin. Staring into the mirror, he thought, "I look like a cadaver with half a neck."

STEVEN J. DEKANICH

Sabbs broke Joey's trance. "It's not as bad as it looks. With time, people won't even notice."

"That's hard for me to believe," said Joey as he refocused on his neck.

What was left of the neck was stained a brownish green from the original prep material. The neatly sewn stitches traversed from the back of his left ear, down the full length of his neck, across his left shoulder, and partially across his right shoulder. Five hideous drain tubes dangled grotesquely from the sutured areas on his neck and shoulder. Nausea drained the color from his face as he stared at the stained pale yellow tubes sticking out of his neck. Closing his eyes, Joey took several breaths and said, "I hope you're right. Because right now, all I need is a couple of bolts in my head, and I could star in a horror film."

Putting on the fresh bandage, Dr. Sabbs said, "I'll talk to someone about getting you a film contract but only if I get a share of the royalties."

Glad the mirror was put away and his neck was once again covered, Joey smiled and said, "Deal."

After Joey's visitors left, Mrs. Schwartz walked into his room with a syringe. His eyes fixed on the needle, Joey asked, "Why am I getting a shot now? I'm not getting operated on until morning."

"This is another calcium shot. We don't want you to freak out on the operating table tomorrow morning. This is easy. It goes in your arm."

Obediently extending his arm, Joey said, "I won't argue with that. How do you think it will go tomorrow?"

"Joey, Dr. Sabbs is one of the best, if not the best. If I was going to be operated on, I would want him. I don't think you'll have much to worry about. From what you've already been through, tomorrow will be a breeze. Do you need a sleeping pill tonight?"

Holding his head and easing back on the pillow, Joey replied, "No, I think I'll be able to fall asleep."

Mrs. Schwartz walked toward the door and reached for the light switch. Before flicking it off, she turned back to Joey and said, "Try not to bleed all over yourself tonight. All right?"

Gripping the blankets with both hands, Joey used his right hand to pull the covers over his shoulders. Opening and closing his left hand several times, he smiled and said, "Okay, I'll be good tonight." ✦

STEVEN J. DEKANICH

Chapter 8

God has a definite plan and purpose for your life.

As if there was such a thing as reruns in life, the morning started as it had several weeks before. About 4:30 a.m., Joey could hear the sound of bottles clinking and feet shuffling. A gentle hand tapped him on the shoulder, and a soft voice said, "Mr. Slunisky, I need to get some blood."

Joey reluctantly opened his eyes. Putting his right hand behind his neck, Joey slowly sat up and yawned. Clearing his throat as the technician rolled up his sleeve, he said, "I'll bet I was the first person on your list."

Clamping the tourniquet on Joey's arm, the technician said, "How did you know that?"

"Lucky guess."

After the technician finished, she put on a compression bandage and said, "Now that you're awake, you can go back to sleep."

The corners of his mouth turning upward, Joey said, "Thanks a lot."

It seemed like his eyes had just closed when an unfamiliar nurse awakened him. "Mr. Slunisky, it's time to get up and get washed."

As the nurse unplugged Joey from the pump, he asked, "What time is it?"

Plugging the tube she had just removed from the pump, she looked at her watch and said, "Five o'clock."

Joey rolled over in bed and thought, "Why do they always schedule these things at such ungodly hours?"

His eyes gradually closing, Joey felt a tingling sweet slumber capture his body as he slipped into peaceful oblivion. Suddenly, he was jarred back to full consciousness. "Young man, don't you go to sleep! I need to get you washed and into this gown."

The gown! That infernal piece of clothing whose sole purpose apparently was to humiliate its helpless victims! The sleep disappearing from his eyes, Joey looked at the nurse's nametag and said, "Mrs. Hall, I've been washing myself for the last few days. If you fill the pan with water, I can get washed and put the gown on."

Nodding, Mrs. Hall filled the pan with water and placed it on the tray table. She dipped a facecloth into the warm water, wrung it out, and handed it to Joey. "If you need any help, let me know."

After washing himself, Joey faced the humiliating garment on his bed. Opening it up from the back, he put his right hand through the ample right armhole. Grabbing the left sleeve, he guided it up his left arm until it reached his shoulder. Try as he may, he couldn't tie the short ties together behind his neck. Pulling on his pajama bottoms, he went in search of Mrs. Hall. He found her in the hallway and asked, "Would you mind tying this?"

Tying the flimsy ties around his neck and waist, Mrs. Hall said, "I thought you said you could handle this."

Joey shrugged his shoulders and turned his head to the left as far as the horse collar would allow. "Guess I was wrong. Remember—it takes a real man to admit that he's wrong."

Watching Joey walk back to his room, Mrs. Hall called out, "Your pants need to come off also. Do you need any help with them?"

Quickening his pace and not turning around, Joey said, "No, I can manage."

At six o'clock, while Joey was talking with his mom, Cheryl Lynn, and Anthony, Mrs. Hall walked into the room and said, "There's been a slip in the schedule this morning, and you won't be going down until eight-fifteen."

Raising his eyebrows, Joey said, "I could have slept at least another hour!"

"That's right, but instead you can visit with your family until it's time to go down."

Mrs. Hall turned to Joey's relatives and asked, "Would any of you like coffee or tea?"

"I'll have some tea, bacon, eggs, toast, and orange juice please."

Shaking her head, Mrs. Hall replied, "Joey, you know you can't have anything until your operation is over."

Joey shrugged his shoulders. "Just thought I'd ask."

Joey and Anthony were discussing a hunting trip when his door burst open. A frantic student nurse came in wielding a syringe. Joey's eyes grew twice their normal size as he asked, "What's wrong?"

Visibly shaken, she blurted out, "I got tied up! You should have had this injection at seven o'clock, and it's past seven-thirty! Oh, God, I'm going to get into trouble!"

The young woman's hands shook while she filled the syringe. With all of her words running together into a barely discernible phrase, she said, "Okay, roll over on your side!"

Holding up his hand and looking at her nametag, Joey said, "Patsy! Wait a minute. Calm down a little before you stick that instrument of pain into my body. This stuff works pretty fast on me, and I'm sure there's plenty of time for me to get relaxed."

Taking a deep breath and exhaling, Patsy said, "I guess I didn't act very professional just now, did I?"

"You were just stressed out. I think it takes a lot of tense moments and experiences to become a good nurse. You're going to do great. Now, let's start over."

Managing to calm down, Patsy checked Joey's ID bracelet and smiled. "Good morning, Mr. Slunisky. I have something here to relax you before you go to surgery. Please roll over on your side." After giving Joey the injection, she leaned over and kissed him on the cheek. "Kathy said you were special," she whispered. "Thanks for the kind words, and good luck."

Waiting for Patsy to close the door, Anthony said, "You really handled that situation well."

"I had to, or else I'd have been stuck twenty times or that needle would have broken off in my butt."

"My brother is a smooth talker," Cheryl Lynn said with a grin.

Looking at his sister, Joey continued, "That may be, but I meant every word. After some of the things I've seen nurses and student nurses put up with, it amazes me how they are still willing to put in the extra effort to help. In my book, these people are worth their weight in gold."

Five minutes after eight, the rattling of a gurney caught Joey's attention. The same orderlies who picked him up for his last operation walked into the room. Joey's heart began to pound as one orderly checked Joey's bracelet and said, "We're here to take you to surgery."

The apprehensive look on Joey's face concerned Mrs. Slunisky. She smiled at the orderly and said, "Let me talk with him."

"Sure."

Squeezing her son's hand, Mrs. Slunisky said in a voice that Joey could barely hear, "Son, I know you'll be all right. God has a definite plan and purpose for your life, and He's not going to let anything happen to you."

The touch of his mother's hand and her calm voice alleviated the nerves that were tying Joey's stomach into knots. With the help of the orderlies, Joey scooted onto the gurney. As they were strapping him down, Joey said, "Dr. Sabbs said this shouldn't be very rough."

No other words were spoken as the orderlies pushed Joey's gurney to the elevator. The lead orderly was about to press the down button when the elevator doors opened, and Aunt Helen rushed out. She dashed past everyone and headed for Joey's room.

Joey called out, "Aunt Helen, we're over here."

Stopping dead in her tracks, Aunt Helen turned her head and saw everyone smiling at her. Her cheeks blushing and her shoulders bouncing as she chuckled, she walked back to the group. With embarrassment still showing on her cheeks, she said, "When I couldn't get my car started this morning, all I could think of was not being here when you went down for surgery. I was so wrapped up in that thought that I didn't see you as I rushed by. What are you still doing here?"

"There was a slip in the operating schedule."

"I'm glad because I wanted to wish you well before you went down."

"Thanks. I'm glad I got to see you too."

The gurney began to move, and the lead orderly said, "Okay, folks, he needs to go now." Before the doors closed, Joey heard Anthony say, "We'll see you in a couple of hours, sport." ✦

STEVEN J. DEKANICH

Chapter 9

Thanks for being there when I needed you.

Staring at the elevator ceiling, Joey was lost in thought when the elevator came to a halt. As the doors opened, he remembered seeing Dr. Braun in this area and reflected on a conversation that his mother had with one of her close friends. "Margo, you should sue that quack for malpractice."

"The thought did cross my mind. But then I started thinking about all of the times he helped my family. I don't know how many times he came to our house when Joey was sick. When Joey had scarlet fever, he was running a temperature between 103 and 105. Dr. Braun came to our home in the middle of the night and was able to break the fever. I could have lost Joey then, but that man saved his life. I'll admit, at first, I was very angry with him and wanted to hurt him for what happened to Joey. I'll never take Joey to him again, but I started thinking what he has done for us in the past and realized that he wouldn't do this intentionally. He's only human, and sometimes people make mistakes."

"But look at all the suffering Joey has gone through."

"That's true. He has suffered, but he was also suffering before, and Dr. Braun helped him. Am I supposed to forget all that and go for a quick buck? I don't think so. I'm a firm believer in what you do will come back to you. Usually a hundredfold."

"My mother may have her ways about her, but she has a pretty good philosophy," thought Joey. A slight bump made Joey take his eyes off the ceiling. Lifting his head to look over his chest, Joey said under his breath, "I'm in line already."

"Yes, you are," said an unknown nurse in green scrubs. "Let's check your bracelet to make sure you haven't changed your identity. Yep, it looks like you are who you're supposed to be."

"Who did you expect?"

"Well, you're not the only person getting operated on this morning. One of the operations is a vasectomy. I don't think you'd want us to get you mixed up with someone else, would you?"

Joey's eyes widened. "No, I don't think so."

Smiling, she patted Joey's shoulder. "I didn't think you would. You'll be going in a few minutes."

Soft cobwebs filled Joey's mind, and his body tingled as sweet slumber enveloped him. Suddenly, the gurney scooted forward, and Joey was shocked out of his sleep. Crimping his lips together, Joey thought, "It's amazing the timing some people have." Joey's feet felt the temperature change first as the gurney was wheeled into the operating room. "Don't they ever turn the heat on in here?" he mumbled.

"No, and I wish they would," said the same nurse who helped him off the gurney during his last visit to the operating room. Taking his hand and double-checking the bracelet, she said, "How are you feeling?"

"No offense, but I'd rather be somewhere else right now."

STEVEN J. DEKANICH

Squeezing his hand, she said, "Compared to your last go-around down here, you'll be out in no time. I'll bet your relaxing shot didn't have much of an effect on you, did it?"

Glassy-eyed, Joey shook his head no.

"Okay, we're still going to help you slide on the table, and this time, we'll make sure your gown doesn't open in the back."

Joey held his breath as he was expertly whisked to the operating table. Once in place, Joey exhaled deeply.

"There. That wasn't so bad, was it?" said the nurse as she prepared the IV.

"No, I guess not."

"Good morning, Joey," said Dr. Sabbs. "Ready for the next hurdle?"

"Ready as I'll ever be. Thank you for the encouraging words last night. They meant a lot to me."

"I meant every word, Joey. If anyone can beat this thing, you can."

An unfamiliar voice said, "Good morning, Mr. Slunisky. I'm Dr. Pratt, and I'll be administering your anesthetic this morning."

Frowning, Joey asked, "Where's Dr. Yeng?"

Inserting the syringe into Joey's IV, Dr. Pratt said, "He was called out on an emergency, and I'll be taking his place." He slowly injected the thiopental sodium. "Okay, Mr. Slunisky, count backward from one hundred."

Still frowning, Joey demanded, "Why? I didn't have to do that before."

His bushy eyebrows lowering and almost covering his eyelids, Pratt said, "Well, you'll need to do it now."

"Why? I ..."

"Joey," said Dr. Sabbs, "try counting backwards from one hundred. I'll bet you don't make it to ninety five."

"Okay. One hundred, ninety ... nine, nimmm ... eig, ni ..."

Total blackness. Suddenly, a feeling of comfort and serenity surrounded his body like a fragile gossamer veil. He could hear something off in the distance. At first, the veil would not allow the sounds to be understood, and Joey was able to stay in his own private comfortable world. Then the words began to punch holes in the veil. "Joey, it's time to wake up. Joey, the operation is over. It's time for you to wake up. Can you hear me, Joey?" After shredding the veil, the words removed it from his mind, and Joey opened his eyes.

Seeing the glimmer in the nurse's eyes and the smile on her face, Joey knew the operation was over and everything was all right.

It was Wednesday morning, and a freezing rain had just started. His right arm leaning against the wall next to the window, Joey rested his head on his right wrist and thought, "I wonder what it would be like in a duck blind right now." Suddenly, the window began to creak, and he could feel a cold draft as gale force winds tried to remove the window from its frame. Stepping back from the window, Joey thought, "On second thought, I'm glad I'm not in a duck blind right now." Mesmerized by the sleeting rain, Joey didn't hear Dr. Sabbs walk in.

"Good morning Joey. It looks like you're doing well today."

Startled by Sabbs' voice, Joey quickly turned from the window. Smiling, he replied, "Yes, sir. I feel great! When can I get out of here? I've been here a month."

"From the looks of your charts, everything seems to be coming along fairly well. You've been off the suction unit for three days now, and I don't see any indications of infection. I'm going to take off your large bandage and—"

"You mean I can get out of this horse collar?"

With a chuckle, Sabbs replied, "Yes, Joey. You'll have something less cumbersome. Now, let's see what I can do about getting this thing off you and getting some of the stitches out."

Not wanting to look at his neck after the sutures were removed, Joey let Sabbs put on the smaller bandage. The lighter bandage was a relief until Joey looked in the mirror. Frowning, he saw his head resting on his left shoulder. Concentrating on straightening his head, Joey brought it to the vertical, but it was very unstable, and when he would relax, it would flop back on his left shoulder.

Walking to the corner of the room, Sabbs watched Joey but didn't say anything.

The whites of his eyes showing, Joey's breath became rapid and shallow. "I ... I can't hold my head up straight. I can concentrate and get it up straight, but as soon as I relax, it flops over. What happened? It didn't do this before."

"Joey, the heavy bandage provided much more support than this bandage. That's why you didn't notice anything. The last time I took the bandage off, you were too shocked from the sight of your neck to notice that your head was lying over your shoulder. The muscle removal has resulted in a temporary situation where your head will hang over your shoulder and your left shoulder will droop. You will need to develop new muscles to support your head and keep your shoulder up. This is something you will have to stay constantly aware of to keep everything symmetrical."

Disgusted, Joey studied the miserable image in the mirror. "Why is it that every time I start feeling good, there's something that tries to knock me down?"

"Joey, that's life. I've seen a lot of other people who have been continuously knocked down get back up—"

"Why do you always have to point out what other people have done? I don't care about other people. I'm concerned about me!"

Waiting a few seconds, Dr. Sabbs made eye contact with Joey and softly replied, "I know." After a few more seconds, Sabbs continued, "Joey, there have been a lot of people who have gone through just as severe if not more severe operations than you. Everyone has pity parties, and some never get over them. Others get on with their lives regardless of what challenge faces them. These people make a decision to carve a path for others to follow if they want to. This path shows a person that if others have done it, they can do it too. But self-centered thoughts will not provide the directions you will need to walk down this path."

"Quit philosophizing with me! Okay? Look, all I can see now is that my head won't stay up, my shoulder droops like I'm a hundred years old, and my arm isn't worth anything. Yeah, it's great to be a pathfinder when you're on top of the world, but damn it … look at me!" With tears streaming down his face, he added, "How can you expect me to be anything when I look like this?"

Sabbs walked over to Joey and gripped him by the shoulders. "Joey, look at me. Look at me."

Breathing rapidly and sniffling, Joey reluctantly raised his tear-streaked face to look at Sabbs. His vision blurred through bloodshot eyes, Joey said, "Dr. Sabbs, what am I going to do?"

Tightening his grip, Sabbs said, "You're going to make it. You're going to deal with this, and you're going to make it. Joey, you're a very special person, and you have a lot to offer other people. What you're going through right now is not insurmountable. With time, you'll overcome this situation. As a matter of fact, I'd venture to say there will be a time when people won't even notice that you had surgery on your neck."

Joey's breathing returned to normal. "Do you really think so?"

A faint smile came to Dr. Sabbs' face as he nodded affirmatively. "Son, I know so."

STEVEN J. DEKANICH

Two days later, Joey was wolfing down his breakfast when Dr. Sabbs walked into the room. "Good morning, Joey," he said with a smile. "It's Friday, the sun is shining, and it's a great day for you to go home!"

"What?"

"That's right. Everything seems to be progressing very well, and I see no need for you to stay cooped up here. I called your mother, and she is on her way to pick you up."

"Dr. Sabbs, that's music to my ears! I can't say that I've enjoyed staying here, but I appreciate everything that you and the others have done for me."

Shaking Joey's hand, Sabbs said, "Joey, I can honestly say I have never had a patient quite like you. There aren't a lot of people who have your ability to bounce back in the face of adversity. Everyone has the potential to bounce back, but very few are willing to make the effort like you have done."

His face reddening, Joey said, "Thank you, sir. What restrictions will I have?"

"As far as I'm concerned, you can do anything you want to do if you feel up to it. I've written a prescription for your hypocalcemia. You will be taking dihydrotachysterol, or hytakerol for short."

The smile disappearing from his face, Joey asked, "How long will I have to take the hytakerol?"

Seeing a familiar look of disappointment on Joey's face, Sabbs said, "You'll have to take it for the rest of your life. Does that bother you?"

"Deep down inside ... it does bother me. I can remember growing up and seeing other people who were dependent on medication to live. I viewed that as a sign of weakness. Now ... I'm one of those people."

Nodding his head, Sabbs said, "I know how you feel because I'm a diabetic and rely on medication every day. I'll admit this reliance troubled me for a long time. Then one day in med school, I was sharing my feelings and concerns with a wise old doctor. I can still picture him sitting at his huge desk, pointing his finger at me, and saying, 'Jim, if you think about it, every person on earth is dependent on something. We all need water and food to live. You just need a more highly processed food than other people.' Joey, when he told me that, I started looking at myself differently. Just because a person is dependent on ... let's call it a more highly processed food ... does not mean they are weak. Weakness is only generated through self-pity."

The last words were like a nail being driven into a board. With his eyes fixed on Sabbs, Joey said, "I think I understand. It really all goes back to attitude again, doesn't it?"

Sabbs smiled and nodded his head again. "That's right. We all go through life with hurts, heartaches, wanting, joy, love, and caring. This kaleidoscope of feelings all mesh together to make us who we are. If a person experiences more of one feeling than another, their kaleidoscope of life may be colored in this way. These feelings may be real or only real in a person's mind. But it is their choice as to how their kaleidoscope is going to look to themselves and others."

"What you're telling me is to keep a bright outlook on life no matter what happens, right?"

Sabbs extended his hand to Joey. "I think you've just framed your life's picture. Joey, if you need me for anything, anytime, don't hesitate to call. I gave your mother my home phone number."

Joey firmly gripped Sabbs' hand and then embraced him. "Thank you again for all that you've done for me."

As soon as Sabbs left the room, Joey heard the door open. Like a delicate silk scarf, her raven black hair softly caressed her shoulders as she walked into the room. Unable to speak, Joey allowed himself to get lost in her eyes. Taking Joey's hand, Kathy said, "I heard you're going home today."

The words shattering her spell, Joey looked down at the floor. Taking a deep breath and with a solemn expression on his face, he looked back at Kathy. "Yeah, my mother is on her way as we speak."

"What's going to happen between us?"

Squeezing her hand, Joey said, "I'm going to share something with you that I have never told my family.... Ever since I've had this operation, I've really had trouble accepting the way I look."

"But, Joey, it doesn't matter how you look."

"I know what you're saying, but right now, it's bothering me like you can't believe. I put on a mask when I'm around my friends and relatives and don't let them see what I'm telling you right now. I really feel like a freak. I guess what I'm hoping for is that someday I will accept the mask that my mind keeps imagining. Until then, I just wouldn't feel right going out with you. I hope you understand because you can't believe how hard this is for me to tell you."

Forcing a smile, Kathy said, "That's okay. I can wait."

Hearing the door open, Joey and Kathy released their hands. With a broad smile on her face, Mrs. Slunisky walked into the room and asked, "Are you ready to come home?"

"I'll see you before you leave," Kathy whispered and walked out of the room.

Solemnly, Joey watched Kathy leave. Forcing a grin, he looked at his mother and said, "More than ready, Mom. I've been waiting ages for this moment."

"So have I," his mother said, the smile not leaving her face. "Cheryl Lynn will be up shortly. She's parking the car." Mrs. Slunisky handed Joey a paper grocery bag. "I brought you a pair of your favorite jeans and a sweater."

Taking the bag, Joey said, "Thanks, Mom. I'll be right out."

Joey walked to the bathroom and shut the door behind him. Setting the grocery bag on the sink, he opened it, and the sweet aroma of his mother's laundry detergent filled the room. "Freshly washed clothes!" Joey thought. "I haven't smelled anything this good in a long time!" Getting dressed was easier than he thought it would be. Sighing deeply, he sat on the commode and stared at the wall. Closing his eyes, he reflected on all of the things that happened to him and thanked God for helping him.

A heavy pounding on the door snapped Joey back. "Joey, are you all right in there?"

"Yes, Cheryl Lynn. I'll be right out."

Joey looked in the mirror. *Street clothes at last!* After wearing pajamas or those wretched hospital gowns for more than a month, Joey was energized by the feel of regular clothes next to his body. Turning to leave the bathroom, he looked out of the window and saw the frozen water puddle where the grade school kids played on their way to and from school. He could remember longingly looking at them and wishing he were out of the hospital. "I don't have to wish anymore," he thought. "I'm going home!" The thought brought a smile to his face as he turned and opened the door.

"What were you doing in there so long?" Cheryl Lynn asked.

Handing the empty bag to his mother, Joey said, "I'll never tell."

"Well, smarty, you've got visitors who want to tell you goodbye."

Joey's face reddened as he looked at the doorway to his room and saw the smiling faces of five student nurses.

STEVEN J. DEKANICH

"That's okay," said Kathy. "It seemed like every time we came in here, Joey was in the bathroom, probably trying to hide from us."

After the laughter from Kathy's joke subsided, Patsy said in a soft voice, "We're really going to miss you, Joey, and we want to wish you the very best." All five student nurses surrounded Joey and gave him a group hug.

After making eye contact with each student nurse, Joey focused his eyes on Kathy. "How can I ever thank all of you for what you did for me?"

"Simple," said Patsy. "Take us all out on a date."

"That sounds like a good idea."

"Yes, it does," said Kathy. "In the meantime, we're going to take you for one last ride."

Joey raised his eyebrows. "What do you mean?"

"We've got a wheelchair here for you."

"Wait a minute. I can walk."

"Sorry, Joey," Kathy said. "It's hospital rules."

"I guess it's hard to fight city hall, isn't it? Okay, just don't pull the chair out from under me!"

Turning to Cheryl Lynn, Kathy said, "Bring your car around to the emergency entrance, and we'll be waiting for you there. The rest of you can help Mrs. Slunisky carry the flowers and gifts."

"What are you going to do?" asked Patsy.

"I'm going to wheel Joey down to the emergency entrance."

"I'm going with you," Patsy insisted.

As Kathy effortlessly guided the wheelchair through the hallways, Joey's mind wandered back to the day he came into the hospital. He was in top physical condition and felt like he could conquer the world. His facial expression sobered as his thoughts shifted to the psychological and physical trauma he experienced. "But I made it, and I'm still alive!" he thought. "People praying for me and seeing me as I could be and not as I was kept me going. They didn't let me feel sorry for myself for very long without getting on my case." Putting his head back against the chair, he closed his eyes and thought, "Everybody had an impact on me getting better."

"Isn't that right?" asked Kathy.

Opening his eyes, Joey's face turned crimson. "I'm sorry, Kathy. What did you say?"

"You haven't heard a word I said, have you?"

"If you'll tell me what you said, I'll tell you if I heard it."

Patting his shoulder, Kathy said, "That's okay. It's really not worth repeating."

Joey thought, "I hate it when women do that."

Seeing the irritation on Joey's face, Patsy said, "I'll tell you what we were talking about. We were just saying that we should kidnap you and keep you around as a model patient. Would you mind?"

"The way you all treated me? I'd love it! Here's a hallway we can turn down!"

The nurses smiled as they wheeled Joey through the automatic doors.

Letting his head rest on the back of his shoulders, Joey looked up at Kathy and asked, "Can I stand up now and walk?"

"No. We're going to carry you to the car!" said Kathy as she playfully punched his right shoulder. "Of course you can get up and walk."

Joey hugged each of the nurses one last time and walked toward Cheryl Lynn's car. Stopping a few feet short of the curb, Joey turned and said, "I don't know where I would be right now if it weren't for all of you. I'll never forget you." Joey opened the rear passenger door of the car and got inside.

Closing the door, Kathy exaggerated her mouth movements so that Joey could lip-read her silent words: "Call me."

As Cheryl Lynn pulled out, Joey asked, "Would you mind if I drive?"

Making eye contact with Joey in the rearview mirror, Cheryl Lynn smiled and said, "Just sit back and relax. I'll be your chauffeur today, but don't expect me to do it all the time."

"You have a wonderful way of saying no!"

Although the temperature hovered at thirty degrees, the day was sunny with wisps of clouds scattered through a powder blue sky. *A day that made you happy to be alive!* Longingly looking at the harvested cornfields for a ring-necked pheasant, Joey barely heard Mrs. Slunisky ask, "How are you feeling?"

Still searching the cornfields, Joey said, "I feel good, Mom. I'm glad to be going home."

The thirty-minute drive home seemed to take only a few minutes. Getting out of the car, Joey looked around the yard and took a deep breath. There were several mammoth blue spruce trees growing in the yard close to the driveway, and their sweet aroma seemed to warm the air with the wonderful fragrance. Joey filled his lungs to overflowing and thought, "Thank you, Lord, for this wonderful day!"

Joey turned to get his suitcase from the car when his mother said, "Don't you dare try to pick that up! We'll get it."

"Mom, it's not heavy. I can do it."

"I'm sure you can, but I don't want you to pop any of those stitches."

"But—"

"Don't argue," interrupted Cheryl Lynn. "She knows what she's talking about."

"Okay. I'll just go inside the house then."

Joey could smell it before he opened the kitchen door. With a huge smile on his face, he turned to his mother. "You made chicken soup! When did you have time to do that?"

"Oh, I guess you can find the time to do anything if you want to do it bad enough. I knew you liked chicken soup."

"Especially your noodles."

"I had the noodles already made, so all I had to do was make the soup before leaving to pick you up."

Joey held the door while Mrs. Slunisky and Cheryl Lynn carried Joey's belongings into the house. He stood in the doorway, breathing in and savoring the wonderful scent of slow-cooked chicken soup. Closing the door, Joey asked, "How much longer before it's done?"

"Just a couple of hours. Why don't you lie down until it's ready?"

"I think I'll take you up on that. I do feel a little tuckered out from the drive and all the excitement. Wake me up when dinner is ready." Joey started down the hallway to his bedroom, but then stopped, turned around, and hugged his mother. "Mom, thanks for being there when I needed you." ✦

Chapter 10

Mom, I think you're overreacting.

Joey was glad to be home and in his own bed. But after two weeks, the walls began to close in on him. Monday morning found Joey pacing from room to room like a caged cat. Walking into his bedroom, he looked at the old white windup alarm clock on his dresser. The large hand was on twelve, and the small hand on eleven. "I've got to get out of here," Joey said to himself.

Spreading the heavy curtains that covered the south window of his bedroom, Joey unlocked the window, placed his palm under the sash, and pushed. Under protest, the old swollen wooden frame resisted. Resting for a few seconds, Joey pushed with all his might. The blood rushed to his head, making his face look like it was scalded. The cracking of the window frame made it sound like it was about to break just before the window yielded and slowly inched its way upward. Feeling the window yield gave Joey strength, and he didn't stop pushing on the window until it was fully opened. The burning muscles in his shoulder felt good.

Then suddenly a horrifying thought came into his head: "Am I bleeding?" Rushing to his dresser mirror, Joey quickly pulled down the front of his pullover and checked his scars—no bleeding. Sighing with relief, Joey walked back to the window, leaned out, and took a deep breath. The brisk air filled his lungs. Joey held his breath, closed his eyes, and tilted his head back to capture the morning sun's rays on his face. Exhaling through his mouth, Joey opened his eyes and stared at the crystal blue sky. Looking across the harvested cornfields, Joey saw the bare trees of the forest beckoning to him like friends in the distance. Readily giving in to the silent invitation, Joey decided, "I'm going hunting!" He quickly put on his brush clothes, grabbed his .410 shotgun, wrote a note, and headed off to the forest behind his house.

Knowing his strength and stamina would be lacking, Joey avoided some of his favorite hunting spots. Cradling the shotgun in his left arm, he held his left wrist with his right hand and leisurely walked through the forest. Looking up in the bare oak trees for signs of squirrels, he saw a flock of snow geese flying south. Mesmerized by the sight of the magnificent birds silhouetted against the clear blue sky, Joey was filled to the brim with the peace and tranquility of nature. The gentle swish of the breeze, as it played with the empty branches of the sleeping giants, created a soft, soothing natural symphony that magically relaxed every muscle in Joey's body. Walking over to a large oak, Joey kicked away the dry leaves at the base of the tree and sat down with his back against the tree. "This is perfect," he thought, then closed his eyes and slept a very peaceful sleep.

Joey was awakened by a cold chill that traveled through his body. Opening his eyes, he realized the sun was setting. He looked at his watch and exclaimed, "Crud! It's late! Mom is home from work and will be mad as a hornet." Hopping to his feet, he began the journey home at a pace quicker than he thought he could maintain.

STEVEN J. DEKANICH

With only starlight guiding him across the final field before his mother's home, Joey slowed his pace to make sure he didn't trip. When he walked into the house, his mother was frantic. Fire in her eyes, she demanded, "Where were you?" Not allowing him to answer, she asked, "What were you thinking? Don't you know you could have been hurt? Your stitches could have come apart, and you could have bled to death."

"Mom, I think you're overreacting."

Her eyes growing twice their normal size and her face turning crimson, she said, "Overreacting? Your sister and I have been worried sick over you." Her voice increased in decibels with each word. "All you did was leave a note saying you were going hunting. You didn't say if you were going with anyone, and you didn't say where you would be. And you think I'm overreacting?"

There was a pause, so Joey knew she expected an answer. "Mom, you're absolutely right. I should have told you where I was going, but I didn't think I would have any problems. Besides Dr. Sabbs said—"

"You didn't think shooting a shotgun would give you any problem?"

"Mom, I didn't take my twelve-gauge. I only took my four-ten, which doesn't kick at all. Besides, I'm right-handed, and the gun would have been on my right shoulder, not my left. Anyways, I didn't see anything."

"Where were you for so long?" asked Cheryl Lynn.

"I was just behind the house."

"If you were just behind the house, why didn't you come when we called you?" demanded his mother.

Trying to inch a smile across his face, Joey said, "I fell asleep and woke up when it was almost dark. I never heard you."

Joey's smile melting the fire from her face, Mrs. Slunisky shook a rolling pin at him. "Next time you do something like this, I don't care how sick you are, I'll coldcock you." A slight grin coming to her face, she added, "Look, I know staying in the house is driving you crazy, but if you decide to do this again, please get someone to go with you. It will save my stomach lining."

"I promise I'll never do anything like this again without letting someone know where I'll be."

"Good. Now go and get cleaned up. Dinner is almost ready."

As he walked past Cheryl Lynn, Joey leaned over and whispered, "I was just behind the house—about a half mile away."

Running the wash water into the sink, Joey began to think about what his mother said and realized she was right. Something could have happened to him, and no one would know where he was. He remembered Anthony talking about how people could stay out of trouble with simple lines of communication.

The holidays came with the festiveness of a Dickens classic. Keeping with a Croatian family tradition, Joey's mother always prepared a tremendous amount of food for Christmas, and this year was no different. After Midnight Mass, about thirty friends and relatives stopped by for a late supper. Oh, how they looked forward to a succulent combination of roast turkey and dressing, roast pork with potatoes, ham, soup, sausage, salads, and delectable Croatian desserts.

After everyone gorged themselves, it was time to open gifts. Sitting on the overstuffed sofa, Joey was removing the carefully wrapped paper around one of his gifts when his godfather, Don, walked up and crouched his massive frame down to Joey's eye level. "How are you feeling?" he asked.

STEVEN J. DEKANICH

"I'm feeling pretty well."

"Your mother was saying you were having problems with the tetany."

"It acts up a couple of times a week, but I think I'm getting used to it."

"Just wondering if you'd be up to going rabbit hunting next week?"

Jumping up from the sofa, Joey exclaimed, "I'd love to! I've been itching to get out."

A Santa Claus laugh coming from his lips, Don straightened his six-foot, six-inch frame and wrapped a thick arm around Joey's shoulders. "I'll bet you are. Have you been out since your last hunting episode?"

Catching his breath from the playful python squeeze of Don's arm, Joey replied, "No. Mom got pretty hot about that, so I decided to stay around the house for a while. How did you know?"

"Let's just say the person who told me about it was the same one who said she thought you were ready to get outdoors."

The evening flew by. Aunt Helen looked at her watch and announced, "It's four o'clock in the morning!"

This caused a chain reaction of everyone looking at their watches and saying, "I didn't realize it was so late. We'd better get our things and head home." One by one, each person hugged and thanked Mrs. Slunisky for the wonderful dinner. Her crimson cheeks highlighted by her snow white hair, Mrs. Slunisky smiled. "Oh, it was no trouble at all. I enjoyed doing it."

Within fifteen minutes, only a few people remained in the house. Enjoying the quietness, Joey, Anthony, and Joey's cousin Rob were content sitting wordlessly on the overstuffed sofa and looking at the twinkling Christmas tree. Rob broke the silence when he tapped Joey on the leg and asked, "When do you plan to start college?"

"I'm starting in the winter quarter, which begins on January 15."

Tilting his head, Rob frowned. "Isn't that kind of early? Do you think you'll be able to handle it?"

Joey shrugged his shoulders. "I won't know until I try. Besides, just sitting around doing nothing but watching TV is really driving me up a wall. Right now, I don't feel like I'm accomplishing anything with my life, and I need to move on." Turning his eyes from Rob and focusing on a burnt-out bulb on the Christmas tree, Joey continued, "Although, I'll admit after seeing the curriculum and hearing the dean of engineering talk, I'm a little apprehensive."

"What did the dean say?"

"It was a very short speech that ended by him asking us to look at the person in front, behind, to the right, and to the left of us. Then he said, 'When you graduate, three of the four people you are looking at will not be in engineering.' After looking at the courses I have to take, I could understand why. It didn't leave me with a real good feeling inside."

Knowing smiles appeared on the faces of the two seasoned engineers. Chuckling, Rob said, "Let me tell you something. Every engineering student has heard the same thing. The dean's statement will actually weed out several people even before they start class. These people, because of their attitude, give up on themselves and their dreams, and I'll guarantee you, they'll be reluctant to do anything else in their lives."

"Why do you think some people have the mindset that makes them quit before they even start while others see things through to the end?"

Entering in on the conversation, Anthony said, "There are a couple of reasons. One has to do with the reinforcement people received during their lives. Another factor is more of an intangible."

Joey asked, "What do you mean, an intangible?"

　　　　STEVEN J. DEKANICH

"It's something that you can't learn. It's a flame from within, and when it burns, you can do anything."

"Do we all have this intangible?"

"It's a free gift from God for everyone to use. When a person decides to be different from the crowd, it's what's inside that determines how successful he will be in his endeavors."

"You know, Joey," said Rob as he got up to get a cup of eggnog, "many people blame other people or events for bad turns in their lives when actually we are masters of our own destinies. When something happens in our life, whether it's as trivial as someone telling you that you have a one-in-four chance of getting your degree or something major like getting cancer, it's our mindset that helps us find a way to successfully get out of any particular situation."

Joey raised his eyebrows. "I don't think a one-in-four chance of getting a degree is trivial."

Pouring the eggnog, Rob frowned as he considered how to respond to Joey's comment. Smirking, he asked, "Did you believe the dean's statement?"

"Sure I did. When I looked around the room, every person looked sharper than me."

"Like I said, every engineering student has gone through the same thing. Even Anthony and me."

"How did you feel?"

"It was a little unnerving at first, but we decided that it wasn't going to be us that failed."

"And you both made it."

"Joey," Rob said, waiting for Joey's eyes to meet his. "Do you think we're any sharper than you?"

"Sure I do."

"Why would you say that?"

"Look at how much you know. Man, compared to the both of you, I'm probably the lowest thing on the food chain."

"You're just uneducated," Rob said, softening the comment with a smile. "You can learn as much or even more than Anthony and me."

Sitting back, Joey said, "Yeah, right."

"I'm serious. Barring a severe mental handicap, if someone wants to learn, they can. It may take some people longer than others, but if they set their minds to it, they can do it." Anthony rose from the sofa and headed for the eggnog. "For a Christmas morning, we're talking about some pretty heavy stuff," he chuckled as he poured himself a cup.

Nodding in agreement, Rob said, "Yes, but I think it's important to get across to this young man the importance of a proper mindset. We are what we think."

"Okay," Joey responded. "You've convinced me that a proper mindset can help you solve a problem, no matter how trivial it is. But what about serious problems like cancer?"

Finishing his eggnog, Rob looked Joey squarely in the eyes. "You should know. You've been through it. What did you learn?"

Sitting back on the couch, Joey looked up at the ceiling and repeated, "What did I learn?" Looking at Rob, he replied, "Although I didn't have control of the cancer, I had control of me."

"What about the times you didn't have control? How did you feel?"

"Lousy! I didn't feel like myself, and it seemed like I disliked everything and everybody."

"How did you feel physically?"

"I don't think I've ever felt worse in my life."

"And when you changed your attitude for the better?"

"I still had a lot of aches and pains, but I could tolerate them and I actually started feeling better."

STEVEN J. DEKANICH

"That's a prime example of what Anthony and I are trying to tell you. No matter what kind of situation hits you, whether it's trivial or serious, your attitude will determine the outcome. When it's something trivial and a person decides to get out of the situation, it will happen. When it's something serious like cancer, and a person decides to overcome it, that person has increased his odds of survival. Even if he succumbs to the disease, his attitude may help someone else survive." ✦

Chapter 11

In life, you'll be judged by your actions and attitudes.

Butterflies filled Joey's stomach as he prepared for his first day at Youngstown State University. An accident on Interstate 80 and limited parking spaces turned the butterflies into buttermilk and soured his stomach. When he finally found a parking space, he had ten minutes to run a quarter mile to the William Rayen School of Engineering Building. He walked in just as class was starting. The professor began by explaining what they were going to do during the winter quarter calculus class. Although Joey had trig-calculus in high school, by the time Dr. James finished discussing his class outline and his expectations, Joey's hands began to cramp, and he was having trouble breathing.

When the class was over, Joey's head was whirling as he made his way out of the building. Negative thoughts began filling his mind. *Am I going to be one of the three people that quit? What makes me think I can do this? I'm not sure I even understood anything Dr. James just said. I'd better drop the class before I really make a fool of myself. I've got chemistry next, and it's not going to get better! Look at me! I'm becoming a physical wreck!*

In the midst of these thoughts, the tetany struck Joey with a vengeance. His hands resembled crab claws and wouldn't open, his breathing was reduced to short raspy breaths, and his cramping stomach almost doubled him over. Joey slowly made his way to a park bench and half-sat/half-laid on the bench. He thought, "Why am I doing this? I could get a job in the mill and not worry about all of this garbage."

Joey sat bewildered for half an hour. Finally, the tetany began to subside, and movement slowly returned to his hands. His breathing still was labored, but he decided to go to chemistry class. After class, he'd go home and tell his mother he was going to drop out of school and get a job at Sharon Steel.

Still experiencing signs of tetany, Joey walked into Dr. Sting's chemistry class. Looking at the floor, he found a seat and plopped down. Dr. Sting was a short, dark-haired man who looked like Will Rogers with a soft-spoken manner that put people at ease. After everyone was seated, he began to call roll. "Adams, Pat ... Horde, Jim ... Kelley, John ..."

Listening to all of these American-sounding names, Joey let his negative mindset take over again and thought, "Why couldn't I have a normal name?" As he was stewing in his negative soup, he remembered a long-ago conversation he had with his Uncle Bill. Joey was twelve at the time and was having difficulty with some of the children in his class. The children told him his name was weird and didn't sound American. He told Uncle Bill how he wished that he had a normal last name like other kids. Joey could remember Uncle Bill grabbing a grease rag, turning around from his tractor, and looking at him. His gray-blue eyes penetrated Joey as he leaned back on his tractor and asked, "What do you think is a normal name?"

"You know, like Smith or Jones. Something people can pronounce."

The greasy rag dangling from his right hand, Uncle Bill crossed his arms. "Oh, you think just because people could pronounce your name will make you … normal or better accepted by your friends?"

"Yeah, I do."

"Let me tell you something, young man. A person's last name doesn't determine what that person is or how he will be accepted. If someone judges you only by what your name is, that person is small and will never go anywhere in life. Stay away from people like that because they will only pull you down." Uncrossing his arms and wiping the grease from his hands, Uncle Bill continued, "I don't know if you'll understand what I'm about to tell you, but listen carefully. Inside of us, we have two people. One person is happy and at peace with himself and is always trying to tell us we can do different things and become the best person we can be. The other person has a sour outlook on life. That person is in constant turmoil with himself and can never see how he can accomplish anything and always tries to tell you that you are worthless. You must learn to stay away from the negative person inside of you because if you don't, he will destroy you."

Joey stared at Uncle Bill without saying a word.

Uncle Bill smiled and grabbed Joey's cheek with a greasy hand. "I don't think you understood what I just told you, but someday you will. Until then, remember this. In life, you will be judged by your actions and attitudes and not your last name."

"Saloozkey? Is there a Joey Saloozkey in this class?"

Flashing back to the present, Joey raised his hand and said, "It's pronounced, Slunisky." A smirk forming on his face, he added, "It's a good American name."

Smiling and nodding his head, Dr. Sting continued, "Smith, Debbie … Tyler, Joe … Vodez, Andrew …"

"Vodez, Andrew," thought Joey as he spun around in his seat to search for the face that went with the name. Andy, slouched in his seat, waved by touching his right index finger to his eyebrow and dropping his hand until his index finger pointed at Joey.

Andy was a year ahead of Joey in high school. Although they didn't have a lot of interaction with each other, the chemistry was there for establishing a strong friendship. To Joey, seeing Andy slouched in his chair was like a thirsty man in a desert seeing an oasis.

The ease of Dr. Sting's nature, reflecting back on what his uncle said, and seeing a familiar classmate put Joey in a different frame of mind. His new mindset changed his attitude and perception, bringing him one step closer to changing his situation.

When class was over, Joey anxiously made his way over to Andy. Extending his still cramping hand, Joey said, "Andy, how have you been?"

Vigorously shaking Joey's hand, Andy replied, "Oh, I've been doing pretty well. Just trying to decide what I want to do for the rest of my life."

"What do you mean?"

"Well, I've messed around for almost a year and changed my major several times. I think it's time to settle down into something productive."

"What are you majoring in?"

An uncontrolled belly laugh rolled from Andy's mouth. "Damned if I know!"

"Buddy, whether you know or not, you don't know how glad I am to see you."

"Oh, yeah? Hey, when you walked in, you looked like a little whipped pup. I never saw you like that. What's up?"

"Man, I felt worse than a whipped pup. This has probably been the worst day of my life."

"What do you mean?"

Joey took in and let out a deep breath before continuing. "To start off with, I left an hour early and ended up running late to my first calculus class. Going into that class, I thought everything was going to be all right because I had a lot of the material in high school—"

"Let's not brag about what we had in high school."

"Believe me, Andy, by the time the professor was done explaining what we were going to be doing and what he expected, my head was spinning, and my body chemistry went all out of whack."

Andy frowned. "What do you mean your body chemistry went out of whack? Are you on drugs or something?"

"No! Nothing like that. I had cancer."

"You what?"

"I had—"

"I didn't know anything about that. When did it happen? How are you feeling now?"

"When's your next class?"

"In an hour and fifteen minutes."

"Mine too. I'll tell you what. Why don't we go get something to eat, and I'll tell you all about it. By the way, what is your next class?"

"Physics."

"No way! Let me see your schedule." Looking at Andy's schedule, Joey said, "This is weird but great!"

"What's that?"

"We're in the same physics class too."

Walking to Tony's Pizza, Joey forgot all about his problems and enjoyed the moment at hand. ✦

Chapter 12

Why is it happening again?

The winter quarter was quite a learning experience for Joey and Andy. Joey was very apprehensive during the first several weeks. He studied constantly and thought he understood the material. However, when he would take a test, he would do poorly. The situation weighed heavily on him, as he had never failed at anything before in his life. Had it not been for Andy, the mental stress combined with his health problems would have turned Joey into a physical wreck.

Andy, on the other hand, was a free spirit. When he started college, his main purpose was to have fun, and he did. That type of approach landed him on academic probation, and his father told him he had better shape up. By the time his second year of college rolled, he realized he would have to settle down and determine a career path for himself. He decided on engineering, mainly because engineers made a lot of money. This decision was an act of fate that put him and Joey in many of the same classes.

It was Wednesday of midterm exam week, and Joey and Andy were studying together in the library. Noticing Joey rubbing his neck, Andy asked, "Are you feeling okay?"

Continuing to massage his neck, Joey replied, "My neck's a little sore. I think it's all the stress of midterms. I'll be all right."

"It may be my imagination, but your neck looks like it's swollen. Are you sure you're all right?"

Solemn-faced, Joey continued to rub his neck and stare at his chemistry book. After several seconds, he raised his eyes to meet Andy's. "You're right. My neck is swollen, but I don't have the time to go to the doctor now."

"When was your last check-up?"

"In January, just before we started the winter quarter."

"Did they find anything?"

"No. Dr. Sabbs said everything was looking good."

"So, you had your check-up in January, and it's the middle of February. Joey, I didn't notice your neck looking like this at the end of the month. When did it start swelling up?"

"About a week and a half ago."

Leaning across the table, Andy attempted a whisper, but he could be heard throughout the library. "You mean you knew your neck was swollen and you haven't been to a doctor yet?"

"If Dr. Sabbs puts me in the hospital now, I won't be able to take my exams and I'll flunk!"

"You're crazy, man! We're not talking about some damn grade here. We're talking about your life. What's wrong with you? Make that appointment!"

"All right. I'll make the appointment for Friday right after my last exam."

"Does your mother know about the swelling?

"No … I haven't told her yet."

Mrs. Slunisky's face turned ashen as the vivid, horrific images of several months ago filled her mind. Through tear-stained eyes, she looked at her son and thought, "Oh, dear God, this can't be happening again." It felt as if her insides were being ripped out. Breathing heavily, she reached for the back of a kitchen chair to keep from falling.

Grabbing her free arm, Joey yelled, "Mom!"

Not saying a word, she embraced Joey, feeling in her heart that if she let him go she would lose him forever.

The test results substantiated their worst fears. The cancer was back! Looking at the test data, Dr. Sabbs couldn't help thinking about a little boy he had just lost to acute lymphocytic leukemia (ALL). Timmy had contracted ALL when he was seven years old. Through chemotherapy, Dr. Sabbs was able to put the cancer into remission for about eight months. Shortly after Timmy's eighth birthday, the cancer reared its ugly head with a vengeance, and nothing could be done except make Timmy as comfortable as possible until the end came. The trauma of Timmy's life being snuffed out and now seeing Joey's positive test results made it difficult for Sabbs to focus. Praying for guidance, Sabbs realized that all he could do with any of his patients was treat them to the best of his ability. After that, he would place everything in God's hands and trust that whatever happened was His will.

Unconsciously wringing her hands, Mrs. Slunisky asked, "Why has the cancer come back? I thought you got it all."

"Mrs. Slunisky, at the time, I said we believed we did get it all," Dr. Sabbs replied. "Cancer is a very complex disease that can arise from a combination of many different factors. Because it is difficult to tell for certain that all cancer cells have been removed, we have scheduled follow-up visits. And Joey was scheduled for another follow-up next week. Now I know you're feeling uncertainty about the success of the initial operations, but I can assure you they were successful. Unfortunately, the type of cancer that Joey has appears to be recurring, and he may be diagnosed with cancer again in the future. That is why the follow-up visits are so important. We can keep close tabs on Joey, and if anything happens, we can respond in a timely manner to treat it."

Unconsciously rubbing his neck, Joey asked, "Since the results of the biopsy were positive, what does that mean for me?"

"Joey, it means another operation."

"What if I choose not to have the operation."

"The cancer could kill you."

Joey gritted his teeth and stared at the floor. Negative thoughts cluttered his mind. *Why, dear God, is this happening again? It's too late to drop classes. How am I going to finish this quarter when I'm in the hospital?* Still looking at the floor, Joey asked, "How soon do I have to get operated on?"

"I'm going to admit you today, and you'll be operated on in the morning."

Joey jerked his head up in surprise. "What? Dr. Sabbs, you know I've already started college, and it's too late to drop classes. If I don't finish this quarter, I'll fail every class. I can't get operated on now."

STEVEN J. DEKANICH

"Joey, you remember what happened the last time when the swelling was allowed to progress for six months."

"Yeah, but—"

"The way I see it, this time the cancer is more aggressive. It's growing faster than the last time. If you don't get it taken care of, you may not be around to go to any classes next quarter."

Not saying anything, Joey continued to shake his head no.

"Joey, do you understand the urgency of this matter? We're not playing games here. What is growing inside you won't wait for you to finish the quarter. It will continue to grow at an accelerated pace. If you don't stop it, it will win."

"What about my classes?"

"The professors should be understanding. I'll write a letter explaining the situation. You can take it to them this afternoon and be back to check in the hospital by four o'clock. By the way, what are you majoring in?"

"Nuclear Metallurgy."

"What did you say?"

"Actually it's a double major in Nuclear and Metallurgical Engineering."

"Sounds too complicated for me."

His forehead wrinkling, Joey said, "With your knowledge, I can't believe you said that. You're just saying that to make me feel good."

Sober-faced, Sabbs said, "Joey, that's out of my field of expertise, so it does sound complicated. I thought you knew by now. I don't make idle comments to try to falsely pump someone up."

Joey found his professors to be much more understanding than he expected. Even Dr. James had a human side to him. They all told Joey that he could make up any missed tests and they would be happy to tutor him if he needed help. Although the professors seemed understanding, Joey wondered, "Even with tutoring, am I still going to pass? This may be a good excuse to drop out for a while. After all, who would blame me?"

Dr. Sabbs intentionally waited until visiting hours were over before he walked onto Joey's floor. Walking past the waiting room, he could see Joey and about fifteen of his friends and relatives. Waving a greeting, he continued to the nurses' station and began reading Joey's chart. After Mrs. Schwartz evicted the visitors and all of the patients were in their rooms, Dr. Sabbs put down the chart and walked to Joey's room. He recalled the first time he saw Joey and how impressed he was with his physical and mental stature. As he looked at Joey now, the physical signs of his ordeal were obvious. However, the physical impairments didn't worry Dr. Sabbs as much as the potential mental impairments. The spark that once burned in Joey's eyes was no longer there. Dr. Sabbs had seen similar things happen before. When patients were continually knocked down, they lost a reason to keep going. Having thought about Joey's situation for several hours, he entered Joey's room believing he had a solution to his problem.

Extending his hand, Dr. Sabbs said, "Hello, Joey. How are you feeling?"

Getting up from the edge of his bed, Joey shook his doctor's hand. "All right, I guess."

"You get a lot of company when you're in here. Is it the same when you're at home?"

"Yes, sir, pretty much. My mother gets annoyed at times, but she gets over it."

"I guess you might say that you have a good reputation with your friends."

His face reddening, Joey replied, "Yes, sir, I guess so."

Motioning for Joey to sit down on the bed, Sabbs sat down in a large stuffed chair, crossed his legs, and grasped his right knee with his hands. Slightly tilting his head back, Sabbs made eye contact with Joey. "Yes, it seems like you have a good reputation. But what kind of character do you have?"

"I beg your pardon?"

"What kind of character do you have?" Sabbs repeated. He uncrossed his legs and leaned forward in the chair, waiting for Joey to answer.

Tilting his head in confusion, Joey asked, "What do you mean?"

"Do you know what I'm talking about when I say character?

"I ... guess so. Isn't it the same thing as your reputation?"

"Not really, Joey. Your reputation is what other people think of you. Your character is what you do and think when you are alone."

Joey glanced sideways at Sabbs and frowned. "What are you leading up to?"

"Joey, with you majoring in a scientific field, you'll find in your studies that everything in the universe is searching for equilibrium. Or, simply put, always seeking its lowest energy level."

"Okay ... but why are you mentioning this to me now?"

"Because, Joey, I think you're considering dropping out of college."

His chin dropping to his chest, Joey blurted out, "How did you know?"

A faint smile came to Dr. Sabbs' lips. "Joey, I've been around the block a few times and seen a lot of people react to illnesses in a way that they feel they have an excuse for not doing what they know is the right thing to do. I think you know what I'm talking about."

His face reddening and his eyes dropping to the floor, Joey nodded in acknowledgment. "It's not fair," he mumbled. "I was doing fairly well in school, and now I'm not sure what's going to happen."

"It would be easier to drop out, wouldn't it?"

Looking up from the floor, Joey said, "Sure it would."

"And no one would blame you if you quit right now, would they?"

"What you just said is what I was thinking today. What are you, some kind of mind reader?"

Chuckling, Sabbs replied, "No, Joey, I'm not a mind reader, but I do understand human nature. When people are frustrated, they respond in different ways. A clean-shaven man may grow a beard or moustache as a silent rebellion against the situation that has been slapped on him. A woman may go on an eating binge because the weight she wanted to lose didn't come off as fast as she wanted it to. Others, when a serious illness comes upon them, will play on emotions of their loved ones. When you're sick, it's easy to get others to do things for you that they normally wouldn't do. Or, it's even easier to get them to accept something less out of you because you're sick. Joey, a person getting trapped in that mode has jeopardized their future and possibly the future of those who look up to them."

"What do you mean jeopardize the future of those who look up to them?"

"Joey, when you're exercising, when are you doing the most good—when it's easy and you're not breaking a sweat or when you feel like you can't do one more pushup or one more lift and something inside you says do it anyway?"

"I'm doing the most good when I push myself to the limit."

"Did you ever quit before you reached that point?"

STEVEN J. DEKANICH

Sighing deeply, he admitted, "Yes, sir, I did."

"How did you feel about yourself?"

"Not very good."

"Did it affect your performance?"

"At the time when I was dogging it, I didn't think so, but it really did."

"What happened then?"

"I guess I not only let me down, I let my teammates down for accepting something that was substandard."

"Joey, with your particular situation, we're talking about the same thing. You have a niece and nephew who are around eight and six, don't you?" Waiting to see an acknowledgment, Sabbs continued, "Your sister said they really look up to you. What kind of an example would you give them if you dropped out?"

His face reddening, Joey said, "I never thought about it. All I was thinking about was how it would affect me and if it was going to be easier."

Joey, life is giving of oneself, no matter what kind of circumstance is slapping you. Be an open, giving person, and be there for the people who really need you. Don't use your illness as a crutch." ✦

Chapter 13

Remember, you have control of you.

Joey was in the hospital for a week and a half and then spent an additional two weeks recovering at home. The conversation that he had with Dr. Sabbs helped him a great deal in coping with his new challenges. Sabbs helped Joey realize that other people's encouragement could influence him to a point, but it was entirely his decision how he would handle a situation. He realized that if he was going to be a success in life, he must be accountable for himself.

A few days after Joey's operation, Dr. Sabbs brought in several books for Joey to read. A frown on his face, Joey asked, "What are these?"

"They are books from some of the masters of the positive attitude—OG Mandino, *The Greatest Miracle in the World*, Dr. Norman Vincent Peale, *The Power of Positive Thinking*, and David Schwartz, *The Magic of Thinking Big*."

"I really don't like to read more than I have to."

"Do you want to find the inner peace I said you could have?"

"Of course I do."

STEVEN J. DEKANICH

"Then you'll read these books. I want you to read them in the order I mentioned them to you. If you do that, you'll see some incredible things happen."

"Like what?"

"You read them and tell me."

During his recovery time, Joey did read the books. The following words from *The Greatest Miracle in the World* helped Joey change how he viewed things.

You have performed the greatest miracle in the world.

You have returned from a living death.

You will feel self-pity no more and each new day will be a challenge and a joy.

You have been born again … but just as before, you can choose failure and despair or success and happiness. The choice is yours.

The choice is exclusively yours.

OG Mandino
"The God Memorandum"

Because of his attitude change, Joey's final grades were, for the most part, acceptable. He got A's in chemistry, physics, and psychology, a B in English, and a D in calculus. Joey thought about taking calculus over, but when he saw how much it would put him behind on his graduation schedule, he decided against it.

In the winter quarter, Joey and Andy had carpooled together and decided to keep it up in the spring quarter. It was Andy's turn to drive the first day of school.

"Joey, Andy's here!" shouted Mrs. Slunisky, looking out the living room window as Andy's beige Chevy Nova pulled into the driveway.

Hurrying to put on his shoes, Joey replied, "I'll be right out."

Mrs. Slunisky watched Andy bounce out of the car and jog up to the front door. A smile came to her face as she thought, "Ah, the energy of youth." Opening the front door, she said, "Good morning, Andy. Are you ready for another quarter of school?"

"As ready as I'll ever be, I guess."

"Joey will be out in a second. Can I get you a cup of coffee or something?"

"No, thanks. How's Joey been feeling?"

"Good. He's had his head buried in some books that Dr. Sabbs gave him."

"What kind—"

"Hello, Andy! How ya doing?" interrupted Joey as he walked into the kitchen.

"I'm doing good. Ready to tackle another quarter?"

"Sure am. Let's go."

Turning toward his mother, Joey kissed her on the cheek and mussed up her hair just before he walked out the door. Getting into Andy's car, Joey sat back, buckled his seat belt, and took a deep breath. Smiling, he looked at Andy and said, "You know what? I feel really good today."

Pulling out of the driveway and onto Sample Road, Andy asked, "Why's that?"

"I guess I'm excited about the new quarter, and I know my way around the campus. Most of all, I have a close friend carpooling with me."

"I feel the same about our friendship. By the way, refresh my memory of what your schedule looks like for this quarter."

STEVEN J. DEKANICH

Opening the front cover of his calculus book, Joey pulled out his schedule and read off the classes and the times.

"How many hours is that?"

"Eighteen."

"Man, you are a glutton for punishment!"

"Why do you say that?"

"Didn't anyone ever tell you that a full load is twelve hours?"

"Yes, but I figured if I took twelve hours a quarter, it would take me more than five years to graduate, and I didn't want to drag it out. Speaking of dragging it out, have you decided what kind of engineer you want to be?"

"No, not yet. I figure I have another quarter to decide since first-year classes are basically the same for all engineers."

"Have you done any reading on what the different professions do or talked with anyone who is an engineer?"

Andy shook his head. "No, not really. Why did you go into engineering?"

"Several years ago, right after my dad died, my mother had a meeting with some manager from Sharon Steel. After they got done talking, he asked me what I had planned on doing with my life after I graduated. When I told him I wasn't sure, he said they needed some good metallurgical engineers. I was fifteen years old at the time, and from that five-minute conversation, I decided I would be a metallurgical engineer."

"Do you know what a metallurgical engineer does?"

"I asked him, and he told me his company makes and rolls different kinds of steel. He talked about huge furnaces that spew sparks and flames and have two hundred tons of molten metal in them. He also talked about red hot steel slabs crashing through different presses and going through a series of rollers and being rolled down into something that can be used in the auto industry, aircraft industry ...

stuff like that. He made it sound interesting enough that I wanted to do it."

"Aren't you planning on doing something with nuclear engineering also? Why would you want to do that?"

"I guess because it's so controversial, I figured there must be something to it, and I wanted to learn more about it."

"You know, you're lucky. You had that guy from Sharon Steel talk to you, and you have your brother-in-law and cousin who are engineers. I wish high schools would have people from different professions and even private business owners come in and talk about what they do. That would give us an idea of what is really going on in the real world. I think reading from a book only gives you a partial picture. I'd rather talk to the people who are out there on the firing line every day and have experience I can learn from. That way, I can make more of an intelligent decision on what I'm going to do with the rest of my life."

Joey was surprised. He had never seen this side of Andy before. "You really mean that?"

"Yes, I do. I'll admit, I was not your model student in high school, but many times I was just bored with the humdrum of book learning. Nobody ever told me or showed me examples of what I would be using trigonometry or chemistry for. Joey, I have no idea what an engineer does, but I guess I'm going to be one."

Joey and Andy got so caught up in their conversation that the forty-five minute drive to Youngstown State University flew by. As Andy pulled into a parking space, Joey asked, "When is your first class?"

"It's the same chemistry class that you have at ten o'clock."

"You mean you got up this early for a ten o'clock class?"

"Hey, what are friends for? I'll see you at the student center after you get out of calculus."

Walking to the William Rayen School of Engineering Building, Joey shivered as his thoughts returned to the uncertainty he had experienced at the beginning of last quarter. He muttered under his breath, "That was one of the worst experiences of my life. Thank God for caring friends and positive-attitude books. Without them, I'm not sure I'd be here. This quarter is going to be different! It's mine, and nothing is going to shake me!" With that thought still in his mind, Joey jogged up three flights of stairs to his calculus class. Seeing only ten people in the classroom, Joey asked if this was Freshman Calculus II. Several students acknowledged that it was, so Joey found a seat in the front row.

One of the students asked Joey, "Do you know anything about this professor?"

"No, I don't. Why?"

"Well, I heard the guy is a real jerk. There were supposed to have been thirty-three students signed up for this class. Most of them dropped it."

"Why? Who is the—"

Joey's words froze in his mouth. Standing in the door was the looming figure of Dr. Fleishkopf. Dr. Fleishkopf stood about six feet, two inches tall, and coldly looked over the class with steely blue eyes. He wore a black broad-brimmed felt hat and black leather overcoat, and Joey couldn't help thinking that the only thing missing from his outer apparel was the insignia of an SS officer.

Not saying a word, Fleishkopf strutted over to his desk, put his books down, took off his hat and coat, and hung them neatly on a nearby coat rack. He looked at his students for several seconds, still not speaking. Finally, standing with his feet spread apart and his arms folded, he asked with a strong German accent, "Do you know why you are here? You are here to learn calculus. From the empty chairs, I see many chose not to come to this class when they found out I was teaching it. It's probably just as well. They most likely would have flunked."

Sitting back in his seat, Joey muttered, "Good grief. This guy does sound like a jerk."

Still standing poker-straight with arms folded, Dr. Fleishkopf continued in a deep ominous voice, "Some of you think you know calculus. I will find out just how much you know. Some of you got a D last quarter … you WILL FLUNK this quarter."

Joey's mind began to go into a psychological tailspin. Those old voices of fear and doubt began creeping in. *You'll never get through this class, you barely made it through the other class. He said if you got a D last quarter, you will flunk this quarter.* Suddenly, a memory of what Dr. Sabbs had said broke through his muddled brain … "Every time you get knocked down, I want you to remember you have control of you. Since you have peace within, there is nothing that can conquer you from without unless you let it. It's all up to you."

Regaining his composure, Joey didn't let Dr. Fleishkopf rattle him. Instead he thought, "Buddy, there is no way I'm going to *flonk* your class."

After a half hour of blatant threats of failure and another half hour of going over the syllabus for the quarter, the class was finally over at nine o'clock. The person whom Joey was talking with before class said, "This guy is crazy! There is no way I'm staying in this class, and if you're smart, you'll get out too!"

Andy, who was standing outside the engineering building, walked over to chat with Joey. "How was calculus?"

"You won't believe it."

"Who's your professor?"

"Dr. Fleishkopf."

"Dr. Fleishkopf!! You have the Ax Man? I've heard more bad things about that guy. He's probably flunked more people himself than the entire YSU faculty put together! Come on. Let's get you out of that class and into another one."

A determined look on his face, Joey said, "The thought crossed my mind about dropping, but I'm going to stick with the class and pass it. By the way, it's not pronounced flunk—it's *flonk*."

With a bewildered look on his face, Andy shook his head. "Man you are a glutton for punishment or a few bricks short of a full load!"

Smiling, Joey said, "Neither, I hope. Andy, it's just when he was talking about how he was going to flunk everybody who got a D last quarter—"

"You got a D last quarter? Mr. Math Brains got a *D* last quarter? I know you were sick, but how did YOU manage to get a grade like that?"

"I—"

"You know something, Joey?"

"Outside of the fact that you always interrupt me, what?"

"Knowing that you got a D in something gives me hope."

"Well, I'm glad that it did somebody some good." The smile disappearing from his face, Joey continued, "When he told us we were going to flunk, it made my blood boil. As long as I'm physically and mentally able, I refuse to let another person rattle me. Besides, I wasn't going to give him the satisfaction of knowing that I didn't have enough guts to stay in his class."

"I think I can find a different word than guts. Think about what that would do to your GPA. Joey, that's a five-hour course you're playing Russian roulette with. Believe me, a bad grade in a course with that many hours could be devastating. I know firsthand."

"My mind is made up. I'm staying in that class and passing it! Now let's walk down to chemistry. I think we have Dr. Sting again."

"I have a better idea."

"What's that?"

"Let's go downtown to McKelvey's and get a hot buttered pecan roll."

Joey tilted his head. "You want to skip the first day of class? You were just talking about your concern for my GPA, and now you want me to skip the first day of chemistry to go get a hot buttered pecan roll?"

"What did you get in chemistry last quarter?"

"An A. What did you get?"

"I got a B."

Still frowning, Joey looked at Andy for several seconds. Suddenly, a slight smile came to his lips. He shrugged his shoulders. "Why not? Let's go get a hot buttered pecan roll!" ✦

Chapter 14

Thank you for letting me see a new perspective on life.

The spring quarter was a hundred percent improvement over the winter quarter. Joey was able to relax with most of his classes and absorb and assimilate the information. His major snag was Calculus II. It was the fifth week of the quarter, and he was only carrying a C average in the class. Unfortunately for most of the other students, it was the third highest grade in the class. One student had a B-, another had a C+, but all the rest had either a D or an F. Several of the students swore that if they ever saw Dr. Fleishkopf on the street, they would run him over. Joey had similar hard feelings, but decided that instead of griping about Dr. Fleishkopf to other people, he would talk to him about his grade.

On Friday morning, he told Andy his plans and that he would meet him in chemistry. Agonizing over what Dr. Fleishkopf's reaction would be, Joey had butterflies in his stomach during the whole class. At the end of class, he tentatively walked over to Dr. Fleishkopf's desk and asked, "Dr. Fleishkopf, may I speak with you for a few minutes?"

The stern Gestapo expression on his face turning colder, Dr. Fleishkopf asked, "What do you want to talk about?"

Clearing his throat, Joey said, "Sir, I'd like to talk with you about my grade."

"Oh. Of course, you think your grade should be higher. Is that what you think?"

"Well ... yes, sir. I'm concerned—"

"That's the trouble with you Americans! You think everything is owed to you! You are not willing to work for anything, but you want everything!"

Stepping back at the outburst, Joey was speechless.

Seeing people from another class coming into the room, Dr. Fleishkopf didn't bother to lower his voice. "Personally I don't see any need to continue this conversation, but if you still want to, you can come by my office at noon today."

Joey knew if he didn't commit to being there, things would only get worse. Regaining some of his composure, he said, "Okay. I'll be at your office at noon today."

"Do not be early and do not be late. Be there at noon or don't come!"

Joey felt dazed as he walked out of the engineering building. "What's wrong with that guy?" he thought.

"Hey, Joey!" Andy yelled from across the street. "I thought you had a meeting after your calculus class."

Walking across the street toward Andy, Joey said, "I did. I have another one at noon."

"That's our lunch hour."

"Yeah, I know. That's probably why he chose the time. Andy, the guy is a real jerk!"

"I told you so."

STEVEN J. DEKANICH

The three-hour wait was agonizing. Joey's insides were tied in knots, and he kept asking himself, "Why am I so nervous?" Unable to answer the question, he felt like a victim going to the guillotine. Joey waited down the hall from Dr. Fleishkopf's office for several minutes, and at exactly twelve o'clock, he knocked on the door. The thick German accent oozed from the door. "Come in!" Taking a deep breath, Joey opened the door, walked in, and closed the door behind him.

Looking at his watch, Dr. Fleishkopf said, "You followed instructions and came precisely on time. Most Americans do not follow instructions."

Dr. Fleishkopf's office was immaculate. There was nothing out of place. Joey thought about his engineering advisor's office, which had books, papers, and broken pieces of metal stuffed in every possible location—on the floor, on his desk, and on every bookshelf. Looking at Dr. Fleishkopf's desk, Joey thought, "Wow! Even his note pad, stapler, and phone are in a perfect line on his desk." Seven pictures of a young woman with three children were placed in strategic locations around the pristine office. Joey asked, "Is this your daughter's family?" as he pointed to the picture on Dr. Fleishkopf's desk.

For a split second, the expression on Dr. Fleishkopf's face seemed to soften. "No," he said. "These are photos of my wife and children."

"You have a very attractive family, Dr. Fleishkopf."

"Had, Mr. Slunisky." His face turning stone cold. "A drunk American driver hit them and killed them all fifteen years ago on Belmont Avenue." Tears welling up in his eyes, he continued, "My wife dreamed of this country for years before we came here. Every night, she would tell our children stories of America." Sighing deeply and looking at the favorite photo on his desk, Fleishkopf's voice escalated. "If I would have known, we never would have come here.

"I'm sorry, Dr.—"

The tears failing to quench the fire in his eyes, Dr. Fleishkopf raised his voice so much that it startled people in the hallway. "You are sorry? You Americans are all alike. Always talking about emotions but never feeling them! What do you know about sorrow and hurting?" Not allowing Joey to respond, he continued, "The day after the accident, I was talking with an American professor and asked him what good is living when all that you love is gone? He told me the kindness, laughter, and special moments of the heart will always be with me and should be cherished. He asked me, 'How could you say they are gone when they are still a part of you and the memories will last forever in your mind?' I broke his jaw! You know nothing of sorrow."

"Perhaps you're right. I probably don't know what true sorrow and hurt are when you lose someone who is very close to you. But from your description, I don't think your wife would have wanted you to torture yourself like you have been."

"You have no right to talk to me like that! What do you know of life? You Americans are very shallow and try to explain away things with empty philosophies that don't mean anything!"

His face getting red and feeling the exasperation clinching his throat, Joey spoke in a voice that he didn't even recognize. It was almost as loud as Dr. Fleishkopf's. "Perhaps they are empty philosophies with no meaning, but with the hate that is built up inside you, what kind of philosophies are you following? You condemn everyone before you give them a chance. You think all of us are the scum of the earth because of what one person did to your family, and it seems like all you want to do is destroy your students for what happened to you fifteen years ago. Yes, Dr. Fleishkopf, I may not know much about life, but I don't think you do either."

STEVEN J. DEKANICH

Fire in his eyes, Dr. Fleishkopf jumped out of his chair, pointed at the door, and yelled, "Get out of my office!"

Joey slept very little that weekend. Sitting at Anthony's kitchen table on Sunday afternoon, he tried to rationalize Fleishkopf's behavior. He asked Anthony, "Why does he act that way? I can imagine what a trauma it would be to lose your family, but why hate other people who didn't have anything to do with it?"

"I don't exactly know, Joey. It may be the only way he knows how to deal with it."

"I don't understand."

"Let me give you an example. Back when I was dating your sister, there were several times that something would happen where you didn't get your way. I remember you pouting and sulking, hoping that acting like that would get you what you wanted. Usually Mom gave you an attitude adjustment, but sometimes you figured out for yourself it wasn't worth the effort to continue the charade."

"Yeah. I can remember some of those times."

"Joey, there were times when I really wanted to blister your bottom."

"Nah!"

"Yes, but I figured it was up to Mom to handle the situation."

Frowning, Joey folded his arms and leaned his elbows on the table. "I'm missing something here. What does the fact of me being an immature brat have to do with the way Dr. Fleishkopf is acting?"

Your actions were immature, but I didn't say you were a brat. If you think back to how you responded to things, most people behave the same way. They will pout and sulk until they get their way. In many cases, people don't know what their way is, and they create a living hell for themselves because they don't know where they are going in life."

"Dr. Fleishkopf sounds like that. The man is definitely unhappy."

"This could also be a case where someone needs to jolt him out of his mindset."

"What do you mean?"

"Remember when Mom got down on you in the hospital for not drinking?"

"Yeah. I felt like a real heel when that happened."

"But it worked, and that is what was important."

"Yeah, but Mom has more guts than me when it comes to things like this. What should I do tomorrow when I go to his class?"

"I would apologize to him and ask to have another meeting with him."

"What? The guy's insane! If I do that, I may wind up with a broken jaw too!"

"I don't think so, Joey. Arguments and hard feelings never get a person anywhere. Even if you think you're right in what you've done, and I think you are, he thinks he's right in what he has done. So who is right and who is wrong?"

"I hate it when you throw these mind games at me. In simple language that I can understand, what are you talking about?"

"You want a better grade and to get on good terms with Dr. Fleishkopf, right?" Seeing Joey nod his head, Anthony continued, "He also thinks you should flunk. Both of you think you're right, so there is a wall of conviction between you. You built half the wall, and Fleishkopf built the other half. The only way you can break that wall down is for you to break your side down first."

"He started it."

"There's a story of a wise old businessman who stood back and listened to his son argue with a good customer about a bill. Before things went too far, the wise old businessman stepped in and smoothed things over with the customer, and the customer left satisfied. His son was irate and told his father that he was right about the bill and he knew it. The old businessman, knowing that his son would one day inherit the business said, 'Over the last few years, that man spent several thousand dollars at our store. His bill today amounted to twenty-seven dollars. Do you think he would have been back if you would have won? Son, let me ask you—do you want to be right or do you want to be rich?' Joey, do you want to feed your ego or do you want to pass? I'm not asking you to compromise your beliefs. Just look at the situation that's before you with an open mind and try to see things through Dr. Fleishkopf's eyes."

Joey was solemn-faced Monday morning when he picked up Andy. Trying to lighten the somber atmosphere, Andy said, "Good morning, Joey! You certainly look like you had a good weekend and have a lot to live for. It looks like you've decided to change your facial expression to match Dr. Fleishkopf's. I must say you're doing a great job at it!"

A faint rise coming from the corner of his mouth, Joey replied, "Very funny."

"Rough weekend, huh?"

"That's an understatement. Andy, I feel like I did before a big football game. My stomach is tied up in knots, and I feel like I could throw up."

"Why? What have you decided to do?"

"I'm going to try to talk to him again today."

"You know, you still have this week to drop the class if you want to."

"Yeah, I know. The thought has crossed my mind, but I made a commitment to myself that I would see this through, and I'm going to do it."

"I still think you're a glutton for punishment."

The spring in Joey's step turned into a plod as he slowly made his way up the stairs to his classroom. Apprehension weighed him down like a ball and chain. Walking into the classroom, he sat down in his usual seat in the front. Dr. Fleishkopf was known for his punctuality. Every day, he walked into the classroom precisely at 8:00 a.m. It was five minutes after, and no sign of Dr. Fleishkopf. Not directing his question to any particular person in the classroom, a student asked, "I wonder where he's at?" At ten minutes after eight, Dr. Fleishkopf walked into the classroom. With an odd look on his face, he apologized for being late and immediately started his lecture. The lecture seemed very strange to the students because the normal arrogant voice and cutting remarks were missing. At the end of his lecture, Dr. Fleishkopf looked at Joey and said, "Mr. Slunisky, I would like to see you after class."

Joey's heart fell into his feet as he thought, "Oh God! Here it comes!" Getting up from his desk, he walked over to Dr. Fleishkopf and asked, "Yes, sir?"

"Mr. Slunisky, if your schedule would allow, I would like to talk with you for a few minutes in my office."

With a nod of acknowledgment, Joey followed Dr. Fleishkopf. As they got closer to his office, Joey imagined the doorway as a guillotine and visualized his head rolling off his shoulders. Not saying a word, Joey sat down and waited for Dr. Fleishkopf to walk around his desk.

STEVEN J. DEKANICH

Dr. Fleishkopf pulled his chair out from the desk and sat down with his head against the back of the chair. His arms resting on the arms of the chair, he clasped his hands together and looked at Joey for a few seconds. Finally he said, "Mr. Slunisky, I owe you an apology."

Joey almost blurted out, "What?" But he contained himself and asked, "I beg your pardon?"

"You heard me correctly, Mr. Slunisky. I said I owe you an apology. After our conversation last Friday, I thought about what you said and did a lot of thinking of what I have done with my life since I lost my family. I realized that in fifteen years, I have not had one person over to my house, except for technical seminars, and I have gone nowhere nor visited anyone. I didn't even have a Christmas tree! That was something that Erika—my wife—thoroughly enjoyed."

With the mention of Erika's name, Joey could see a faint smile. Relieved that things were progressing as they were, Joey kept quiet and let Dr. Fleishkopf continue.

"For fifteen years, I was an empty shell of a man who was filled with hate because of what fate dealt me. Because I was so miserable, I wanted to make everyone else miserable. I drove away all the friends that I had. I kept telling myself that my work was more important than people, and I buried myself into it. My work was substandard because I just thought of me. It makes me sick to think what I had become. Fifteen years ago, I promised myself that I would never be hurt again. Do you know what a person does when he makes a promise like that?"

Mesmerized by the conversation, Joey shook his head no.

"When a person makes that kind of promise, he is also promising to never love again. He becomes cold and self-centered. He despises being around happy people because he is envious and resentful of their joy. Over a period of time, he becomes a walking, festering mass of malignant flesh that is growing out of control, and he tries to infect everyone he comes in contact with. You see, Mr. Slunisky, your words last Friday made me take a long, hard look at myself. For the longest time, I did not want to deal with the person I had become because I hated him. Because I hated me, I hated everyone else. With this mindset, I lost all rapport with my students and the faculty. I'm surprised this university kept me on the staff—especially since the person who heads the mathematics department is the one whom I punched fifteen years ago. I was put on probation last quarter for flunking too many students. I guess, subconsciously, I was trying to drive myself out of a job. I rationalized if that happened, I would kill myself because I would have nothing left."

Joey's eyes widened in shock as he listened to Dr. Fleishkopf.

"You seem surprised at my words. Mr. Slunisky, I can assure you there are many others out there who have the same feelings. People who have been beaten down by life and think, because no one cares, it's easier to give up than go on. If these people don't have someone come into their life, as you came into mine, and help them realize they are still worth something, to themselves and to society, they become lost souls. Joseph … may I call you Joseph?"

"I prefer Joey."

"Okay, Joey. You may not realize what you did for me. You were the catalyst that got me to thinking that God has a plan and a purpose for all our lives, and He gives us the free will to follow His plan on a road to happiness or to follow our own plan on a road to destruction. Thank you for getting me back on the right road."

STEVEN J. DEKANICH

The next morning, Dr. Fleishkopf walked into class precisely at 8:00 a.m., took his coat off, and hung it neatly on the rack. He walked over to his desk, but instead of sitting at the seat, as he normally did, he half-sat, half-leaned against the front of his desk. In tune with his normal nature, he didn't say anything for several seconds. This time, however, there wasn't the usual foreboding. Dr. Fleishkopf had a peculiar smile on his face and a slight twinkle in his eye.

Standing up from the desk, he said, "Class, I have a very important announcement to make. I evaluated your grades and the type of examinations I have given you, and I have determined the tests were much too difficult for this level of calculus. Therefore, I have decided to grade you on a curve. To find out what your midterm grade is, raise the grade that I reported to you last week by one and a half. That is, if you had a B-, you now have an A, if you had a C, you now have a B+, etcetera."

"Dr. Fleishkopf, are you feeling all right?"

"Mr. Smith, I couldn't feel better! Now let us resume our lesson."

At the end of class, Joey walked up to Dr. Fleishkopf and said, "I want to thank you for re-evaluating the grade situation."

"No, Mr.... Joey. It is I who thanks you. Without our discussion, I would still be headed for certain personal destruction. I thank you for letting me see a new perspective on life. Oh, by the way, remember the person I told you about whose jaw I broke? I am having lunch with him this afternoon!" ✦

Chapter 15

I'm young, I'm ambitious and I've got drive!

The B+ in Calculus helped put Joey on the honor roll at the end of the quarter. Now, a new challenge lay before him—getting a summer job. He could get a job at Donald's Golden Dawn, but he wanted to generate a more substantial income than a grocery store could pay. Brooding at the breakfast table about his problem, his mother brightened his mood by asking, "Why don't you apply at Sharon Steel?"

"That sounds like a good idea! Do you think they're hiring?"

"You won't know until you find out."

As he drove down Roemer Boulevard, the steady hum and vibration from the old brick street gave Joey a queasy stomach. Parking his car, he looked at the employment building and saw a large group of young men milling around. When he entered the building, it seemed there were just as many young men on the inside as there were outside—only these guys were either waiting to get an application or filling one out. Apprehensively, Joey walked to the end of the line to get an application. After filling it out, he handed the completed application to the receptionist. She thanked him but would not make any comments regarding his chances for being hired. Joey walked to his car and thought, "Now what am I going to do?" Retracing his route, he had never noticed, until now, how gray the old brick houses had become from the mill smoke.

Studying her son's facial expression as he emerged from his car, Mrs. Slunisky knew he had been defeated. Opening the front door, she asked, "How did it go?"

Joey sighed deeply as he walked past her and said, "Not very well."

"What do you mean?"

Plopping into a chair next to the kitchen table, Joey ran his hand through his hair. "Mom, in just the period of time I was there, there were over a hundred other guys wanting a job."

"So?"

"What do you mean, so? The lady who took my application said over two thousand people have applied for jobs in the last two weeks. How can I beat them out since they were there before me?"

"I realize it won't be easy, but do you want a job?"

"I want it so bad I can taste it."

"So who cares if you're number two thousand and one? Go after it!"

"How would you propose I do that?"

Mrs. Slunisky poured herself a cup of coffee and sat at the table with her son. "Remember how you got the job at Donald's Golden Dawn in the summer of your junior year in high school?"

"I just applied for it, didn't I?"

"Yes, you applied for it, but you went back every week, sometimes two and three times a week to see if they had any openings. That showed them you were serious about getting a job. I think you should do the same thing now."

Chuckling, Joey said, "I almost forgot about that. Okay. I'll go and fill out another application tomorrow."

Joey was true to his word. He returned to Sharon Steel to fill out another application—and then another and another. He would go in at different times, hoping to see a different receptionist so it wouldn't seem so strange that he was asking for another application. It was Wednesday of the following week when the receptionist saw the name on the top of the application and asked Joey to please wait. She picked up her phone, dialed a number, and said, "Mr. Moody, the person who filled out all of those applications is here."

Joey's heart jumped into his throat when he heard the words. "All right! Mom was right," he thought. A short, rotund, balding man with thick glasses came to the reception area and held his hand out to Joey. "I'm Paul Moody. Please come back to my office."

When Joey was seated in the office, Mr. Moody said with a chuckle, "I must say we have never received so many applications from one person in such a short time. It is quite evident you want a job."

"Yes, sir. I do want a job."

Suddenly the smile disappeared from Mr. Moody's face. "Believe me, son, nothing would please me more to say you've got a job here. We could use more people with your enthusiasm and persistence, but I'm afraid I have to say we can't find a place for you."

Feeling like he had been punched in the stomach, Joey asked, "Why? I don't understand."

"Son, with the kind of hard and dangerous work we do around here, we're concerned your handicap would get you hurt."

"My handicap? What kind of handicap do I have?"

"Reading your application, we see that you have had severe bouts with cancer and had a lot of muscle tissue removed from your shoulder and neck. We feel you would be in danger working here."

STEVEN J. DEKANICH

Joey shook his head, crossed his arms, and sat back in the chair. "I don't believe this," he muttered. With the veins bulging from his forehead and neck, Joey glared at Moody and said, "What you're telling me is that you don't think I am physically able to cope with the kind of work that goes on here, right?"

Mr. Moody meekly shrugged his shoulders. Hearing someone walk by Mr. Moody's office, Joey turned and saw a familiar face. Jumping out of the chair, he ran out into the hallway. "Mr. Lennon!" he called out. "Can I talk with you?"

Startled by an unfamiliar voice, Mr. Lennon stopped and turned around. "What can I do for you?"

Hurrying into the hallway, Mr. Moody said, "I'm sorry, sir. I was just telling this young man that we couldn't hire him."

"Yeah! He was telling me that I was handicapped and couldn't work here! Give me one minute with him on a wrestling mat, and I'll show you who's handicapped!"

With a brief smile betraying his amusement, Mr. Lennon put his hand up. "Easy there, young man. We're not getting into any wrestling matches. Come into my office." Winking at Mr. Moody, Mr. Lennon said, "I'll take it from here, Paul."

Sitting down at his desk, Mr. Lennon took a better look at Joey, "You go to Saint Anthony's Croatian Catholic Church, don't you?"

"Yes, sir. I've seen you there many times and heard you do the readings. Mr. Lennon, I'm sorry that I spoke out of line to Mr. Moody, but it's really important to me that I get a job here."

"Why do you want a job here?"

"I can make the most money here, and that will help me with my schooling."

"Is that a fact? What kind of contribution can you make to this company, and why do you think I should hire you instead of someone else?"

"Well, sir, I would be one of the best workers you ever hired. I'm young, I'm ambitious, and I've got drive!"

Standing up from his desk, Mr. Lennon looked at Joey for several seconds. "Very well put. I may be putting my neck on the line from an insurance standpoint, but I believe things will work out. Come in tomorrow morning for your physical. My secretary will give you the time to be here."

A big smile forming on his face, Joey could barely contain himself. Springing out of his chair and reaching across the desk, he vigorously shook Mr. Lennon's hand. "Thank you, Mr. Lennon! I can't tell you how much this means to me. I won't let you down!"

Joey's physical was scheduled for eight o'clock Thursday morning. He was sitting in the dispensary at 7:30 a.m. After taking a long, hard look at Joey's shoulder and neck, the examining doctor said, "Son, it looks like you've been through the ringer. How do you feel?"

Knowing that what he said might determine whether he got the job, Joey felt uneasy as he saw his reflection in the mirror on the wall. Sitting on the examination table stripped down to his waist, the disfigurement seemed more grotesque than before.

"Son, how do you feel?"

The doctor's voice snapped Joey out of his trance. He turned his face from the mirror and looked the doctor squarely in the eyes and said, "I feel great!"

"Have you had any problems with your neck or shoulder or with the movement in your left arm?"

"Sir, I would be lying to you if I said there were no problems. I have overcome a lot, and I feel I'm strong enough to do any of the work out here."

STEVEN J. DEKANICH

"Let me be the judge of that. Now relax and let's see what we've got." The doctor moved Joey's shoulders and arms through some weird contortions. After several minutes, he looked at Joey and said, "You still have quite a bit of restricted movement in your left arm and shoulder, but I think if we could get you placed in the proper work environment, you shouldn't have any problem."

A sigh of relief escaping from his lips, Joey stood up and said, "Thank you for giving me a chance."

"You're welcome. You may want to thank Mr. Lennon too."

After his physical, Joey signed several papers and was given his employee badge—Badge Number 6843. "Now I'm an official Sharon Steel employee," he thought as he fingered the badge. He was told to report to work at seven o'clock on Monday morning, at which point he would be assigned to the millwright crew on a blast furnace. At first, it didn't register, but as he was walking to the car, it hit Joey: "That's where my neighbor, Will Fueler, works." With that thought in his mind, he couldn't wait to get to work on Monday. ✦

Chapter 16

You only have one chance for a good first impression.

To Joey, the millwright shanty looked like a godforsaken building. As he entered the shanty, Joey's nostrils flared from the heavy smell of oil and grease that hung in the air. Quickly assessing the shanty interior, Joey saw huge tool chests with padlocks, massive pockmarked grease-soaked wooden tables with vices, worn and battered benches, well-used come-alongs stacked against one wall, and a multitude of other tools that he had no idea what they were used for. As he was wondering if he had done the right thing, he heard a gruff voice. "Well, hello there, young fella. I'm glad you could make it."

At the sound of the voice, Joey spun around on his heels and looked into the eyes of his neighbor. Although he stood only five feet, nine inches, Will was a giant of a man. Tipping the scales at two hundred and forty-five pounds, he didn't have an ounce of fat to be found on his body. Will's physical stature, coupled with his close-cropped hair and steely eyes, created an aura that commanded respect from everyone who worked with him, including management. His massive shoulders and arms made him look like an NFL All-Pro center. Joey remembered Will single-handedly picking up the back end of a Chevy Malibu and pulling it out of a large ditch by his home. One day, Joey asked him what workout equipment he used. Will laughed and said his secret was good, hard farm work.

Putting his arm around Joey's shoulder and playfully squeezing it, Will said, "Today, you and I are going to work on the pig machine."

Will's arm constricted Joey like a giant snake. "The what?" Joey asked, trying to catch his breath. After Will released his playful hold. Joey rubbed his chest and said, "Oh, I get it. The next thing you're going to ask me for is to go find a skyhook, right?"

"He's not kidding," said a tall, lanky millwright walking through the door. "Along with pigs, we have monkeys, salamanders, and a bunch of other things around here you'll get to know about." Putting his hand out, the man said, "The name's Payton Jones."

Shaking Payton's hand, Joey said, "Hi. My name's Joey Slunisky."

"I know. Will told us all about you."

"I hope he lied and said good things."

Payton tightened his grip on Joey's hand and looked him intently in the eyes. "I think you'll do all right over here."

Payton was right—Joey did do all right. Because of his easygoing nature and not being afraid to work, Joey immediately fit in with the millwright crew. He found he actually enjoyed and looked forward to going to work. The millwright shanty, which he initially found so deplorable, became a second home. Because of the money he was making, Joey contemplated quitting school, but Will was quick to dispel those ideas. Joey found out they weren't kidding about the different animal names. There really were such things as pig machines, monkeys, and salamanders.

Every day brought a new experience. Because he was teachable, Joey learned a lot from Will and the other millwrights. Time passed quickly, and it wasn't long before the summer was coming to an end. Thinking of how his income would likewise be coming to an end, Joey began wondering what he could do to maintain his solvency. He approached Will and several other millwrights, asking, "Is there any kind of program here where I could work and go to school at the same time?"

Rubbing his chin, Will said, "The only thing I can think of would be the Chem Lab."

"What do they do there?"

"They test metals coming out of the furnaces to make sure all the material has been added in proper amounts."

Another millwright said, "Yeah, I heard it's a gravy job."

Joey, his eyes bright with the prospect of having a job while he was going to school, said, "That sounds great! I'm off tomorrow. I think I'll check it out."

The next morning, Joey introduced himself to the receptionist and asked if he could see Mr. Lennon. A puzzled look on her face, she said, "You know, that's really strange because Mr. Lennon just asked me to call you and set up an appointment to see him."

"How about that! May I see him now?"

Picking up her phone, she said, "Let me check.... Yes, Mr. Slunisky, Mr. Lennon will see you now."

Mr. Lennon greeted Joey at the door of his office and invited him to come in and have a seat. "You're probably wondering why I wanted to see you," Mr. Lennon said as he settled himself behind his desk.

STEVEN J. DEKANICH

"Well, sir, I guess you probably heard that I was interested in a job in the Chem Lab."

"No, I don't have anything open in the Chem Lab," Mr. Lennon said. "But I do have another opportunity for you. Joey, I've checked with your boss and some of the people you've worked with and heard good reports from them all. I have something that will be better for your career. There is an opening in the Metallurgical Lab. Do you want that job?"

Stunned by the offer, Joey stammered, "Sh … sure I do!"

"Great! I thought you would. I have an interview set up for you with the chief metallurgist, Mark Fallingwell, next Tuesday at one-thirty."

"Mr. Lennon, I appreciate everything you've done for me, but I don't understand why you've gone out of your way to help me."

"To be honest, Joey, I liked your attitude from day one. You don't always find that in young people nowadays. I thought you had a lot of potential, and the reports I received from your boss and fellow workers just confirmed it. I think you'll do well here." Sitting back in his chair, Mr. Lennon smiled. "Besides, with you being Croatian, I figured you could use all the help you could get!"

They both chuckled for a few seconds. Then Lennon's face becoming serious, he said, "There is one thing I want to tell you before your interview."

"What's that?"

"Whenever you talk with someone, you only have one chance to make a good first impression. Keep the same attitude that you have and make sure you wear a suit for your interview."

"Okay. I'll make sure I do that."

"If you don't mind me asking, what color is your suit?"

"It's a lime green leisure suit."

His hand hiding an uncontrolled smile, Mr. Lennon waited to compose himself. He moved his hand from his face and said, "Son, I don't think a lime green leisure suit would be the proper thing to wear. Did you save any money?"

"Yes, sir. I banked most of it."

"Good! I want you to realize I'm not trying to tell you what to do. I'm merely trying to optimize your chances of getting the job. Do you understand?" Seeing Joey nod his head, Mr. Lennon continued, "Take some of that money and invest it in a black, gray, or navy blue business suit. Buy a new white shirt, and get a red or burgundy silk tie."

"But I don't know how to tie a tie."

"Come back to my office, and I'll show you. Joey, I'm serious about this. If you dress properly for an interview and have the right attitude, you'll make a good first impression. If you don't, you won't, and the job could go to someone else. It's as simple as that." ✦

STEVEN J. DEKANICH

Chapter 17

New page in his life.

The following Tuesday, the chief metallurgist's secretary was scheduled to pick Joey up from Mr. Lennon's office at one o'clock. Kate, a pleasantly plump, dark-haired, dark-eyed woman in her fifties, always met everyone with a smile on her face and a twinkle in her eye. Her nature reminded Joey of a close friend's grandmother, and he was immediately put at ease. Extending her hand, she said, "Hello, Joey, I'm Kate Carrello, Mr. Fallingwell's secretary."

Shaking her hand, Joey replied, "Pleased to meet you."

"My car is just outside, so why don't we drive over to the Met Lab?"

Getting into an immaculate black Olds 98 with black leather interior, Joey asked, "Did the company give you this car?"

Chuckling, Kate answered, "Oh, no. This is my car. You'll find the managers, engineers, and secretaries can drive into the plant and park next to the Met Lab. Unfortunately, the students' parking lot is one hundred yards from the lab. But it's still better than parking in one of the big outside lots. You'd have almost a half-mile walk."

Pulling out of the parking lot, Kate drove across railroad tracks and through the main entrance, waved at the guard, and turned right.

Joey was never on this side of the plant. He was all eyes as they drove by a long gray building with hundreds of steel slabs stacked outside. The doors of the building were opened, and Joey caught glimpses of men burning steel slabs with oxygen torches. Fascinated with all the sparks spewing from the slabs, Joey asked, "What are they doing?"

"It's called scarfing. They do that before the steel is rolled. Mr. Fallingwell will explain it to you in more detail."

Rounding a bend in the road, Kate drove past one of the employee parking lots on the right. On the left, Joey saw more steel slabs and coils—thousands of them. "Is all of this stuff sold?" asked Joey.

"Most of it."

"Wow! I'll bet there's a lot of money sitting here."

"I don't know exactly how much, but I'm sure it's in the millions," Kate said. Crossing another set of railroad tracks, Kate pointed at a dingy brick building and said, "That's the managers' office building on the right."

"Is that where the Met Lab is?"

"No. We have a ways to go yet."

As they came to a blind corner, Joey was surprised to see a red traffic light hanging from the side of a building. "There are traffic lights in the plant?"

Stopping her car, Kate answered, "Yes, there are, usually at blind intersections like this one. You always want to obey the signs because you never know what will be coming around the corner."

Almost like it was planned, a gigantic vehicle came roaring around the corner.

Wide-eyed, Joey asked, "What's that?"

"That's a straddle carrier. They carry slabs of steel around the plant."

As the carrier roared by Kate's car, Joey thought, "Look at that! The wheels are higher than the car. If that thing hit us, it would be all over."

The light turned green, and Kate cautiously drove around the corner. Traversing through a labyrinth of long alleyways and dusty gray buildings, they finally came to a dingy brick building that said "Met Lab" on the door. Getting out of the car, Kate said, "It's not a national lab, but we do a lot of good work here."

Mr. Fallingwell, a slight-build, graying man in his mid-sixties, was sitting at his desk reading a report when Kate and Joey walked in. Putting the report down, he smiled, got up from his desk, and walked over to Joey. Extending his hand, he said, "You must be Joey Slunisky. I'm Mark Fallingwell. Please, have a seat. Would you like a cup of coffee?"

Joey didn't drink coffee, but he remembered Mr. Lennon's advice: "When you're at an interview, if someone offers you something to drink, accept it because it puts both people at ease." Smiling at Mr. Fallingwell, Joey replied, "I'd love some, with cream and sugar please."

"Kate, would you mind getting us two cups? Thank you." Waiting until Kate left the room, Mr. Fallingwell continued, "She's a great secretary and really keeps me straight. In your career, you'll find that a good secretary, like a good wife, is a critical part of a successful organization. I've been arguing with top management for years to increase secretary salaries. Oh, well, enough of my rambling … young man! You have a very impressive work record! I personally know your past employer, Jed Donald, and I must say I never received a recommendation like the one he gave you. If you're half as good as he said, you'll be the best student metallurgist we've ever had."

With his face reddening, Joey said, "Mr. Fallingwell, I appreciate your confidence in me, and I give you my word I will not let you down."

Mr. Fallingwell's thin face turned solemn. "That's a phrase you don't hear very much these days. It used to be a man's word was his bond. Now we have to sign things to keep us all honest." Spinning his chair around and turning his back to Joey, Mr. Fallingwell pensively stared at his massive bookshelves overflowing with vintage books on steelmaking and processing. Mr. Fallingwell's mind was transported back almost fifty years where he was given a summer job as a laborer on an open-hearth furnace. Fascinated with steelmaking, he decided to make it his career. Going on to get a metallurgical engineering degree and coupling it with good practical experience, he worked his way up to one of the top managers in the company. He thought, "It's been a long time since I've seen such enthusiasm and eyes that were hungry to learn. This young man seems to have exactly what I'm looking for in a student metallurgist."

Staring at the back of the old metallurgist's head, Joey thought, "I wonder what he's doing?"

It only took Mr. Fallingwell a few seconds to formulate his thoughts. Spinning his chair back to face Joey, Mr. Fallingwell leaned forward, placed both elbows on the edge of his desk, and folded his hands. With his hands clasped together and his shoulders slightly rounded forward, Mr. Fallingwell looked like a news commentator. "Joey, I was planning an in-depth interview with you because I'm very particular about the students we hire. However, I've decided to forgo the formalities. You've got the job if you want it."

"Of course I want the job!" Joey blurted out.

A faint smile coming to his thin lips, Mr. Fallingwell said, "Excellent! Now, let me tell you what you'll be doing here."

Mr. Fallingwell spent forty-five minutes with Joey, telling him about his new job responsibilities and giving him a tour of the lab. Joey had a good feeling about everything. Sure, he would be starting with all the crud jobs that no one else wanted. Mr. Fallingwell told him that before a person is given big responsibilities, he needs to prove to himself and others that he can handle little responsibilities.

As they returned to Mr. Fallingwell's office, the chief metallurgist didn't bother to sit down. "How soon can you start?" he asked.

"Well, sir, I asked my boss at the blast furnace how long he would want me to stay on if I got an offer from the Met Lab, and he asked if I could work through Sunday. I'll be finishing up on the day shift."

"Excellent! You can plan on starting here at eight o'clock on Monday morning. You'll be reporting to Ford Fromme. I would have introduced you to him, but Ford is off today. Now, let's get with Kate, and she can make arrangements for getting you a blue sticker for your car so you can drive into the plant to the students' parking lot."

Kate arranged for the sticker, and then Mr. Fallingwell asked her if she could drive Joey back to his car. Before parting ways, Mr. Fallingwell firmly gripped Joey by the shoulder and said, "I look forward to having you join our team. If there's anything I can do for you, my office door is always open."

Joey shook the older man's hand and said, "Mr. Fallingwell, thank you for your time. I look forward to being on your team."

Driving back to Joey's car, Kate said, "It sounds like the interview was a success. You know, Joey, I've been Mr. Fallingwell's secretary for over ten years, and I have never seen him hire anyone on the spot like he did with you."

"Everything has happened so fast," Joey said. "I just hope that I'll be able to make a positive contribution."

"With your record, I don't think you'll have anything to worry about. Where are you parked?"

"It's the blue Pontiac Tempest on the end, Mrs. Carrello."

"Call me Kate."

"Kate, thank you for the ride."

"You're quite welcome. Oh, by the way, several of the secretaries thought you looked very handsome in that black suit and red tie."

Day shifts at the millwright shanty were always busy, so time flew by. At eleven-thirty, most of the crew went on lunch break. Pouring a steaming cup of black coffee from his dented steel vacuum bottle, Will said to Joey, "So this is your last day with us."

"Yes, it is. And you know, I'm really going to miss this place.

"I'm not your boss, but why don't you take the last couple of hours and say goodbye to the rest of the crew on the furnaces. We'll cover for you."

"Will, that sounds like a good idea. I think I'll take you up on that."

At two-thirty, everyone met back in the millwright shanty and got ready to hit the showers. Talking and shaking hands with the whole crew, Joey wasn't sure if he wanted to turn the new page in his life. "You guys taught me so much. I'll never forget you."

Sitting on a workbench and propping his elbow on the giant vice anchored to the table, Payton said, "Yeah, you weren't too bad to work with yourself. One thing to remember—don't get too smart."

Walking to the change house, Joey asked Will, "What did Payton mean by the statement, don't get too smart?"

With a smile, Will said, "Oh, I think he was trying to tell you not to get a big head because you're going to be an engineer."

After showering and getting dressed, Joey looked around the change house. Knowing that this part of his life was coming to a close gripped his insides with mixed feelings of joy and sweet sadness. Memories of the past few months hung in his mind like morning clouds over the Great Smoky Mountains. Still lost in his thoughts, Joey didn't hear Will come around the corner. "Well, young fella, are you ready to go?"

After one more quick glance around, Joey took a deep breath and said, "Yeah, let's go." ✦

Chapter 18

Please don't let this be happening again!

Joey probably slept no more than an hour and a half the whole night, but enthusiastic restlessness seems to be almost as therapeutic as sweet slumber. Long before his alarm went off, Joey bounced out of bed like he was on springs. Humming, he busied himself by getting out the clothes he would wear that day. By the time he got all his clothes, his mind was fully focused on the song he was humming. Opening his bedroom door, the T-shirt in his left hand became an imaginary electric guitar, and he half-danced, half-skipped down the hallway. Happy with his performance, he bowed to an imaginary audience and exited stage right into the bathroom.

Flicking on the light, he lay his clean clothes on top of the hamper. Still humming, Joey opened the medicine cabinet and took out his razor and shave cream. After shaking the shave cream can, he dispensed an egg-sized amount of the rich lather in the palm of his left hand. Taking his right hand, he began applying the shave cream to the left side of his face. Suddenly, with his eyes widening, a raspy whisper crept from his mouth. "Oh, my God, no! Please don't let this be happening again!"

Just below his left earlobe, Joey saw a small lump protruding from his neck. He stared in disbelief. Five minutes later, he snapped out of the trance when Mrs. Slunisky knocked on the bathroom door and asked, "What would you like for breakfast? You've got plenty of time to eat."

"Mom, I'm not very hungry this morning," Joey replied with false cheerfulness.

"Son, you've got to eat something."

"Okay then. I'll have bacon and eggs."

"Good! They'll be ready by the time you come out."

Joey tried blocking the thought of the lump out of his mind and finished getting ready. Mrs. Slunisky called out, "Your breakfast is ready," just as Joey walked around the corner and into the kitchen.

Mussing his mother's silver-gray hair, Joey said, "Good morning, Mother! Breakfast smells really good!"

Fixing her hair, she said, "Thank you. Are you ready for your first day on the job as a student metallurgist?"

"I was awake most of the night thinking about it."

"I figured you would be. That's why I wanted to make you a good breakfast."

Not sure how long he could keep up the front or if his mother would notice the lump on his neck, Joey wolfed down his breakfast. He brushed his teeth, grabbed his lunch bag, kissed his mother, and was out the door at seven.

Watching her son pull out of the driveway, Mrs. Slunisky felt troubled but didn't know why.

What should have been a momentous exciting day brought forth a mixture of feelings for Joey. He was excited about his job, but when he looked in the rearview mirror, the lump on his neck overshadowed the excitement with a foreboding sense of dread. Hearing of other cases where people were let go from their jobs because of illness,

Joey thought, "Before I say anything, I think I'll wait to find out what this is." The decision made, Joey concentrated his thoughts on his new job.

Seeing the blue sticker on the back of Joey's rearview mirror, the guard signaled Joey to proceed. Joey parked in the students' lot and said a prayer before he opened the car door. Walking into Ford Fromme's office, Joey saw three students. Sitting with his feet propped up on a desk and his arms folded across his chest, Stan Shredder was the first to speak. "You must be the new student."

"That's right. My name's Joey Slunisky."

Joey walked over and shook hands with Harry Luftman, Ray Poole, and Stan.

Easing back in his chair, Harry said, "It's good to have you with us."

Ray threw an empty crumpled paper coffee cup at Harry and jokingly said, "Yeah. Now you won't have to do all the crappy jobs around here."

"Every student who worked here knew someone in the lab," Stan said. "How did you get the job?"

Joey shrugged his shoulders. "Your guess is as good as mine. I had an opportunity for an interview, and I guess things just worked out."

"How long was your interview with Fallingwell? I don't think anyone of us got out in less than an hour. It felt like being interrogated by Admiral Rickover for a position in the Nuclear Navy instead of just a student metallurgist's job."

"My interview didn't—"

"You must be Joey Slunisky," said Ford Fromme, walking into the room and extending his hand.

Spinning around, Joey looked into the smiling face of his new boss. "Yes," Joey replied, shaking his hand. "And you must be Mr. Fromme."

STEVEN J. DEKANICH

"Call me Ford. I see you already met some of the other students. Just hope they haven't corrupted you." Noticing the confused look on Joey's face, Ford continued, "Just joking, of course. They're all a good group of student engineers."

Getting up from his chair and stretching his six-foot, seven-inch frame, Ray interrupted, "We pay him to say things like that."

"How do you like that? You try to pay these rummies a compliment, and they slam you!"

Smiling as he walked out the door, Ray said, "Well, now that I've upset you, I'm going to work."

Stan hopped up from his chair and said, "Me too. Walt has me working on a failure analysis that has to be completed today. I'll see you later, Joey."

Ford nodded at the last of the trio remaining in the room. "Harry—"

"Yeah, I know. You want me to show him the ropes."

"That's right. We've got numerous orders for pipe tests that Eddy has to run today."

With a sinister smile forming on his lips, Harry turned to Joey. "Come on, rookie. You're in for a treat!"

Joey followed Harry out of Ford's office. They turned left and then trotted down a stairway. At the bottom of the stairway, Harry led Joey through a door. The entrance led into a well-lit lunch area for the technicians. Not seeing anyone, Harry said, "Looks like everyone is working already." As they walked around a corner, Joey saw several technicians dressed in beige lab coats busily preparing their work for the day. After introducing Joey to the technicians, Harry explained how to prepare the samples for testing. "See all those stacks?"

Harry indicated pieces of steel lying in stacks on a large metal work bench. Each piece was twenty inches long by fifteen inches wide and ranged from one-sixteenth of an inch to a quarter inch in thickness. There were three to five pieces per stack, and the customer information was taped to the top piece.

Joey nodded, and the sinister smile returned to Harry's face. "Well, these are all yours! What you need to do is set the shear for a half-inch and cut five samples from each piece. Make sure you keep track of all the orders. Here—let me show you how to set the shear."

Harry took one of the thicker pieces, pushed it into the stops, got his hands out of the way, and pressed a button. Within a matter of seconds, mechanical arms came down to hold the steel in place, and the massive shear blade cut through the quarter-inch piece of steel like a hot knife through butter. Picking up the cut piece, Harry said, "One more thing— be careful. One slip, and you could lose a finger or a hand."

His ears ringing from the crashing sound of the thick metal shearing, Joey said, "You bet I'll be careful. I have a personal relationship with my body parts."

"After you cut the steel, put the cut pieces in this cart, mark the rest of the pieces with the order number, and put them in the bin over there. I'll be back to see how you're doing, and then I'll tell you what needs to be done next."

Two technicians, Jim Stanlan and Carl Yacob, shook their heads and smiled as they watched Joey cut the samples from each piece. With an inquisitive look on his face, Joey asked, "Am I doing something wrong?"

"Not really," said Jim with a slight grin on his face. "But you may be making several unnecessary movements. Let us show you our system for cutting samples. It'll speed things up and be just as safe."

Jim and Carl showed Joey their techniques by cutting several samples. Joey could see how he was wasting time by doing things that didn't lead to productivity. Thanking them, Joey continued with his work.

STEVEN J. DEKANICH

Harry was surprised when he returned forty-five minutes later and found Joey cutting his last piece. Patting Joey's shoulder, Harry said, "You done good! I expected you to be here for a while."

"The kid learns quick," Jim said. "Of course, we gave him expert instructions. Joey, I've always heard, if you want to learn how to do something right, ask a technician. Don't ask an engineer." With a big smile coming to his lips, Jim looked at Harry. "Especially a student engineer."

His face getting red, Harry asked, "Oh, yeah? Where have you always heard that?"

"We're always saying that down here."

With a forced smile coming to his face, Harry grumbled something under his breath and then turned to Joey. "Okay, rookie, let's take the cart to the back room, and I'll show you what to do next."

As he slowly rounded a corner with the cart top-heavy with samples, Joey heard, "Hey, Joey!"

Stopping the cart, Joey turned toward Jim. "Yes, sir?"

"We'll be back in a bit to show you how to do it right."

Shaking his head, Harry said, "Those guys joke around a lot, but they're a good group of technicians." Looking at the cart full of samples, Harry continued, "What you'll need to do is grind both sides of the cut edges. Start out on the coarse wheel and go to the finer wheel. After you grind the surface, they'll be sent upstairs to the second floor where Eddy is going to run the etch test like Ford talked about."

"Didn't he call it a pipe test?"

"It's the same thing. The samples are put into hot hydrochloric acid, pulled out, and examined to see if any chemical segregation is present. I'll grind a couple to show you how it's done, and you can do the rest." The sparks flying from the piece looked like firework sparklers bound together and burning at the same time. Flipping up the face shield, Harry handed the sample to Joey. While Joey examined the perfectly ground surfaces, Harry said, "It's all yours."

"This doesn't look that difficult," Joey thought. When he got done with the first sample, the ground surface had bevels going every which way. Shaking his head "no" as he looked at the sample, Harry said, "It's not as easy as it looks, is it? Just keep working on it. We have plenty of stock if the samples get too thin."

"Thanks for the words of confidence."

Patting Joey's shoulder, Harry said, "Don't mention it. I'll be back to get you before lunch."

Joey had been grinding the steel samples for almost two hours when Harry flicked the lights. Joey still had his protective face shield on when Harry reached him. He was quite a sight to behold. Covered with a light metal dust, he looked like an old mannequin that had been forgotten in some remote corner of an attic. Frowning, Harry remarked, "The guys said you didn't take any breaks while I was gone."

"No. You said you'd come back for me at lunch, so I figured you wanted me to work straight through. I really didn't mind."

"This isn't a straw boss operation. If you need to take a break, you can do so and not be ostracized for it."

Joey couldn't resist. "What do ostriches have to do with it?"

"What?" Shaking his head, Harry laughed. "Very funny! Take your face shield off, and go upstairs in the bathroom and wash up for lunch."

There is something very distinctive about the acrid aroma of burnt or ground metal. Like cigarette smoke, it clings to your body and clothes. Trotting to the top of the stairs, Joey passed Ford's office on the way to the bathroom. Noting the aroma, Ford looked up and saw Joey. "Hey, Joey, come here for a second," he called out.

STEVEN J. DEKANICH

Already halfway down the hall, Joey stopped in his tracks. He spun around and jogged back to Ford's office. "Yes, sir?"

"Just wondering how things are going." His eyes scanning Joey's body, Ford smiled as he noted the metal dust covering Joey's lab coat. "It looks like Harry really has you working. What do you think of it so far?"

"Actually, there's a little bit of a pyromaniac in me, and I'm really enjoying grinding the steel and seeing the sparks."

"You mean you're actually having fun?"

"Yes, sir. It's a fact that I have to do the job, so I look for a reason in my mind that makes me want to do the job. If I make it a point to find something good in anything that I do, it helps me do better work. And if I really enjoy something, I lose all track of time."

With a puzzled look on his face, Ford remarked, "I've never heard anyone say they enjoyed grinding steel before, but if you like it, that's all that matters. Let's get together this afternoon before you go home."

"Okay. What time?"

"Let's make it three-thirty."

"Sounds good to me. See you then."

Walking into the bathroom, Joey could see the gray metal dust on his hair and shoulders. He could also see where his face shield had been because it was the only clean part of his face. "No wonder Harry said to go and get cleaned up," Joey said to himself as he shook out his lab coat. After washing up, Joey was headed down the hall and passing the file room when he heard a secretary talking. "Did you see his neck? It's really hard for me to look at him." Turning around, she saw Joey standing in the doorway. Her face turning white and then crimson, she said, "Oh, I am so sorry."

Joey's initial response was to retaliate. Sure, his neck wasn't the best thing to look at, but she wasn't a Miss America either. However, by reading the positive-attitude books Dr. Sabbs had given him, he learned that even when you want to, there's no need to argue or verbally slam people. We all have deformities of some sort, and other people may not understand you because they don't know you. If you retaliate negatively to a statement, all it does is create hard feelings and alienates you from a person who might otherwise have been a good friend. Instead of attacking the person, address the situation and get it resolved.

"I think it looks pretty gross myself, so there's no need to apologize." The positive-attitude books taught Joey that there is no better medicine for an awkward moment than a smile. Letting a real, unforced smile come to his face, he extended his hand and said, "Hi. I'm Joey Slunisky."

Immediately taking his hand, she responded, "I'm Nancy Booker, and this is Jean Sharp."

"It's a pleasure to meet you both," he said. He glanced at the clock. "I've got to meet Harry. We have some pressing business to attend to…. Actually, it's lunch. I look forward to working with you."

Still smiling, Joey walked out of the file room. He never heard Nancy say, "What a nice person."

After lunch, Harry inspected the completed orders. Pleased with what he saw, he placed the orders on a dumbwaiter and sent them to the second floor. Joey returned to his grinding and lost all track of time until the lights flicked. He turned to see Harry and Ford walking toward him.

Looking at the finished sample stacks, Harry commented, "Looks like you've done well your first day on the job."

Joey took his face shield off and smiled. "Thanks."

Ford picked up a piece and examined the ground surface. He raised his eyebrows and nodded his head in approval. "I agree with Harry. These specimens look good. Joey, go get cleaned up. Harry

STEVEN J. DEKANICH

will send the completed orders up to Eddy, and you can finish the rest tomorrow."

"But I thought these had to be completed today."

"You'll learn the one thing that is constant around here is change. There were a few priority changes since this morning."

Shrugging his shoulders, Joey answered, "Okay."

After cleaning up, Joey walked into Ford's office. Ford put aside the report he was working on and motioned toward a chair. "Have a seat. How was your first day?"

"Most enjoyable!" Joey answered. "I think I'm going to like it here."

"You know, when we talked earlier, I thought you were trying to hand me a line of bull, but you weren't, were you?"

"No, sir. When I'm hired to do something, it's a fact that the job has to be done, so I find a reason to enjoy it."

Smiling, Ford asked, "How old are you?"

"Nineteen, sir. Why?"

"Oh, I've got some forty- and fifty-year-olds who I wish had your work philosophy."

"My work philosophy?"

"Never mind about that. I wanted to talk to you about our student program. Are you familiar with co-op programs?"

"A little."

"This isn't one of them. In a co-op program, you work a certain period of time and go to school a certain period of time. Here, you work and go to school at the same time. You'll have a flexible schedule and can arrange your work schedule around your classes."

"How many hours can I work?"

"As many as you want as long as it doesn't affect your grades. Also, I want a copy of your grades at the end of each quarter."

"How low can a grade go?"

"In your major, we don't want to see anything lower than a B. By the way, bring in a copy of your last grade transcript tomorrow. Some students work twenty hours a week, and others forty hours a week. When classes start, you'll be able to judge what you can do." Looking at the clock, Ford continued, "It's about time you punch out. I don't want to have to pay you overtime on your first day."

Joey walked with the other students to the parking lot. Everyone was joking, and Joey felt on top of the world. Still smiling and waving to the others, he got behind the wheel of his car, looked in the rearview mirror, and saw the lump. ✦

Chapter 19

Just once, I'd like to have things go my way.

When Joey told his mother about the lump, his words were devastating to her. However, she realized the importance of staying calm. After the initial shock, she managed to regain her composure. She took a deep breath and said, "I'm going to call Dr. Sabbs and ask if he will take you first thing in the morning."

"Mom, let's see if he can take me after work."

"I think—"

"Mom, please. I don't want to jeopardize my job by taking off on the second day that I'm working there. It's only a matter of a few hours. Let's see if he'll see me around five."

After another eventful day at the Met Lab, Joey drove directly to Dr. Sabbs' office. Pulling into the parking lot, he saw his mother and sister waiting for him. Waving, he pulled into the space next to Cheryl Lynn's car. "I didn't know you were coming," he told his sister as he emerged from his car.

"What kind of sister would I be if I didn't come?" she said. "Besides, you'd do the same for me."

Putting his arms around his sister's and mother's shoulders, Joey answered, "I think you're the best family a person could ask for."

When they arrived in the waiting room, there were several people waiting to see Dr. Sabbs ahead of them. The trio found seats together and waited for Joey's turn.

About five-thirty, a nurse called Joey into an examination room. She asked him to remove his shirt and have a seat on the examining table. A few minutes later, the door opened, and Dr. Sabbs appeared. Extending his hand, he said, "Hello, Joey. What seems to be the problem?"

Shaking Dr. Sabbs' hand, Joey answered, "I have another lump on my neck."

"You know, if you keep coming back like this, we should put a zipper in your throat."

"Very funny."

Dr. Sabbs' expert hands probed the lump and the area around the lump. "The lump feels intact and isolated to the area where you see it."

"Does it have to come out?"

"Yes."

More irritated than concerned, Joey asked, "Why is it that every time something good happens in my life, I get clipped?"

"That's the way life is. What makes you think it should be any different for you?"

"Just once, I'd like to have things go my way."

"I think things are going your way. How can you explain the movement in your left arm coming back or not losing your voice? Also, your mother tells me you just got a job with the Metallurgy Laboratory at Sharon Steel."

"That's true, but I wouldn't have had to worry about my physical ability if I never had cancer."

Dr. Sabbs remained silent for a few seconds, thinking of a different approach. "Joey, it's a law of nature that says when something is afflicted, if it survives, it'll be stronger because of the affliction. The insecticide we use to kill mosquitoes this year will have a lesser effect on them next year because they develop a tolerance to the poison. It's the same way with human beings. Any affliction, if a person can survive it both mentally and physically, will make that person stronger in the long run."

"I don't see how, but you've been right every other time, so I'll take your word for it. How long will I have to be in the hospital?"

"Since you're just starting a new job, I'd say you're concerned about losing time at work."

"Yes, sir."

"I'll be able to do your operation in my office. We'll plan on your surgery at five o'clock on Friday. That'll give you the weekend to recover."

"Why can you do this one in your office but I had to go to the hospital for the others?"

"Because of the location and nature of the lump. I should be able to excise it using only a local. Don't worry. We're close to the hospital if something should go wrong."

"With you doing the operation, I'm in good hands. I guess you can say I'm willing to stick my neck out for you."

Chuckling, Dr. Sabbs said, "That was almost as bad as the zipper in your neck. Oh, one other thing. It would be a good idea to tell your boss about your operation."

Somewhat relieved the operation was going to be done in Dr. Sabbs' office, Mrs. Slunisky was still concerned about waiting until Friday. Dr. Sabbs assured her everything would be all right.

Driving into work early Wednesday morning, Joey thought, "I guess I'm going to find out just what kind of employer I have."

As Joey expected, Mr. Fallingwell was already busily at work when he knocked on the door. "Mr. Fallingwell, may I speak to you?" Joey asked.

Setting his work aside, Mr. Fallingwell smiled. "Good morning, Joey. Come in and tell me what's on your mind."

Joey took a seat, and the expression on his face turned Mr. Fallingwell's smile into a look of concern. "Mr. Fallingwell ... I don't know exactly how to tell you this ... I have to have another operation."

"I see. You seemed reluctant to tell me about your situation. Why?"

"Well, sir, I've heard of cases where an employer let an employee go because of health situations."

"I see, and you were concerned we were going to fire you. Is that correct?"

"Yes, sir."

"Joey, first of all, that would be illegal, and we wouldn't think of it. Let me retract that statement. We have had a few cases where we let employees go for excessive absenteeism, but those people also had atrocious work records. They felt the company owed them a living and they shouldn't have to do anything for their pay. I don't see that in your case. Did your doctor say how long you would be off work?"

"He knew my concern about taking off and said he could do it after-hours in his office on Friday. I should be back to work on Monday."

"That won't put you in jeopardy, will it?"

"Oh, no, sir. He seemed very confident in what he was doing."

"Who's your doctor?"

"Dr. Sabbs."

"I know him. He's a good man."

"I agree with you a hundred percent. I owe that man my life."

STEVEN J. DEKANICH

Joey was relieved with the support he received from both Mr. Fallingwell and Ford. "They're human too," he thought. Their attitude and support resulted in a conviction that Joey would always go the extra mile for them.

Joey was so busy with work that Friday came quickly. His mother and sister pulled in the parking lot the same time as Joey. Seeing their sullen faces, he smiled and said, "I guess we all made it here in the neck of time."

Her solemn expression not changing, Cheryl Lynn said, "That's not funny."

Sighing and looking forlorn, Joey replied, "Yeah, I guess these remarks are a real pain in the neck."

A fragile smile coming to her face, she playfully punched Joey in the shoulder. "You're something else, you know that?"

They entered Dr. Sabbs' office, and his nurse, Nancy, directed Joey to the examination room. While she prepped his neck, Nancy asked, "Have you ever been awake during an operation?"

"Not intentionally. I woke up one time during an operation. That was quite an experience."

"I'll bet it was. As you know, Dr. Sabbs is one of the best, and I just wanted to say there isn't anything to worry about."

"Hello, Joey," said Dr. Sabbs as he walked into the room. "How is the new job treating you?"

"Very well, thank you. I think I'm going to like it there."

"I think you will too. I know Mark Fallingwell and talked with him a few days ago. He'll do you right if you do a good job for him. Ready to get started?"

"Yes, but I must admit. This is certainly different than the other operations. I don't even have on one of those wretched gowns."

Smiling devilishly, Nancy said, "We can make arrangements for you to put one on if you'd like."

Blushing, Joey emphatically shook his head. "No, thanks! I'll pass."

Smiling as he scrubbed, Dr. Sabbs said, "I thought you would. Now, I need you to lie on your stomach."

"Wouldn't it be easier for you if I stayed sitting?"

"Have you ever fainted before?"

"I've come close when I overexerted myself. Why?"

"I don't want to take the chance that you may decide to black out on us."

"But I've got a strong stomach."

"Case in point, I was operating on the hand of a person who also had a strong stomach. We covered the hand with towels and exposed only the area that was to be operated on. When he asked me why I was covering the hand, I told him so he didn't get sick. He laughed and said that wouldn't happen to him. He was sitting upright while I operated on him, and we were carrying on a good conversation. Right in the middle of a sentence, he blacked out and keeled over. I didn't even know it was happening until Nancy grabbed him to keep him from banging his head on the floor."

"Okay, I'll lie on my stomach."

"As you lie down, I want you to fold your arms in front of you and rest your chin on your forearms. What I'm going to do now is deaden the area to be excised." While they were waiting for the anesthetic to take effect, Dr. Sabbs said, "Remember our conversation a few days ago when I mentioned to you the more something is afflicted, if it survives, it will be stronger in the long run?"

Pivoting his head to look at Dr. Sabbs, Joey answered, "Yes, sir."

"I want to share a brief story with you of a distinguished psychiatrist named Viktor Frankl. Frankl was a survivor of unspeakable atrocities at the hands of the Nazis in one of their concentration camps. He wrote a book, *Man's Search for Meaning*, in which he said, 'Everything

STEVEN J. DEKANICH

can be taken from a man but one thing: the last of the human freedoms—to choose one's attitude in any given set of circumstances …' Frankl said that learning this kept his mind free and alive even while he was languishing in the death camp. Joey, I want you to remember that attitude is an intangible that comes from within. It can keep us free, even fairly cheerful, regardless of our hardships. Unfortunately, each person must learn for himself how to find his own inner peace and freedom."

"If I have to find it out for myself, why did you tell me about it?"

Smiling and shaking his head, Dr. Sabbs answered, "A typical teenage response. I thought you might need some steering in the right direction." Letting his smile fade into a serious expression, he answered, "Because Frankl's afflictions didn't kill him. They made him stronger. Another thing he said was, 'Fear makes come true that which one is afraid of.' If we dwell on things we don't want, we're sure to get it. If people feel sorry for themselves and think life has dealt them a lousy hand, they're going to get lousy hands all their life…. Now, you should be numb enough to start."

Putting his chin back on his forearm, Joey thought, "While Dr. Sabbs is talking, I have no idea what he's saying, but by the end of the conversation, everything makes sense."

Joey could hear Dr. Sabbs and Nancy talking. He felt pressure on his neck but no pain. As Dr. Sabbs was making the initial incision, Joey heard a gristly sound, almost like cloth tearing, and he felt some blood run down the side of his face. While Nancy was wiping the blood, Joey's head began to swim. "Oh, God, I'm getting sick!" he thought. He quickly distracted himself by thinking about a song, and the nausea began to leave.

About fifteen minutes later, it was all over. Pale-faced, Joey was unsteady. Nancy helped him sit up and asked, "So, you weren't going to get sick?"

"Did I say that?"

Interrupting their conversation, Dr. Sabbs held up a small vial. "Want to see what your problem was?"

Looking at the vial, Joey saw a white mass with roots. "Oh, yuck! It looks like a jellyfish."

"We'll send this to be analyzed. We'll know if it is malignant next Tuesday. I want you to take it easy the rest of the weekend. If you have any problems, call me."

Putting his shirt back on, Joey shook Dr. Sabbs' hand. "Thank you for all you've done for me. My mother said you were a godsend, and I agree." ✦

Chapter 20

As long as it's in my head, it's very real to me!

The growth was malignant. However, because of its nature, Dr. Sabbs felt additional surgery was unnecessary. Joey was put on a four-week checkup cycle with strict orders to immediately come in if he noticed any swelling. Joey was free to spend his energy concentrating on his new job. Because of the understanding and support he received from Mr. Fallingwell and Ford, Joey carried out his unspoken commitment to them. Not realizing they were the source of Joey's commitment, Mr. Fallingwell and Ford commented many times during Joey's career at Sharon Steel that they never saw anyone work harder or have as much enthusiasm.

Joey was so engrossed in his job that the weeks just flew by. It was the Monday before school started, and he was getting ready to leave the Met Lab for the day when Ford called out, "Joey, you have a phone call."

A puzzled look on his face, Joey picked up the phone. "Hello."

"Joey! How ya doing?" said an excited voice on the other end.

"Andy! Long time no talk! What have you been doing with yourself?"

"Like you, working. I've been helping my dad in his garage this summer, and it seems like time has really slipped away. Why don't we get together?"

"Sounds good! When and where?"

"Let's go to the Seafood Express on Connelly Boulevard. They've got good food and even better-looking waitresses. I'll pick you up at six."

"Sounds great! See you then."

At ten minutes to six, Joey heard his mother say, "Joey, Andy's here."

As he finished up in the bathroom, Joey could hear his mother giving Andy a hard time. "Well, stranger, it's been a long time since you've graced our home with your handsome face."

"It has been a long time. This summer flew by, and next week classes are starting again."

"Joey tells me you've been working for your father."

"That's right. He's a real slave driver too."

"You don't look any worse for wear. It's about time you kids learned the meaning of work."

"Hello, Andy!" said Joey as he came into the kitchen.

Smiling, Andy responded, "How's it going, guy? You ready to pig out?"

Mussing his mother's hair as he walked by, Joey replied, "Let's go!"

Joey and Andy used the drive to the Seafood Express to catch up on the happenings of the last few months. As they walked across the parking lot to the restaurant, Andy said, "That new job of yours sounds really interesting. Do you think I might have a chance of getting hired there too?"

"There's probably a chance, but you need to be a metallurgical engineering major before you can get in."

"Funny you should mention that. I was planning on switching to a two-year technical degree in metallurgy."

"I think you'd be better off with the five-year degree."

"I know, and I'll switch after I get my grades up, but I think this is a sure way of doing it."

"Hello. May I help you?" asked a dark-haired, dark-eyed hostess with striking facial features.

Lost in their conversation, the two didn't hear the young lady's question. Still not letting the smile escape her ruby red lips, she repeated, "Good evening, gentlemen. May I help you?"

Temporarily rendered speechless by her attractiveness, Joey and Andy just smiled at her. Frowning slightly, she cocked her head and asked, "Are you two all right?"

Andy was the first to recover. "You'll have to excuse my friend. He's been working hard, and it's been a long time since he's seen a beautiful woman."

She blushed slightly at the familiar line and then turned toward Joey. "Where have you been working?"

Before Joey could respond, Andy interrupted, "He's been working on an offshore drilling rig for the last several months, and that kind of job is very hazardous and isolated."

Raising her eyebrows, she turned her chin into her shoulder and looked at Joey from the corner of her eyes. "That sounds interesting.

Perhaps we could talk about your adventures later on. Would you like smoking or non-smoking?"

Stammering, Joey said, "Non-smoking please." As the hostess directed them to their table, Joey elbowed Andy in the ribs. "Oil drilling rig, my foot!"

The hostess handed them their menus. "Your waitress will be Chris. Enjoy your meals." Before walking away, she squeezed Joey's shoulder and said, "Looking forward to hearing about your adventures."

Smiling an acknowledgment, Joey waited for her to get out of earshot before he snapped at Andy, "Great! Now what am I going to do?"

"You'll think of something. What do you want? It's my treat tonight. The steaks are great, and so is the shrimp scampi."

"We're having a special on our steak and lobster entrée," said their waitress.

Shifting his gaze from the captivating gray-blue eyes of their waitress to her name tag, Andy asked, "Chris, how much is it?"

"It's $13.33."

Joey's eyes widened. "Is this a whole meal or a cut-down version?"

"Oh, it's a full meal," Chris said with a smile. "I can assure you, you'll have enough."

"I don't know," said Andy. "You're looking at a couple of guys who can eat a large pizza apiece."

"If you're still hungry, you can always order something else."

Looking at Joey, Andy asked, "What do you think?"

Joey shrugged his shoulders. "Sounds good to me."

"How would you like your steak?"

"Medium."

Assuming his most authoritative look, Andy said, "Chris, we'll have two specials with the steaks done medium."

STEVEN J. DEKANICH

"And on your salads?"

"Ranch. Also, please bring us a couple of colas."

"I'll bring your colas and salads right out."

Watching Chris' lithe body make her way around the tables to the kitchen, Andy absently asked, "Are you dating anyone?"

His eyes falling to the floor, Joey replied. "No, not yet. When it comes to dating, I guess I'm self-conscious about the way I look, and I'm concerned what might happen."

"What do you mean? What might happen?"

"Andy, you know there are times when, for no reason, I start choking, and other times, my hands start to cramp up and I look like I have a pair of crab claws. I'm afraid something like that will happen when I'm on a date, and I don't want to put someone through that."

"But you don't mind putting me through that?"

"It's different with you. You're my close friend, and I can be myself with you. Regardless of what happens to either of us, it will not affect our friendship. Ya know, Andy, I did call some girls up to ask them for a date, but I've become so self-conscious about everything, I had to write notes of what to talk about on the phone."

"I can't believe what I'm hearing! Mr. Positive Attitude is talking like a real down-and-outer. Man, I think you're blowing everything out of proportion. It's all in your head."

"That's right, and as long as it's in my head, it's very real to me."

Chris returned to the table with a tray. "Gentlemen, here are your salads and colas," she said as she laid the food and drinks before them.

Putting his elbow on the table and his chin in the palm of his hand, Andy looked up. "Chris, this isn't meant to be a come-on, and it's just a hypothetical, but if one of us asked you out, would you find us physically attractive enough to go out with?"

Chris looked at Andy and Joey for a few seconds. "Yeah, I'd say you'd both qualify to take me out." Looking at Joey, she continued, "I understand you've been working on an oil drilling rig. I'd like to hear about it sometime."

Joey's mouth fell open as she walked away. A triumphant smile flashing across his face, Andy exclaimed, "See! It's all in your mind!"

The meal was wonderful. Joey told Chris that he didn't work on an oil rig but shared some of his blast furnace stories with her. Because Joey was so explicit with his details, Chris hung on his every word and didn't leave the table for almost ten minutes. For a brief moment, Joey forgot about his hang-ups and enjoyed himself.

As they pulled into his driveway, Joey extended his hand. "Andy, I really enjoyed this evening. Thanks a lot."

Shaking Joey's hand, Andy said, "Don't mention it. It was a lot of fun. I thought you would have asked Chris out, though."

"Talking a few minutes with someone is a lot different than spending several hours with that person. There was a beautiful student nurse who I met when I was in the hospital, and I was planning on asking her out, but I wasn't quite ready. I'm still not sure I'm ready, but thanks to you, I'm on the right track." ✦

STEVEN J. DEKANICH

Chapter 21

Man, I've never felt like this before.

Driving to Youngstown State, Joey and Andy talked about their schedules for the upcoming quarter. As they pulled onto Belmont Avenue, Joey said, "There are probably going to be times this quarter that I'll need to drive myself because I'll be going to work right after classes."

"That's another good reason for me to get a job there. We could save a lot of money by arranging our class and work schedules together."

"I wasn't going to tell you yet, but—"

"But what?"

"I talked with Mr. Fallingwell about you and told him of your interest in getting a job with the student program at Sharon Steel."

"What did he say?"

"He said if you were really serious about working there and your grades reflected it this quarter, he'd consider hiring you."

"What kind of grades is he talking about?"

"He didn't say. But knowing Mr. Fallingwell, I'd say straight A's."

As they drove down Fifth past Spring Street, Andy appeared deep in thought. He remained quiet until he parked the car and then turned toward Joey with a serious expression. "You know, Joey, I believe I can get those grades."

"I believe you can too."

"As long as I believe it, that's what matters. After seeing the way I've been in the past, what makes you think I can do it now?"

"Because you've got a reason now. I'm reading an interesting book Dr. Sabbs loaned me entitled *Man's Search for Meaning* by a person named Viktor Frankl. Frankl was an Austrian Jew who had been in Dachau and Auschwitz during World War II. In his book, he talks about some of the survivors of the camps. Many of these people shouldn't have lived, but they did, even though their bodies were pulverized from beatings. Frankl came up with an interesting deduction that, regardless of the challenges in life, when a person is able to find meaning or a 'why' in their life, they can endure almost anything. Right now Andy, you've got a why, and that's the reason I believe you'll make the grades."

"You and your books! But you're right. I've got a reason why."

"Along these same lines," Joey continued, "Dr. Sabbs was talking to me about a thing called a *Why Factor*."

"A what?"

"A *Why Factor*. He heard a motivational speaker talk about it. When he first mentioned this to me, I didn't know what he was talking about. After thinking about it for several days, I called him up and discussed it at length with him, and it made a lot of sense."

"You mean he lets you call him up and ask him questions?"

"Yeah. Why?"

"I've never heard a doctor do that before."

"He's not your average doctor. Andy, this guy not only saved my life, he helped direct my life."

"So what is this *Why Factor*?"

"Let me ask you. Do you know why a lot of young people get old before their time and why some old people never seem to get old?"

"I haven't the foggiest idea."

"It's because few people learn in life that there's only one way to never get old, and that's to have a definite goal in your life," Joey explained. "That's the *Why Factor*. Did you ever wonder why some people who know so little do so well, and other people who know so much do so little?"

"No, not really," Andy admitted.

"It's because people who know how to do something sometimes only think about doing it and then get discouraged because they never did it."

"Like being all talk and no action?"

"Exactly! The other group knows why they have to do something but may not know how to do it. But because they know why they're doing something, they'll figure out how."

"Come to think of it, when we go to college, we're always learning how, but I've never had anyone ask me why I was going."

"That's hard to answer. 'Why' is like love and faith—you can't explain it, but you know when you have it. It's as real and tangible as this car. When you have a definite why, nothing will sway you from your goal. It doesn't matter if a crisis slaps you in the face; knowing why will keep you going."

Joey had never seen anyone work harder than Andy at studying and doing extra credit. The quarter was also going very well for Joey, and for once, it seemed the cancer would not interfere with his life.

However, fate was about to change Joey's life in a marvelous and unexpected way.

On a cool brisk October evening, Joey was walking to his car after work when a thought suddenly hit him: "It's Cheryl Lynn's birthday next week, and I didn't get her anything yet!" Instead of heading home, he stopped at The Red Barn for a hamburger, cola, and fries. He called his mother from a pay phone to tell her he wouldn't be home for a while and then headed to the Shenango Valley Mall. "What can I get for a very special sister?" he wondered as he parked his car. When nothing came to mind, he decided to browse through the stores to see what he could find.

He was walking through JCPenney when he saw her—a radiant blond hair and blue-eyed beauty dressed in a red-and-white striped uniform. Her name was Angelynn Dolder. She went to the same church as Joey, and he was always attracted to her, but for some reason, he never got up enough nerve to say more than "hi" to her. There was something about this moment, however, that compelled him to talk with her.

"Hello. Looking for anything in particular?"

The startled look on Angelynn's face transformed into a warm smile. "Yes. I'm looking at some Polaroid cameras, hoping that I'll get one for my birthday."

"Really? When is your birthday?"

"October 28. I'm going to be sixteen."

A thought flashed through Joey's mind: *She's only sixteen!* But the conversation seemed so natural that he dismissed that thought from his mind. "I see you work at the hospital."

With a puzzled look on her face, she said, "No, I don't."

STEVEN J. DEKANICH

"Isn't that a candy-striper outfit that you have on?"

"No. I work at Morgan's Kentucky Fried Chicken, and this is my uniform. Don't I smell like chicken?"

Joey raised his eyebrows and smiled. "Come to think of it, I was wondering where that wonderful aroma was coming from. Speaking of food, it's been a long time since I've eaten. Would you like to get something to eat?"

"I'd love to, but we need to ask my mother first."

"Where's she at?"

"I'm supposed to meet her and my grandmother at the front of the store. Let's walk out and see if she's there."

As they walked side by side, Joey's hand brushed Angelynn's hand, and the adrenaline rush he felt was like getting a shot of epinephrine. His heart felt like it was going to pound a hole through his chest. "Man, I've never felt like this before," he thought.

Exiting JCPenney into the main part of the mall, they saw Angelynn's mother and grandmother sitting on a nearby bench.

"Mom, you remember Joey Slunisky?" Angelynn said.

"Oh, yes," her mother answered. "He goes to our church, and he used to carry my groceries out at Donald's Golden Dawn. Hello, Joey. I haven't seen you for a long time."

Smiling, Joey replied, "I've been going to college and working in the Metallurgy Lab at Sharon Steel."

"That's nice. It sounds like you're working hard." Turning to her daughter, she said, "Lynn, Oma and I need to run to Sears for a few minutes. Then we'll be ready to go."

"Mom, Joey asked if he could treat me to a cola at Grant's. Would you mind if we went there while you and Oma go to Sears?"

"Of course not. We'll meet you here a little bit later."

Relieved that Angelynn could go, Joey asked, "What time do you want us back?"

Mrs. Dolder looked at her watch. "The mall closes in an hour and a half, so why don't you plan on being back in an hour."

"Great! We'll meet you here at eight-thirty."

As they strolled through the mall toward Grant's, Joey inquired, "Your mother called you Lynn. I thought your name was Angelynn?"

"It is, but I don't like the name Angelynn, so I go by Lynn."

After being seated at their table, Joey remarked, "My mother used to work here. They have decent food. What would you like?"

"Really, all I'd care for is a cola."

"Are you sure?"

"I'm positive."

As they chatted, Joey thought, "Lynn is the easiest person to talk with that I have ever met." Lynn talked about her job at Morgan's and what she was doing in high school, and Joey talked about his courses and the work he was doing at the Met Lab.

After hearing about Joey's job, Lynn said, "I'm glad to hear you're working in a laboratory. Working at the mill is dangerous."

"It's not that bad. I worked all summer at the blast furnace."

A pained look coming to her beautiful eyes, Lynn said, "Last month, my grandfather was putting belt dressing, whatever that is, on some piece of machinery. His arm got caught in a moving belt and twisted around several times. He had to have his arm amputated."

"I'm sorry to hear that."

"It shocked our whole family. So you be careful when you're out there."

The sincerity and concern in her voice surprised Joey. Getting lost in her eyes, he thought, "I wonder if she's feeling the same way about me as I am about her?"

His thoughts were interrupted by the waitress. "Can I get you anything else?"

STEVEN J. DEKANICH

"No, thanks," Joey said. Looking at his watch, he exclaimed, "It's eight-forty! We need to go!"

Joey and Lynn hurried back to the benches in front of JCPenney. Just as they arrived, they saw Lynn's mother and grandmother walking back from Sears. "Good. They're just coming now," Lynn said.

"Sorry we're late," Mrs. Dolder said. Time just slipped away."

Glancing at Joey, Lynn replied, "That's okay, Mom."

"Well, young lady, it's time we head home. Joey, it was good seeing you again."

Lynn extended her hand to Joey. "I had a really nice time. Thank you."

Taking her hand with both of his, Joey felt his heart quicken as he said, "It was my pleasure. Hope you get that camera."

Joey stood and watched as Lynn walked away. "This was really a great night," he said to himself. "And I didn't need any notes to talk with her! I wonder what will come of it?" Walking to his car, he wondered, "When did she say her birthday was? I think it was October 28. Yeah, that's it. I need to mark that down on my calendar.... I think I'll surprise her and send her flowers for her birthday." Joey opened his car door and sat behind the wheel with his mind racing. "This was really an amazing night. I'm glad I came.... Oh, crud! I didn't get Cheryl Lynn anything!" ✦

Chapter 22

Precious and few.

The next day, Andy noticed something different about Joey, but he didn't know what it was. Finally, walking to chemistry class, he grabbed Joey's arm. "All right, what's the deal? You're acting like you're starstruck."

A twinkle in his eye, Joey replied, "Andy, I had a great experience last night. I'll tell you after chemistry."

After class, Joey headed over to Andy. "We've got an hour until the next class. Why don't we go down to McKelvey's and get a hot buttered pecan roll? I'll treat."

"Sounds good, and with you treating, it sounds even better."

They had walked almost a hundred yards without Joey saying anything. Suddenly Andy stopped and exclaimed, "That look you have is driving me crazy! What is going on with you? We're not leaving this spot until you tell me!"

"All right. I met a girl."

"It's about time. Tell me about her. What does she look like? Where does she go to school?"

"Andy, she's beautiful! And she's a freshman."

"What's she majoring in?"

"She's a freshman in high school."

"She's what! Aren't there laws about things like this?"

"What do you mean?"

"About being underage and all that. It's called robbing the cradle."

"Yeah, but what a baby!"

"This person really has you starstruck, doesn't she?"

"Yes, she does. You know what I'm going to do? Her birthday is October 28. I'm going to send her flowers."

"You don't even know her."

"Can you think of a better way to get to know someone?"

Yes, Joey was starstruck. He never had a girl take control of his thoughts like Lynn had. During class, instead of taking notes, he found himself thinking about her and writing her name. October 27 came, and Joey ordered a dozen mixed carnations from Gibbs Flower Shop. After he ordered the flowers, old thoughts of fear and doubt began creeping into Joey's mind: "I wonder if she'll like them and if they'll make a difference? Is she too young? Maybe Andy was right. I don't really know her, so should I be sending her flowers?" Luckily, these thoughts came after he placed the order.

For the rest of the week and into the next week, Joey's work and class schedule had him leaving at seven in the morning and coming home at twelve-thirty at night. His mother was also working evenings as a head cook at the Holiday Inn. Since no one was home to answer the phone, he didn't know if Lynn even got the flowers. On Saturday, Joey was picking up the mail when he saw a blue envelope addressed to him. Opening the envelope, he pulled out a letter that was on the same color stationery as the envelope and read:

November 4, 1970

Dear Joey,

I tried several times to call you to invite you to a party that I was having last Friday night but never got an answer. So, knowing how busy you are, I thought I would write you a thank-you note for the flowers! I was working on my birthday, and when my mother picked me up, she didn't say anything about the flowers. We had a few of my relatives over for cake and coffee. After they left, she said I had one more present, took me back to my bedroom, and opened the door. There on my bed were the flowers with your card! I didn't know what to say! I've never been surprised like that in my life! Thank you! Although we didn't get together for my party, I would like to see you and show you my new camera!

Your friend,

Lynn

Joey was in another world as he read the letter over several times. Suddenly the blare of a car horn brought him back to reality. "I'm standing in the middle of the road!" he exclaimed as he jumped out of the way of the oncoming car. Watching the car disappear off in the distance, Joey thought, "Man! I've heard of people having a crush on someone, but I've never heard of anyone being crushed for thinking about someone!"

On Saturday evening, Joey decided to call Lynn. For some reason, the negative thoughts of "what am I going to say, is she going to want to talk to me, or do I really want to call her," never entered his mind. The phone rang a few times, and then Joey heard the impish voice of Lynn's younger sister, Tina. "Hello. Dolder's."

"Hello. Is Lynn there?"

STEVEN J. DEKANICH

"Just a minute please." For a second, Joey didn't hear anything. Then as if Tina was holding the phone next to her mouth, Joey heard her yell, "Hey, Lynn! I think it's that guy that likes you!"

In the background, Joey could hear thumping sounds of an attitude adjustment that only a big sister could administer to a little sister. After a few seconds, he heard a voice that made his heart race and put a lump in his throat. "Hello."

After a few seconds, Joey answered, "Hello. Lynn?"

"Yes."

"This is Joey. How are you doing this evening?"

"Just fine. How are you?"

"Doing great! I must say, you've got an interesting sister."

"Yes, I do, don't I? She's a good kid, but sometimes she can be a real snot. As a matter of fact, my grandmother calls her Rotznase."

"She calls her what?"

"That's German for snot-nose, but enough about my sister. The flowers were beautiful! Thank you."

The conversation between Joey and Lynn flowed effortlessly from one subject to another. It lasted for almost forty-five minutes before her mother broke in and said she needed to get off the phone. Before he hung up, Joey made it a point to ask Lynn out. "I'll be tied up until next Saturday. Would you like to go out?"

After asking her mother, Lynn replied, "I'd love to. What time?"

"I'll be there at six-thirty. How do I get to your house?"

After giving him her address and directions, she said, "I'm looking forward to seeing you, and thank you again for the beautiful flowers."

Joey had a smile on his face as he hung up the phone. Walking into the kitchen, he glanced at the calendar. "November 14 is going to be our first date," he thought. "It's going to be like Valentine's Day in November."

Although he was extremely busy during the next week, time still seemed to drag. Finally, Saturday came. Joey spent most of the day cleaning his car. Several months before, Harold Loore, a car salesman friend from Stupka Pontiac, called Joey's mother and said he had a really clean car for Joey. It was a white two-door 66 Pontiac Catalina with a blue interior. The car was massive, but when Joey saw it, he immediately wanted it. Mrs. Slunisky, having a reputation for being able to squeeze blood out of a turnip, got Joey a deal that would have been the envy of any negotiator. This being his first car, Joey was very proud of it and kept it clean, but because it was a very special day, he wanted it immaculate.

After slipping on the tie his brother-in-law had just tied for him, Joey put on his suit jacket and walked into the kitchen. His mother looked at him and said, "My, don't you look handsome!"

"Thanks."

"What time do you think you'll be back?"

"I don't know. There's a double feature playing in Youngstown that I want to see, and then I want to take Lynn out for supper."

"Just remember. I don't think her family would want her out too late."

"It shouldn't be that late."

Checking to make sure he had an extra pack of breath mints in his pocket, Joey got in his car and proceeded down Sample Road. His mind racing as he wondered how the evening would turn out, Joey unconsciously consumed half the pack of mints by the time he got to Lynn's home, only a few miles away. Turning into Lynn's driveway, Joey stopped the car and trotted up the front steps. He rang the doorbell and was met by Mrs. Dolder. "Hello, Joey," she said, "Lynn will be out in a few minutes. Please, have a seat."

Joey sat down and watched Lynn's mother and her aunt Kate working on a new set of draperies. A few minutes later, Lynn came into the room. "Hello, Joey. It's good to see you," she said.

Springing up from the couch, he turned his eyes toward hers. "It's good to see you too. Shall we go?"

Joey helped Lynn with her coat. They said goodbye to Lynn's mother and aunt and walked to the car. After holding the door open for Lynn as she settled into the passenger seat, Joey walked behind the car and popped another mint just to be sure. Driving toward the interstate, Joey asked Lynn, "I noticed several deer antlers mounted in your foyer. Does your dad hunt?"

"No, not really. Actually someone gave him the antlers, and he thought they would look good in the foyer."

Once again, the conversation flowed from one subject to another with ease. Before they were about to pull off I-80, Lynn asked Joey, "What is your favorite singing group?"

"My favorite singing group? I haven't really given it much thought. I guess I just listen to a song, and if I like it, I'll leave the station on. If I don't, I change it. As a matter of fact, the song coming on right now, I really like."

"That's one of my favorite songs too. The title is *Precious and Few* by Climax."

The two were silent as they listened to the lyrics. Joey glanced over at Lynn as she was looking out the window. Her golden hair softly caressed her rosy cheeks, and her blue eyes were highlighted with just the right amount of eye shadow and mascara. As he looked at her, he thought, "Her facial features are like a model's." Lynn turned toward him and smiled. The smile made him melt inside, and he almost missed the turnoff.

Holding onto the armrest as they sped down the exit ramp, Lynn calmly asked, "What movie are we going to see?"

"Actually it's a double feature, *Bonnie and Clyde* and *Bullitt*."

"Oh … I heard they're really good movies."

After parking his car, Joey hopped out and opened the door for Lynn. They walked arm in arm into the Southern Park Cinema. The movies lasted longer than Joey anticipated, and they didn't leave the theater until eleven o'clock. As they were leaving, Joey had some problems with his left arm while putting on his topcoat. With a disturbed look on his face, he said, "I still have a few situations with my arm."

"Considering what you've been through, I think you're doing great."

The initial embarrassment of not being able to move his arm was immediately erased by Lynn's comment. She didn't look at him with contempt for not being able to do a simple thing like putting on a coat. Nor did she look at him with pity for being partially handicapped. She looked at him with amazement and acceptance for being able to do the things he could do. Even if he had trouble believing in himself, through her belief in him, Joey was able to surmount any obstacle that was put before him.

Opening the car door for Lynn, Joey said, "I know it's late, but I'd really like to take you out for supper."

"I'd love to."

"I was hoping you'd say that! We're going to Schuster's Steak House in Brookfield. They have some fantastic steaks there."

The romantic atmosphere of Schuster's topped off a perfect evening. Neither looked at their watch until they were driving down Madison Street. A panicked expression coming to his face, Joey said, "Do you know what time it is?"

"No. What time is it?"

"It's past two-thirty! Great! This is going to make a wonderful impression on your parents!"

As he pulled into the driveway, Lynn reached out and took Joey's hand. "Joey, I had a wonderful time," she said.

　　　　　　　　　　STEVEN J. DEKANICH

With her face dimly lit by the lights from the dash, Joey could see the twinkle and sincerity in her eyes. He cautiously put his arm around her shoulder and drew her toward him. Not receiving any resistance, he kissed her gently on the lips and said, "Lynn, this was a wonderful evening, and I'd like to see you again."

Smiling, Lynn replied, "I'd like that very much."

Hopping out of the car, he opened the door for Lynn and walked her to the side garage door. Lynn's father was waiting for them at the doorway. Looking into the steel blue eyes of Mr. Dolder, Joey thought, "Oh, God, what's going to happen? How would I feel if my daughter went out on her first date and some young punk brought her back at two-thirty in the morning? I'd probably take his head off!" Expecting the worst, Joey walked up to the door.

An expressionless look on his face, Mr. Dolder asked, "Do you know what time it is?"

"Yes, sir, we—"

Mr. Dolder pointed a warning index finger at Joey. "Let me tell you something, young man, I was young once. Don't do it again. Understand?"

The look on Mr. Dolder's face told Joey that he meant business, and Joey instinctively replied, "Yes, sir." He extended his hand.

Shaking Joey's hand, Mr. Dolder said, "Good." He turned to his daughter. "Now, young lady, it's very late, and you need to get to bed." With a frown directed at Joey, he added, "And you, young man, need to go home."

Driving home, Joey smiled as he reflected on the evening. As he turned onto Sample Road, the song *Precious and Few* came on the radio, and suddenly it meant everything to him. Pulling into his driveway, one word kept coming into his mind—perfect. This was a perfect evening. ✦

Chapter 23

Harmony.

Because of his work and school schedules, Joey was only able to see Lynn on Saturday evenings and sometimes on Sunday. He always made a point to call her every day, and they always had something to talk about.

Before they knew it, the Christmas season was in full swing. Walking through the mall one Saturday evening, Lynn asked Joey, "Have you seen Kraynak's Christmas Santa Land display?"

"No. What's it like?"

"Joey, it's like a dream world. Why don't we drive over there and see it?"

Joey pulled his car into a space at Kraynak's parking lot and hopped out of the car to open Lynn's door. Suddenly, he felt a cool tingling sensation on his cheek. Looking up into the dark sky, he could see half-dollar-size snowflakes lazily drifting out of the heavens. A smile forming on his face, he opened Lynn's door and said, "Wait until you look at the sky!"

Joey and Lynn were mesmerized for several minutes as they watched and felt the flakes gently caress their face and hands. Joey's eyes met Lynn's, and she melted in his arms. They both felt the glow of their yet unspoken love. For a brief moment in time, like two figurines in a glass water globe with snow swirling around them, they were suspended in their own little world where the only thing that existed was the two of them.

Hand in hand, they walked through the front doors of Kraynak's. The sounds of a string recording of *What Child is This?* floated gently through the air. It seemed to encircle Joey and Lynn and touched their very beings as they followed the signs to the display.

Lynn was right. The Christmas tree and character displays rivaled a Disney production. Walking through the displays made it seem like they were in a dreamland. The displays were beautiful, but what really caught Joey's attention was the fascination in the children's eyes as they watched a snowman come to life right before their eyes or saw one of Santa's elves skate effortlessly over a pond. Joey tapped Lynn's shoulder and pointed at a beautiful blue-eyed little girl in a red snowsuit with white fur trim. "Look at her," he said. "There's enchantment written all over her face. If everyone could look at each other like she's looking at that tree, we wouldn't have any fights in this world."

Squeezing Joey's arm, Lynn replied, "I think you're right."

As they neared the end of the marvelous display, Joey asked, "Why don't we go to Morgan's and get a piece of strawberry pie?"

"Okay. That way, I can check and see when I'm scheduled to work next week."

As they walked into Morgan's, several people who worked with Lynn said hello. Seated at a back table, Lynn looked into Joey's eyes. "This has been a wonderful evening. Thank you."

His heart again feeling a thrill, he replied, "It is I who should thank you. Lynn, maybe it's the season, but I never remember feeling this good about life until I met you."

Blushing, she squeezed Joey's hand. "I feel the same way."

The mood of the moment was interrupted by Lynn's friend Debbie. "Would you like a menu?"

Still holding Lynn's hand, Joey shifted his gaze from Lynn to Debbie. "No. We already know what we want. Two pieces of strawberry pie and two glasses of milk, please."

"Coming right up."

Softly caressing Joey's hand, Lynn said, "Tonight was perfect. Being with you, seeing the snow, and the Kraynak's display, I don't know how it could have been better. Have you ever thought of what a perfect Christmas would be like?"

Thinking for a moment, Joey replied, "Actually, my perfect Christmas would start on Christmas Eve. I would hire a sleigh drawn by two Clydesdale horses. The horses would have big red ribbons tied around their necks and sleigh bells attached to their harnesses so you would be able to hear them long before I got to your house. About seven o'clock, I would knock on your door, and you would open it dressed in your Christmas best. I would help you with your coat and walk you out to the sleigh. The sleigh would be made of hand-rubbed walnut, and the steel runners would glisten in the moonlight. Around the outside of the sleigh would be red and green bows, and the seats would be lined in white velvet. I would help you into the sleigh, and we would cover up with a blanket.

"As we started off, a full moon would appear on the horizon, and the snow-covered ground would make it seem almost like daytime. We would spend several hours riding around looking at all the beautiful decorations, and about eleven o'clock, we would head to the church for Midnight Mass. During the church service, the parishioners' expressions would all look like that little girl's face that we saw tonight. The whole congregation would be filled with love, and anyone walking in could feel the electricity of the moment.

"After mass, we would invite my sister and brother-in-law, Aunt Helen, and Uncle Bill to join us in the sleigh. We would ride through several neighborhoods, looking at all the beautifully colored lights. Then, as we came down Sample Road, the full moon would be directly overhead and would light up the snow-covered fields. Lynn, the fields would sparkle like billions of diamonds had been scattered over them. The breathtaking sight would leave us speechless because what we were beholding seemed to signify the true meaning of this night.

"When we reached my home, I would help you, my sister, and my aunt out of the sleigh, and we would go inside for a midnight dinner like we've never had before. As usual, there would be about thirty or forty people in the house, and each person would be filled with the love and joy of the season, and all of them would be reluctant to go home because they would want to hold onto this special feeling they had never felt before. Later, I would take you home just before sunrise, and together, we would watch the new day dawn, and there would never be a more beautiful sunrise than the one we beheld.… That would be my perfect Christmas."

Tears welling up in her eyes, Lynn was silent for several seconds. "Joey, that is one of the most beautiful things I've ever heard—"

"Here we go, two strawberry pies and two glasses of milk. Is there anything else I can get you?"

The smile leaving her face, Lynn said, "No. I think you've done all you can do."

"I'm glad you're pleased 'cause I'm expecting a good tip."

Joey and Lynn looked at each other, shook their heads, and laughed.

At two o'clock in the afternoon on Monday, December 28, Joey was busily grinding etch specimens when Harry flicked the lights and called out, "Joey, you have a phone call in Ford's office."

Wondering who it could be, Joey removed his face shield and trotted up the stairs to Ford's office. Picking up the phone, Joey said, "Hello."

"Joey! Did you get your grades yet?" asked an excited voice on the other end of the line.

"Not yet, Andy. Why? Did you get yours?"

"You bet I did!"

"What did you get?"

After a short pause, Andy said, "Joey, I got all A's!"

"Andy, that's fantastic!"

"I know! Now, like we talked before, when do you think I can have the interview with Mr. Fallingwell?"

Andy's friendship was very important to Joey, and when Andy asked when the meeting could be set up, there was no question in Joey's mind that he would do it. Joey answered, "I saw Mr. Fallingwell earlier today, so I'll go right now and arrange the meeting with him."

"Thanks, buddy."

"What are friends for? You'd do the same for me. I'll talk with you later."

Walking to Mr. Fallingwell's office, Joey saw Kate. "Kate, is Mr. Fallingwell free to talk for a few minutes?"

"I'm sorry, Joey, but he's tied up until at least five-thirty. Would you like to see him tomorrow?"

"Actually, Kate, if it's okay with him, I'll punch out and wait for him."

Kate raised her eyebrows. "This must really be important. Let me check with him." Appearing a few seconds later, Kate told him, "He said five-thirty would be fine."

At five-thirty sharp, Joey knocked on Mr. Fallingwell's door. Mr. Fallingwell opened the door and said, "Joey, please come in. Well, young man, what's so important that it couldn't wait until tomorrow?"

"Well, sir, remember the person I was talking about who wanted to get on the student program?"

"Oh, yes. You said he was on probation, but that he was a good friend of yours and that he had a lot of potential."

"Yes, sir. You mentioned if his grades were good enough this quarter, you'd consider interviewing him."

"Go on."

"He called me today and said he got all A's."

"Very impressive. It sounds like he is serious."

"Mr. Fallingwell, I've never seen this side of Andy. When I told him that you would consider giving him an interview if he got all A's, he had more focus on where he was going than any person that I've ever known."

"But I didn't tell you all A's."

"I know. I just wanted to give him a high goal to shoot for. Dr. Sabbs told me of a speech that he heard from Dr. Norman Vincent Peale. A statement Dr. Peale made about setting goals was, if I can remember the words, 'Shoot for the moon! Even if you miss, you'll still end up among the stars.' It sounded like a good philosophy to use, so I tried it on Andy."

"And your friend hit the moon."

"Yes, sir, he did."

A thought crossing his mind, Mr. Fallingwell looked intently at Joey and asked, "Joey, if I could tell you something that would help you in the long run, would you want me to?"

Looking intrigued, Joey replied, "Yes, sir, I would."

Mr. Fallingwell sat back in his chair, placing his elbows on the armrests and folding his hands in front of him. "Joey, you and your friend each have a goal that you are striving for," he said. "That is to get a degree. The university gave you an outline of what has to be done each year and each quarter. When you get to class, your professors break it down further by telling you what has to be done each week and each day. You decide how to spend each hour to get your assignments completed so, in the long run, you will have done what was required to earn your degree. Is that not so?"

"Yes, sir. That pretty well sums it up."

"Joey, in this particular situation in life, the plan for achievement was given to you in outline form. Unfortunately, after people graduate, many forget what it took to get the degree. They wander aimlessly through life and wonder what happened when they try to accomplish something else." Leaning forward in his chair and pointing a thin arthritic finger at Joey, Mr. Fallingwell continued, "Joey, a person must have a plan of action in anything he does in life. As the old saying goes, 'If you don't know where you're going, you probably won't like it when you get there.' That cliché may seem very obvious, but the majority of people never heed its warning and they wonder why they're never blessed with other achievements and success. Remember—when a person is not prepared, success is a very illusive and taunting animal that will harass a person until the day he dies. Am I making sense to you?"

Mesmerized by the conversation, Joey nodded and said, "Now I know that you and Dr. Sabbs are friends because you think so much alike."

A big smile coming to his face, Mr. Fallingwell said, "Yes, I guess you could say we share a common philosophy of life.... Well, so much for the ranting of an old man." Mr. Fallingwell turned to look at his calendar. "My schedule looks clear at two o'clock Wednesday afternoon. I'll have Kate make the necessary arrangements to get Andy in here for the interview. Because of his past grades, I can't promise you that I'll hire him, but I will keep an open mind."

"Thank you, sir. That's all anyone can ask for. Oh, by the way, what you just shared with me was far from ranting, and I really appreciate it. If more people knew or practiced what you just told me, it's almost scary to think of all that could be accomplished."

"Yes, Joey, a lot could be accomplished, but something even more could be obtained as a by product of the process."

"What's that, sir?"

"When a person doesn't know where he is going or hasn't any desire to achieve anything in his life, that person is usually filled with frustration, fear, anxiety, and possibly hate. When you know where you are going and what you need to do, there is an excitement and yet an internal calm that allows you to cope with any situation. This calm provides a person with fulfillment, courage, security, love, and inner peace that can be summed up in one word."

"What's that?"

"Harmony." ✦

Chapter 24

What am I going to do?

Mr. Fallingwell was impressed with Andy and gave him a job. As Andy had said, this turned out to be a great thing for both him and Joey because the two of them were able to carpool to school and to their jobs.

As Joey proceeded with his sophomore and junior years, he became frustrated because he was plagued with several bouts of cancer. The cancer always struck at the most inopportune times for Joey. Invariably, it would rear its ugly head during midterms, finals, or critical periods at work. But Joey had more of a reason than he ever had before to overcome the cancer and move on with his life. That reason was Lynn. Lynn provided a balance in Joey's life like he had never felt before. It was not a crush or puppy love scenario but the kind of relationship that lasts through all eternity. Joey and Lynn were not only in love with each other, they were best friends.

Joey wanted to quit school in his sophomore year, get a full-time job as a technician, and marry Lynn. He felt that he could make a good living as a technician, and he and Lynn could enjoy their lives together. Fortunately, Lynn wouldn't have anything to do with Joey's idea. "Did I just hear you right? You want to give up all the schooling you have to get a job as a technician?"

His eyebrows furrowed, Joey responded, "A technician's job isn't so bad. As a matter of fact, it's a lot of fun."

"But, Joey, you've worked so hard. Don't throw it all away."

"I'm not going to throw it all away. I'll still go to school part-time and get my degree. By the way, there's a guy I work with who is a technician and has a family and is just about to get his degree."

"How long has he been going to school?"

"I think he's been going about eight years."

Shaking her head no, Lynn pleadingly looked into Joey's eyes. "Joey, please don't do this."

"Don't you want to marry me?"

"Of course I want to marry you! And I will marry you. But promise me you'll get your degree first. Do you think Mr. Fallingwell would approve of this?"

Although Lynn was younger than Joey, she was not as spontaneous as he was in many situations. Joey smiled and took her hand. "I guess you're right. I'll get my degree first, but as soon as I do, that ring is going on your finger!"

Relieved, Lynn hugged Joey and whispered in his ear, "I can't wait!"

Joey's goal to get married spurred him to take an average of twenty hours a quarter while also working forty hours a week. Some people said he was crazy and was going to burn himself out. Although it was a hectic schedule, Joey actually enjoyed it. Mr. Fallingwell was right when he said, "When you know where you're going and what you need to do, there is an excitement and yet an internal calm that allows you to cope with any situation."

It was a very demanding schedule, but Joey didn't forget why he was doing it. Although their conversations weren't as long, he still made a point to call Lynn every day and see her on Saturday evenings. Because he kept a balance in his life, things seemed to progress better than he expected.

The beginning of the spring quarter of their junior year, Joey and Andy were walking past the Schwebel Auditorium in the William Rayen School of Engineering Building when Andy asked, "Have you thought about where you want to work?"

"Not specifically, but I do want to get into a nuclear-related field. How about you?"

"I think I'm leaning more towards the steel industry."

"Sounds good."

"Did you know there are several companies that are interviewing right now on campus?"

"No! Where at?"

"I think it's somewhere downstairs. Let's go check it out!"

They found the area that had been set up for interviewing. Talking with an attractive blond receptionist, Andy asked, "What does a person need to do to get an interview?"

Putting her elbows on the desk and folding her hands in front of her, she said, "It may be too late. We sent out a memo to all engineering departments informing them of these interviews."

"Oh, great! I think we may have had a failure to communicate here."

While Andy and the receptionist carried on a conversation, Joey looked at the pictorial displays of the companies that were being represented. Like a magnet, his eyes were drawn to a set of pictures that showed a fall setting and three giant plants nestled in a picturesque landscape. "Where is this place?" interrupted Joey.

Looking at the pictures, the receptionist answered, "That's the Nuclear Division of the Union Carbide Corporation located in Oak Ridge, Tennessee."

A sparkle came into Joey's eyes as he pointed his finger at one of the pictures. "That's where I want to be."

"You're too late. They interviewed yesterday."

"Did they leave any material behind?"

Looking through a stack of papers, she pulled out a brochure. "For some reason, I only have one brochure on Oak Ridge."

"May I look at it?"

She smiled and handed the brochure to Joey. "Honey, you can have it."

"Thanks!"

Walking to Crystallography class, Joey was completely engrossed in the brochure. Had it not been for Andy pulling him out of the way, Joey would have stepped on a student sitting on the steps in the lobby. "Put that brochure down," Andy said. "You're going to hurt somebody."

Ignoring Andy's comment, Joey exclaimed, "Andy, this place sounds great! They have three facilities in Oak Ridge—a gaseous diffusion plant that produces uranium fuel for nuclear power plants, another plant that has diverse responsibilities in programs related both to national defense and to peaceful applications of nuclear energy, and the Oak Ridge National Laboratory, which is one of the world's largest and most diverse research and development centers!"

"Sounds interesting."

"There's more! Not only do the plants sound exciting, the area sounds ideal! Listen to this: 'Oak Ridge lies along the southern slope of Black Oak Ridge in the valley between the Cumberland and Great Smoky Mountains. This is a region of clean air, abundant water, and outstanding natural beauty.' Andy, look at these pictures!"

"Easy there, fella! You sound like you're getting ready to go ballistic."

"I think I just might be. This place looks and sounds great!"

From his junior into his senior year, Joey couldn't get the thought of Oak Ridge out of his mind. Although it was not a wise decision, because he felt so sure about getting a job in Oak Ridge, Joey sent out very few resumes to other facilities involved with nuclear energy. Many people ridiculed him for that and advised him that he needed to keep his options open and be willing to take advantage of other opportunities not involved with nuclear energy.

Oak Ridge did not interview at Youngstown State in the spring quarter of Joey's senior year. When he asked why, he found there was a government freeze on hiring. This news, along with a couple of letters of rejection from other facilities, put a damper on Joey's spirits. Not sure if he was making the right decision, he made an appointment to talk to Mr. Fallingwell.

Noticing Joey didn't have the usual spring in his step as he walked into the office, Mr. Fallingwell sensed something was wrong. Shaking Joey's hand, he said, "Please, have a seat and tell me what's on your mind."

Joey sat down and leaned forward in the chair. "Mr. Fallingwell, last year when I mentioned to you about Oak Ridge, the dream of going there seemed so real there was no doubt in my mind that I would be there. I just found out they aren't hiring, and I'm getting ready to graduate in August."

"I see. Have you sent out other resumes?"

"Yes, sir," Joey said. Dejected, he looked at the floor. "They all came back with the same answer—thanks but no thanks."

"Joey, there may be a reason for the turndowns. I think since Oak Ridge isn't interviewing, it's a pretty good indication of the current condition of the nuclear industry. You may have had the wind taken out of your sails, but don't let it get you down. Resolve yourself to become so good at what you do that those companies that turned you down will regret it. One other thing—you know you can have a job here any time you'd like."

"Yes, sir, and I really appreciate it, but there's something in me that won't let the thought of Oak Ridge out of my mind. There's a lot of people who think I'm crazy, and they're all telling me to forget this ridiculous dream and look for a different job."

"Joey, all your life, you're going to have experts telling you what you should or shouldn't do." Trying awkwardly to lighten up the moment, Mr. Fallingwell smiled and said, "Don't let these people 'should' on you." Chuckling to himself and becoming a bit embarrassed at his feeble attempt of humor, a serious Mr. Fallingwell cleared his throat and continued, "Like we talked before, you know where you want to go, but the way that you thought would take you to Oak Ridge is closed. The thing to do now is to figure out another way to get there. Look at this as a challenge to see just how serious you are about going to Oak Ridge. Remember—when you are seriously searching for something, the way will make itself available."

Walking out of Mr. Fallingwell's office, Joey thought, "I sure hope he's right. I've read similar things in positive-thinking books. It sounds good, but this is real life and is it really going to work this time? Lynn and I set our wedding date for August 10. If I don't get a job, what's going to happen? What am I going to do?" ✦

Chapter 25

Things seemed to fall into place.

It was a low period in Joey's life. He felt like everything was turning against him, making it difficult to rebound. Because of his change in attitude, he lost his focus and another area began to fall apart—his thesis.

Andy walked into the lab just as Joey flung his test data sheets across the table.

"My, aren't we in a good mood?"

Joey stared at Andy with a crazed look on his face.

Andy raised his hands, palms facing Joey. "Easy. I was only kidding. What's wrong?"

Plopping into a chair, Joey leaned back and covered his face. "Andy, nothing's going right."

"What do you mean?"

Joey took his hands from his face and leaned forward in the chair. "First of all, I don't have a job yet."

"Neither do I."

"But you've had several offers. You just haven't made a decision yet."

"As I recall, you have a standing offer to work at Sharon Steel any time you want the job."

"I know that, but I want to get into a materials development and a nuclear-related field."

"What else is bothering you?"

Looking at the data sheets scattered over the desk and floor, Joey answered, "Nothing's going right on my thesis. I'm supposed to be studying the effects of neutron radiation on a lead tin alloy and on low-carbon steel. I'm trying to get the lead tin alloy to harden to give me a baseline, and nothing is happening like it should. I don't know what I'm doing wrong. Andy, this is really getting to me. Look at my hands!"

Joey's hands had become so gnarled and twisted that they resembled crab claws. Andy thought, "I haven't seen him like this since the first day of his freshman class." Sitting down next to Joey, Andy asked, "How long have you been working like this?"

"Since the fall quarter."

"No. What I mean is, how much sleep have you had in the last week?"

Sitting back in the chair, Joey tried to think. "For the last week, between classes, work, and this damn thesis, I've probably averaged an hour to two per night."

"Any catnaps?"

"If I did, I don't remember them."

"You probably haven't eaten anything for a while, have you?" After Joey shrugged his shoulders, Andy continued, "Look man, you're killing yourself. Nobody can survive on only an hour of sleep per night, and I know you can't function without food. Right now, your brain is short-circuiting so badly, you wouldn't recognize a solution even if it yelled out, 'Here I am!' You know what? You're going to skip the rest of your classes today, and I'm going to report you off work tonight. You're going to go home and get a good night's rest."

"But—"

"No buts about it. I'll help you pick up these data sheets, we'll grab a bite to eat, and then I'm going to take you home so you can get caught up on your rest."

"Andy, I don't have the time. I've got to get this done."

Grabbing Joey's arm, Andy said, "Look, don't argue with me. I'm bigger than you are, and if you don't watch it, I'll be forced to sit on you. Do you want me to do that?"

Shaking his head as a fragile smile formed at his lips, he told Andy, "I guess you're right. Let's go get a hamburger."

The next morning, Joey felt refreshed and invigorated, and all of the symptoms of tetany were gone. He was still getting ready when his mother let Andy in the front door. He heard his mother say, "Good morning, Andy. Would you like some breakfast?"

Sitting down at the table, Andy replied, "I'd love some. How is Joey doing this morning?"

"He seems to be in a much better frame of mind this morning, thanks to you."

"Yeah, he looked like death warmed over yesterday."

"He's been driving himself too hard lately trying to get his thesis done."

"Yeah, I know."

"Are you two having fun talking about me?" asked Joey as he walked into the kitchen.

Andy smiled and lifted his coffee cup in the gesture of a toast. "Of course we are."

　　　　　　　　STEVEN J. DEKANICH

Sitting down to a breakfast of bacon and eggs, Joey said, "You know, I hate to admit it, but you were right. Even though my problems aren't solved yet, I feel a whole lot better."

After breakfast, Joey and Andy bid Mrs. Slunisky adieu, and they were off. Pulling onto I-80, Andy asked, "Just what are you trying to do on your thesis?"

"Okay, you know how low-carbon steel will harden over a period of time?"

"Yes, the hardening process is called aging isn't it?"

"Right. I wanted to see if I could accelerate age the low-carbon steel using the energy from neutron radiation from a californium source. The energy going into the steel matrix should make it harden faster than the normal aging process."

"Sounds logical. So what's the problem?"

"Dr. Smith also wanted me to study a lead tin alloy. What I've been trying to do for the last several months is get the alloy to harden so I can have a baseline to work from."

"And it's not hardening?"

"No. In fact, it's getting softer. I'm going to talk to Dr. Smith today and ask for help."

"That's a good idea. There has to be a logical explanation for it."

Several hours later, Joey was walking into a lab the metallurgy students used as a hangout when he heard Andy call his name. "Joey! What did Dr. Smith say?"

Joey gave Andy a smile, an expression that had been missing from his face for quite a while. "Andy, you're not going to believe this. We searched through numerous reference books and found something very interesting. The lead tin alloy is self-annealing at room temperature. It gets softer instead of harder when it sits out."

"So, what are you going to do now?"

"Dr. Smith said it would be okay to use only the steel for the thesis."

"Are you going to have enough time to finish it before graduation?"

"I hope so."

Joey attacked his work with new vigor. He interviewed with other steel companies and got offers from them all. This was a boost to his ego, but the thought of Oak Ridge was still strong in his mind, and he turned the offers down. However, even with the boosted ego, August was rapidly approaching, and Joey's thesis was going to require at least another month's worth of work. Without the thesis, he wasn't going to graduate. This thought weighed heavily on Joey's mind when Andy walked into the lab. "Joey, how's everything going?"

Thinking of all the work that still had to be done, Joey answered, "Not very well. Andy, I'm not going to have the thesis done before graduation."

Andy sat down beside Joey and put his hand on his shoulder. "Before you decide to flip out and your body goes weird on you, go and talk to Dr. Smith. Perhaps there's a way you could report on the work you've done and pass it on to another student."

His eyes widening, Joey looked at Andy. "Great idea! I think he's in his office. I'll talk with you later."

Finding the door to Dr. Smith's office open, Joey poked his head inside. "Dr. Smith, do you have a few minutes?"

Dr. Smith invited Joey to have a seat and asked, "What can I help you with?"

"It's about my thesis. There's still so much to do and so little time to do it in."

"I know, and I've been thinking about your situation. Joey, I've never done this before and probably won't do it again. So that you can graduate, I'm going to give you your thesis grade before it's done if I have your word you'll finish it after graduation."

STEVEN J. DEKANICH

Not believing what he just heard, Joey was speechless for a moment and then stammered, "Of … of course I'll finish it."

"I was hoping you'd say that. How's it coming?"

"Dr. Smith, after your offer, it couldn't be going better."

That evening, as Joey and Andy were walking toward the Met Lab, Mr. Fallingwell called out, "Joey, can you come into my office?"

Tossing Andy his lunch bag, Joey walked into Mr. Fallingwell's office. "Yes, sir?"

"Have a seat. There's something I want to talk to you about. Joey, because of your interest in the nuclear field, you've turned Sharon Steel down. I know you've turned down several other steel companies as well and still don't have a job."

Uncomfortable with this blunt summary of his situation, Joey shifted in his seat but answered, "Yes, sir."

"I'm going to offer you something that I have never offered a student. If you don't get a job before you graduate, I will allow you to stay with the student program for two months after you graduate until you find a job or decide to come with Sharon Steel as an engineer."

For the second time that day, Joey was speechless for a few seconds. "Mr. Fallingwell, I don't know what to say."

"A simple thank-you will suffice."

Springing out of the chair, Joey enthusiastically shook Mr. Fallingwell's hand. "Thank you!"

Although Joey was given more time to resolve two major issues in his life, he refused to postpone the most important one—his marriage. A few weeks before their wedding, Joey and Lynn found a nice apartment on Erie Street in West Middlesex. Cleaning the apartment before their furniture arrived was an enjoyable experience. Taking a break from their work, Lynn surprised Joey with a picnic lunch. They spread a blanket on the kitchen floor to eat and enjoy each other's company.

Lynn took a deep breath as she looked around their apartment. "Can you believe this?" she asked, her face breaking into a radiant smile. "We've been looking for an apartment for how long?"

"Several months at least."

"Right. And not one place looked good to us. Now with only a few weeks left before our wedding, your cousin's father-in-law had this vacant apartment. And it's perfect!"

"Yes, it is. I had a good feeling the minute I walked in here, and we didn't even have to sign a lease. Ya know, Lynn, God really has been good to us. I don't know why, but things seem to be falling into place."

"You know when I think things started working out for us?"

"When?"

"That day that Andy brought you home early and made you get some sleep. Joey, before that, you didn't seem like you."

"Why didn't you say something?"

"Would you have listened to me?"

"Probably not."

"That's why I didn't say anything. I just prayed something would happen to release you from whatever it was that was tormenting you."

"That's a good way to put it, Lynn. It was a mental torment. I thought I was focused on where I was going, but I wasn't. When I was in that frame of mind, I didn't know what I was doing, and everything seemed to be against me. I created a living hell in my mind, and it spread through my whole being."

STEVEN J. DEKANICH

"But you turned it around."

"I didn't do it myself. Lynn, it was your prayers and support and the support of several others that helped get my mind right. After that, things seemed to fall into place. For a while there, I questioned what Mr. Fallingwell, Dr. Sabbs, and those positive-thinking books said about attitude. But they were right all along. When you are seriously searching for something, the way will make itself available." ✦

Chapter 26

The dawn of a new era.

For most people, August 10, 1974, was just another day. But for Joey Slunisky and Lynn Dolder, the first rays of the morning sun streaking across a cloudless sky signified the dawn of a new era. For on that day, these two people would be bound together in holy matrimony. Joey and Lynn had a special relationship, and they would continue to work at keeping it special. Their respect for each other grew each day, and they never developed the practice of undermining each other in public or in private.

Looking at the clear morning sky and feeling the cool breeze coming through his window, Joey was glad he didn't let his friends take him out for one more night of freedom. As he got dressed, he chuckled as he remembered the bachelor party for a friend. "I don't think Dave remembered his wedding, let alone what kind of morning it was. I'm glad Cheryl Lynn made me promise not to go."

"Joey, are you up?" he heard Anthony ask from the hallway.

"Sure am. C'mon in, best man."

"Well, young fella. Today is the big day. Still want to go through with it?"

"There's no doubt in my mind."

"I'm glad to hear you say that. We need to be at the church by ten, so we'll leave here about nine-thirty."

"I wonder why we need to be there so early. The wedding isn't until eleven."

"You'll be surprised how fast time will go. Go ahead and get ready."

After shaving and showering, Joey looked at the tuxedo. The black trousers and white dinner jacket trimmed in black looked sharp just hanging on the hanger. After putting on his white ruffled shirt and pulling on his trousers, he tried to tie his bowtie. Not having any luck, Joey called out to his mother, "Mom, is Anthony still here?"

"I thought you might need some help with the bowtie, so I stuck around," came the reply from the kitchen.

Anthony tied the bowtie. Joey slipped on his jacket and walked out into the kitchen. "Wow! Aren't you the cat's meow!" said a very expressive Aunt Helen.

His face turning red, Joey smiled and said, "Thanks." Looking at his mother, Joey asked, "Mom, are you all right?"

Suddenly the tears his mother was trying to hold back poured forth.

"Mom, what's wrong?"

"Don't you know?" asked Aunt Helen. "She's losing her little boy today."

Wiping the tears from her eyes, Mrs. Slunisky said, "After all these years, it's hard to see your only son grow up and get ready to walk out the door. Wait until you have some of your own, then you'll understand."

Hugging his mother, Joey said, "You're probably right. But for now, dry those tears … or I'll mess your hair up."

A devilish smile spreading across her face, Mrs. Slunisky said, "After paying twenty dollars to have my hair done, if you mess it up today, so help me, I'll kick you in the shins. And if you don't believe me, just try it."

Joey's eyes widened. "I believe you. Your hair is off-limits today … at least for a little while."

At the church, Joey and Anthony knocked on the door of the rectory and were met by Father Jerome. "Well, young man, today is the day!" Father Jerome said in a jovial voice. "Still want to go through with it?"

"People keep asking me that. Yes, sir, I'm positive."

After meeting with Father Jerome, Joey and Anthony walked into the church to check out the pre-wedding preparations. They listened for a while as Lynn's cousin Dee played the organ and Joey's cousin Kutchie and Rudy sang the Chicago hit *Color My World*. With a big sigh, Joey looked at Anthony and said, "Ya know, I really feel good about this. So many times, I've heard of people having second thoughts just before the wedding. I don't feel any of that. Am I weird?"

Smiling, Anthony put his arm around Joey's shoulder. "No, Joey, you're not weird. You're very fortunate to feel that way." Looking at his watch, he said, "It's about twenty minutes to eleven. Let's walk back into the sacristy."

Gazing around the church, Joey said, "I thought there would have been people here by now. I guess we're not going to have a very large crowd."

A few minutes before eleven, Joey, Anthony, and Father Jerome walked out. Joey's eyes almost came out of his head when he saw that the church was full! He looked at Anthony and asked, "Can you believe this?" Just then, the organ began to play, and Joey's eyes shot to the back of the church. The bridesmaids and groomsmen made stunning couples as they made their way down the aisle. Joey smiled, and his heart filled with pride, as he watched his niece and nephew walk down the aisle as flower girl and ring-bearer. Suddenly, there was a pause in the music. Joey's eyes once again shot down the aisle just as the wedding march began to play.

The papers would describe Lynn as: "carrying a bouquet of cascading roses and wearing a slipper-length coat ensemble of white silken organza, styled with a sleeveless empire dress and an A-line skirt and removable coat highlighted by full bell sleeves and ending in a chapel train. The portrait lace headpiece is holding the bouffant veil of silk illusion." But what Joey saw was the most beautiful woman he had ever met. Although there was the excitement of the moment, he still felt the same calm he had always felt when he was around Lynn, and she felt the same way. These feelings provided a rock solid foundation for their relationship.

When Lynn and Mr. Dolder reached the altar, Joey took Lynn's hand. Her hand seemed to be trembling as Joey took it. He then realized it was not Lynn who was trembling, but Mr. Dolder.

It seemed like in no time at all the wedding ceremony was coming to a conclusion. As the mass ended, Father Jerome asked Joey and Lynn to turn and face the congregation. "Ladies and gentlemen," he said, "I'd like to introduce you to Mr. and Mrs. Joey Slunisky!" The whole church applauded. Joey never felt as good in his life as when he and Lynn walked down the aisle. Just before they reached the back of the church, their photographer appeared and said, "Kiss each other," and they were happy to oblige.

They spent the rest of the afternoon taking pictures at Buhl Park and visiting older relatives who had trouble getting out. At six o'clock, the wedding party went to Saint Michael's Center for the reception. And what a reception it was! Because of all the relatives and friends on both sides, the final guest list was six hundred fifty people! Talking with one of the caterers, Joey asked, "How's everything going?"

A rather frazzled-looking middle-aged woman tried to smile and answered, "Mr. Slunisky, we've been serving continuously for two hours, and according to our count, we estimate eight hundred twenty-five instead of six hundred fifty."

"I thought there were a lot of people here."

"Not only are people eating at the tables, they're eating out in the hallway too!"

Hugging the woman, Joey said, "Yeah, but they seem to be enjoying themselves, so I'd say you're doing a great job."

Looking Joey squarely in the eyes, she said, "Mr. Slunisky, we've never had this many people in here before." Shaking her finger at him, she continued, "And I hope we never do again!"

The music played on into the night. The food and drink flowed freely, and everyone was having a great time. It reminded people of an old-style German/Croatian wedding that lasted for days. People of the Shenango Valley would talk about Joey and Lynn's wedding for years to come, and each time they did, it made Joey's mother and Lynn's parents burst with pride.

One of the most emotional moments for Joey was seeing Lynn dance with her father. After that came the bridal dance, and Joey stepped in line to be the last person to dance with Lynn. Facing each other, they stood on the threshold of their new life—a life that would be filled with struggles and triumphs, tears and happiness, and sicknesses and health. But because they were together, it didn't matter what happened. Taking Lynn by the hand and looking into her blue eyes, Joey felt as if they were once again standing in the parking lot of Kraynak's with the snow gently falling around them and they were two figurines in a crystal snow globe. Only the loud applause of the huge audience brought them back to the reality of the moment. Smiling, Joey asked, "Are you ready to go?"

All it took was seeing the twinkle in Lynn's eyes, and Joey whisked her off her feet and carried her out of the hall.

Joey and Lynn spent a glorious week at Paradise Stream in the Pocono Mountains. They had planned on touring some of the New England states, but unexpected job interviews brought them back early. The interviews were with two foundries and a small steel company in Erie, Pennsylvania. All of the companies offered him a job, but Joey didn't accept any of them.

Just before they got married, Lynn went to work for Donald's Golden Dawn because it offered better pay than her previous job. Ten days after the wedding, Lynn was still at work when Joey got home from Sharon Steel. Inside the mailbox, amidst the junk mail, were his grades for the quarter. His hands shaking, he opened them. "I don't believe this!" he exclaimed. Picking up his car keys, he raced to Donald's to see Lynn. Standing behind a register, she smiled as he walked through the front door. "Hello, handsome. I didn't expect to see you until I got home."

With a serious look on his face, Joey said, "I just got my grades and wanted to talk with you about them."

Frowning, Lynn asked, "What's wrong?"

Joey's face broke into a smile. "Dr. Smith gave me an A for the thesis!"

"Are you serious?"

"I sure am! Do you think you can get off early?"

"It's been pretty slow. Let me ask."

Coming back with a smile gracing her face, Lynn said, "Harold said I could leave. What did you have in mind?"

"Let's go out to eat and celebrate. We'll pick your car up when we get back."

"Where did you want to go?"

"Why don't we try Schuster's?"

Sitting at the same table as they did on their first date, Lynn took Joey's hand. "So much has happened to us since our first date, and it seems to be getting better and better each day. You've worked so hard for everything, and now you'll be getting your degree." Her eyes filling with tears, she said, "Joey, I'm so proud of you."

Joey squeezed her hand. "Lynn, I couldn't have done it without you. There were a lot of times that I would have quit had it not been for you."

With a quizzical look on her face, she asked, "What do you mean?"

"There were times when the stress of everything seemed to be crashing down around me, and I wasn't sure I could handle it. You provided a balance for me. When I was with you, everything seemed all right, and I could think straight. Yes, my lady, you don't know what an important role you played in me getting this degree and I thank you for it." Looking deeply into her eyes, Joey was quiet for a few seconds, and then squeezing her hand again, he said, "There aren't words to describe how much I love you."

Graduation day came, and Joey and Andy were all decked out in their caps and gowns. Sitting with the graduates from other disciplines, Joey looked around, turned to Andy, and said, "I think there were over two hundred that started out with me in engineering. There are only seven of us graduating today."

STEVEN J. DEKANICH

With a nod of agreement, Andy said, "Yeah, there was quite a weeding-out process. A lot of those people changed their majors or quit. I'll say one thing. I don't know if I would be here right now if it hadn't been for you."

"Buddy, I feel the same way about you. We were good for each other in this experience, and if I had it to do all over again, I'd want it to happen just like it did."

After the ceremony, there was a lot of laughter, happy tears, and picture-taking. Pride beamed from Joey's mother and his Aunt Helen. Walking over to them, he said, "Well, I done did it. I are an engineer."

Hugging Joey, Aunt Helen said, "And what a great one you're going to be!"

Lynn had a surprise graduation party for Joey at their apartment. She had Anthony invent a reason for taking Joey out, and when they came back, a lot of Joey's friends and relatives were there to congratulate him. That evening, after the majority of the guests had left, Joey said to Anthony, "This has been a whirlwind month! Getting married, going on a honeymoon, and now graduating. All I need now is a job."

Lynn came up behind Joey and put her arms around her husband. "I'm not worried at all. I know something will come that you'll be happy with."

At work the following Wednesday, Andy walked up to Joey and said, "I just interviewed with the Metals Division of Union Carbide in Ashtabula, Ohio."

"Ashtabula? Never heard of the place. What do they do there?"

"It's Union Carbide's ferro alloys plant where they specialize in making ferro silicon alloys."

"Are you going to take the job?"

Andy shook his head. "No, I don't think so. I think I'll stay with Sharon Steel. I did tell them about you, though, and they want to talk to you."

"You think they'll have something to offer me?"

"I do. Because it's Union Carbide, there's a potential door to Oak Ridge."

His eyes lighting up, Joey shook Andy's hand. "Who should I contact?"

"Here's his card. His name is Ken Thoms, and he expects to hear from you today."

"You were sure I'd be interested?"

"If there was anything that would give you the opportunity to get to Oak Ridge, I knew you'd be interested."

Excited, Joey called Mr. Thoms and scheduled an interview for the following Monday. After touring the plant and talking with several superintendents, Joey thought it would be an interesting job. Mr. Thoms explained that the company would put him on a six-month training program, which would give him an opportunity to work in each area of the plant. Then he would be assigned as an engineer on one of the furnaces. The job wasn't exactly what he had in mind, but it was with Union Carbide, and he felt it put him closer to his dream of eventually getting to Oak Ridge. So, he accepted the position.

That evening, when Joey returned home, Lynn was waiting for him. "Well?" she asked. "How was it?"

"Good. As a matter of fact, I was offered the job."

"And?"

"We're moving to Ashtabula on October 1! Mr. Thoms set it up for us to meet with a Realtor to look at apartments next Monday."

"Joey, that sounds great! Oh, by the way, Dr. Smith called to see how you were coming on your thesis."

A blank look on his face, Joey said, "Oh, crud, with everything going on, I forgot all about it. I guess I was hoping Dr. Smith would have too."

Jerking her head backwards and furrowing her eyebrows, Lynn snapped, "Joey Slunisky! I'm surprised at you! You gave that man your word. He trusted you and gave you an A!"

Joey dropped his eyes to the floor and then looked back at Lynn. "You're right." With a determined look on his face, Joey promised, "It'll be finished before we move to Ashtabula." Hugging Lynn, he whispered, "Thanks for keeping me straight."

Lynn's eyes softened, and she cupped his face with her hands. "We all need a little nudge sometimes."

For the rest of the week and weekend, Joey focused his attention on the thesis and completed a substantial portion of it.

Early Monday morning found Joey and Lynn driving on Highway 11 North to Ashtabula. "I wonder if we'll find something?" asked Lynn.

"Time will tell," Joey answered. "But I think it's going to be a lot of fun."

Meeting with the Realtor, they began their search for an apartment. Some were nice, but none gave Joey and Lynn that special feeling they got when they saw the apartment in West Middlesex. It was getting late in the day, and they still hadn't found anything. A bit frustrated but impressed, the Realtor said, "You've got to be one of the most cautious young couples I've ever met. Most newlyweds will buy or rent the first thing they see. I'm glad to see you're not like that."

After thanking her for the compliment, Joey said, "You see, Mrs. Thomas, Lynn and I have been together for four years, and we know the things that will make us happy. So, if something doesn't give us that right feeling, we won't take it just for the sake of taking it."

"You don't act like a lot of the other baby boomers I've met who have the philosophy of 'I want what I want when I want it.'"

"Oh, I'd say we do that to a point, but we try to keep it in check. All through my life, I've been warned about impulse buying. I have always been told to wait a few days, and if I still want something as much as I did the first day, chances are I could use the item. If not, I didn't really need it. So, Mrs. Thomas, that's the philosophy that I normally use. However, Lynn and I seemed to have developed a sixth sense, if you will. When something feels right to the both of us, it's usually a good decision to make."

Casting an admiring look at them, Mrs. Thomas said, "You two have an interesting way of approaching things. Before we part today, let me make a phone call to my office. I may have a place that will give you a good feeling." After making the call at a phone booth, Mrs. Thomas hurried back to the car with a smile on her face. "Good news! The apartment is vacant and clean. Let's take a quick look at it."

As they pulled into the parking lot of the Normandy Apartments, Joey said, "They look new."

"They are. They were built within the last year. We're going to look at Apartment Number Three." Walking into the two-bedroom apartment, Mrs. Thomas knew by the looks on their faces that this was going to be Joey and Lynn's new home.

Joey and Lynn signed the papers and put down an advance payment. They then thanked Mrs. Thomas and headed back to West Middlesex. As he turned onto Highway 11 South, Joey looked at Lynn. "Well, Mrs. Slunisky, what do you think of our new home?"

Looking at the address on their copy of the contract, Lynn smiled and answered, "Well, Mr. Slunisky, I don't think we could have found a nicer place than 1124 Pennsylvania Avenue, Apartment Number Three. This is truly the beginning of a new life for us."

STEVEN J. DEKANICH

Lynn was working when Joey finished his thesis, so there were no other sounds in the apartment. Joey sat for several minutes and stared at the stack of papers that was the handwritten manuscript of his completed thesis. Laying the papers on the table, Joey reflected on his life, thinking, "Even with all my illnesses, I have so much to be thankful for. My friends and relatives have shown more love and concern for me than I'd have ever thought possible. And now, the most beautiful girl in the world has chosen to spend her life with me." Tears came to his eyes as memories flooded his mind, and he quietly said, "Dear Lord, I don't know what I did to deserve your blessings, and I don't deserve them, but I thank you from the bottom of my heart."

The ringing of the phone snapped Joey from his thoughts. "Hello."

"Hi, Joey. I was wondering when you were going to bring your thesis over."

"As a matter of fact, Cheryl Lynn, I was on my way out the door. I'll be pulling in your driveway in about fifteen minutes."

Joey's last day at the Met Lab was very similar to his last day at the blast furnace. There was an excitement about moving on, yet a certain reluctance to letting go of that which was familiar. Joey spent most of the day saying goodbye to people. He called Mr. Lennon to thank him for all he had done for him, but he was not in his office. So, Joey got Mr. Lennon's secretary's word that she would pass on his appreciation to him. The last person he saw that day was Mr. Fallingwell.

With a big smile coming to his thin face, Mr. Fallingwell said, "Come in, Joey, and have a seat. Well, young man, so this is your last day with us?"

Looking at a man he deeply respected, Joey replied, "Yes, sir, and I want to thank you for everything. I not only learned a lot about metallurgy from you, I also learned a lot about life."

Mr. Fallingwell very rarely let his feelings show. However, his face reddened for a few seconds after hearing Joey's comment. Sitting back in his chair and folding his arms in front of him, Mr. Fallingwell said, "Joey, you're going to learn about life every day that you live. Don't ever become stagnant."

"What do you mean?"

"There are times when people achieve something significant in their lives and they think they have really made it. The way I visualize a person like that is … like a ripe tomato on a vine. The next stage is it gets rotten. There are other moments to seize, and we must move on with our lives. After a major accomplishment, many people cannot pull themselves out of what I call a glory rut. Their mind lingers on that one accomplishment, and they never do anything else for the rest of their lives. Let me read you something that one of my professors read to me the day I graduated." Picking up a dog-eared King James Bible on the edge of his desk, Mr. Fallingwell turned to Luke, and read, "And I will say to my soul, soul, thou has much goods laid up for many years; take thine ease, eat, drink, and be merry. But God said unto him, 'Thou fool, this night thy soul shall be required of thee."

"Why did he read that scripture to you?"

"Because I graduated at the top of my class and I thought I was really something. That scripture shows how fragile we humans are. Even with our great accomplishments, we all still die. What he did was to indelibly etch in my mind never to gloat or look down on people because of my accomplishments. Ultimately, Joey, we are all here to help our fellow man. And, if God has blessed us with other achievements, be thankful for them, but always remember—to whom much is given, much is expected."

"That's a strong statement."

"It's also exciting when you know that God will never give you something more than you can handle." Realizing he was lecturing, Mr. Fallingwell smiled and sat back in his chair. "You came in to say goodbye, but instead you wound up once again listening to an old man ramble." Getting up from his chair, Mr. Fallingwell walked over to Joey and shook his hand. "Joey, you've been one of the best students I've ever had in the program, and although it saddens me you're not staying with us, I want to wish you and Lynn the very best."

"Thank you, Mr. Fallingwell. Anything you say means a lot to me, and like I said before, I've learned so much from you."

"Joey, I haven't said anything to your mind that you didn't already know in your heart." ✦

Chapter 27

Joey, is your neck swollen?

By four o'clock, September 30, the movers hired by Union Carbide had finished packing and loading the truck. They told Lynn they would see her at the apartment in Ashtabula at eight o'clock the next morning. After the movers left, Joey and Lynn quietly looked around their empty apartment. A deep sigh escaping his lips, Joey put his arm around Lynn's waist. "Kind of sad, isn't it?"

Leaning against Joey, Lynn put her hand on his and replied, "Yes, it is. This was our first home."

Lost in their thoughts, Joey and Lynn stood arm in arm for several minutes until Joey squeezed Lynn's hand. "I think it's time we finished loading the cars, tell the family goodbye, and get on the road."

It was almost eight o'clock when they finally left. A light rain began to fall as they merged onto Highway 11 North from I-80. The closer they got to Ashtabula, the harder it rained. Looking in his rearview mirror, Joey could barely see Lynn's car as it made its way through the downpour. A scowl forming on his face, Joey said to himself, "This kind of weather is not what I had in mind for an ideal start to a new life."

STEVEN J. DEKANICH

They proceeded slowly through the raging tempest and finally pulled into the Holiday Inn parking lot at eleven-thirty. Scrunching his shoulders to keep the rain from going down his neck, Joey ran to Lynn's car and shouted so his voice could be heard above the howling wind. "Some weather, isn't it? Hon, why don't you stay in the car while I check in? There isn't any point in you getting wet."

After they checked in, both took a hot shower to warm up, and by one o'clock, they were in the harbor of each other's arms. The inclement weather was forgotten, and everything seemed right with their world.

It seemed as if their eyes had just closed when the phone was ringing with their wake-up call. Excited about the new day, Joey walked over to look out the window. The rain had stopped, and the sun was beginning to appear on the horizon. Turning to Lynn, Joey said, "It looks like it's going to be a beautiful day. Let's get dressed and have a quick breakfast."

After breakfast, Joey walked Lynn to her car. Holding her hands and getting lost in her eyes, he said, "Well, my dear, today is truly the start of a new life for us."

Squeezing his hands, Lynn replied, "Yes, it is, and I'm really excited." She threw her arms around Joey's neck. "Well, Mr. Slunisky, have a great day. I'll be waiting for you in our new home when you come from work."

Joey spent the first day meeting several managers and receiving a general plant orientation. The people he met were very personable and more than willing to help. Toward the end of the day, Mr. Thoms called Joey into his office. "How was your first day on the job?"

"Outside of feeling that I didn't contribute anything, it was most enjoyable."

"Don't you worry about the contribution stuff just yet. This is a little different than the steel industry, so get your feet on the ground, learn about the plant and how it operates, and keep associating with the experts we have around here. If you do that, I can assure you your contributions will be significant. Now, on a lighter note, have you talked with your wife today?"

"No, sir, I haven't. Our phone isn't hooked up yet."

"With all the rigors of moving, she's probably going to be dragging when you get home. I want you to take her out to eat tonight at the company's expense."

"Thank you, Mr. Thoms."

"Call me Ken. A restaurant that I highly recommend is the Stage Coach Inn. They have excellent steaks."

"Mr.... Ken, thank you again. Lynn will be pleased."

Although for a young wife, moving is exciting, toward the end of the day, Lynn was getting tired. But when Joey walked through the door with a dozen carnations and the news of going out to eat, her energy was rejuvenated. Hugging her husband, she said, "I have baked chicken in the oven, but that's okay. We'll have it tomorrow."

"You are a remarkable lady. With all you had to do, you still made dinner."

Pulling into the parking lot of the Stage Coach Inn, Joey parked the car and turned off the lights. Suddenly Lynn exclaimed, "Joey, look!"

Lazily drifting down were half-dollar-size snowflakes. This was the first snowfall of the year. Joey hopped out of the car and opened Lynn's door. For several minutes, they stood arm in arm and beheld nature's beauty. Once again, it seemed as if they were two figurines in a crystal snow globe. The peace of the moment filled their hearts as they walked hand in hand into the restaurant.

It seemed like in no time at all, the month-and-a-half training/orientation program was completed. Joey was assigned as an engineer on #20 furnace in the Number Four Alloy Department. Mr. Thoms was completely right. Making ferro silicon alloys was different than making steel, but much of it was still the same environment. Both processes include intense heat, dust, smoke, and noise. Being somewhat of a pyromaniac, Joey enjoyed the environment and especially seeing the furnace taps. Even after seeing hundreds of them, Joey was always mesmerized.

The excitement of getting to know each other, living in a new area, and meeting new friends made time fly for Joey and Lynn. Saturday evening, February 22, 1975, found them sitting on their couch looking at photo albums. As she closed the album of their honeymoon in the Poconos, Lynn said, "So much has happened in our life since then, but I still feel like we've just been married."

Joey put his arm around her and pulled her close. "I feel the same way. Lots of couples drift apart after they've been married for a short time. I guess we decided not to participate in that program."

Snuggling in Joey's arms, Lynn whispered, "I'm glad we didn't."

Enjoying the moment together, neither said anything for several minutes until Joey asked, "Why don't we go for a walk?"

"Okay."

The sun had already set when Joey and Lynn stepped out of the apartment. The ten-degree temperature made the snow sparkle as if diamonds had been scattered over its surface. Taking Joey's hand, Lynn said, "Oh Joey, this is just beautiful, and with no wind, it doesn't even seem that cold."

The two walked through the harbor area for over an hour. Suddenly they found themselves in front of a friend's home. "Let's see how Ernie is doing," suggested Joey.

Hearing Joey's knock on the door, Ernie opened it. "Well, this is a surprise," he said. "Come on in."

Ernie and Joey started about the same time with the Metals Division. Since they both enjoyed guns, hunting, and fishing, it was natural for them to become close friends.

After enjoying a cup of hot chocolate, Joey said to Lynn, "Well, my dear, I think it's time we headed back. Ernie, thanks a lot."

Walking to the door with his guests, Ernie looked out at the street and asked Joey, "Where's your car?"

"We walked here."

"You what? In ten-degree weather and the temperature dropping? You're two miles from your place. Let me take you home."

"No, thanks. We enjoyed walking over here, so we should be all right going back."

"I think you're crazy."

"Love makes a person do crazy things," Joey said. He slapped Ernie's back. "See you at work Monday."

The first mile and a half back was wonderful. The stars were out, the snow glistened, and there was no traffic to disrupt the winter silence. As Joey and Lynn made their way down Main Street, however, clouds began to blank out the sky, and the wind picked up. Before long, they were walking through a raging blizzard that made it difficult to see even a few feet in front of them. Like a ravenous gray wolf, the wind lashed at their faces and tried to rip the very coats off their backs. Desperately pulling his collar around his neck, Joey thought, "I wish I had taken Ernie up on his offer." When they finally reached their apartment, it felt like their hands and feet were frozen. As they stumbled through the door, the warmth of their home never felt so inviting. Taking off his snow-laden coat, Joey looked at Lynn and said, "Your complexion looks beautiful."

"Thank you, but there are easier ways of getting a good complexion other than going out in a raging blizzard."

They warmed themselves with a cup of hot tea and reflected on the night. They agreed it was a lot of fun except for the unexpected blizzard. After finishing their tea, they were getting ready for bed when Lynn's eyes widened. "Joey, is your neck swollen?" ✦

Chapter 28

We are made or unmade by the thoughts we think.

Monday afternoon found Joey and Lynn traveling back to Sharon and wondering what Dr. Sabbs was going to say. Was it swollen glands, or was it cancer again? Up to this point in their marriage, life had been good to Joey and Lynn, and the happiness they shared was like something found in a fairytale. Unbeknownst to them, the cancer, like a sinister creature of the dark, would soon be entangling Joey in its web of pain and suffering.

The look on Dr. Sabbs' face told them the story. "I'm sorry, Joey, but this operation must be done in the hospital."

"Do you think it is cancer?" asked Lynn with an expression that Joey had never seen before.

"Lynn, we won't know until we perform a biopsy on the removed growth."

"But do you think it is?"

"Knowing Joey's past history, there's a good possibility that it is."

Seeing the deer in the headlights expression on Lynn's face, Joey recalled what his mother looked like when he had his other bouts.

Noting his furrowed eyebrows, Dr. Sabbs asked Joey, "What are you thinking?"

"Nothing."

Not letting his eyes leave Joey's, Dr. Sabbs continued to look at Joey until Joey finally said, "Okay. I was thinking of the mental hell that I put my mother through, and now I'm putting the most important person in my life through the same thing. When something like this happens, why can't it affect only the sick person instead of the whole family? I wish she would never have seen the swelling."

"How could you keep that from her? Then if it was cancer and it killed you, what would that do to her? Worse yet, if she found out you knew about it and never told her, how would that make her feel? Joey, that's not what love is. Love is not only for good times. It's especially there for us when we have trouble making it on our own. Be thankful and not regretful that you have people who care and are concerned about you. That's a blessing you can't put a price tag on."

"But this still causes so much mental anguish."

"Agreed. Something like this will always do that." Pointing his finger at Joey, Dr. Sabbs added, "But if you let it cause mental anguish through your own pity party, YOU, not the cancer, are the reason for the mental anguish. Like we talked before, it's the hard times that build character and relationships—that is, if you let them. It's your decision."

An expressionless look on his face, Joey said, "It all comes back to choice again."

"That's right, Joey. You're free to act however you want. Feel sorry for yourself and pull everyone down. Or accept the fact that you may have cancer again and, if you do, you're going to do whatever it takes to overcome it."

A faint smile coming to his lips, Joey asked, "You'll never cut me any slack, will you?"

Chuckling, Dr. Sabbs answered, "Not in your case, Joey. Now, let me outline what we're going to be doing in the next few days."

Admitted on Tuesday morning, Joey was once again subjected to a multitude of tests. "I almost forgot what it was like to be jabbed, probed, and zapped by man and machine," he told Lynn on Wednesday afternoon while they waited for Dr. Sabbs to come with the results.

"You'll be all right," she told Joey, squeezing his hand.

Dr. Sabbs appeared in the doorway. "Good afternoon, Joey. How are you feeling?"

"Aside from being a little sore from all the needle pricks, I feel great."

Sitting down on the side of Joey's bed, Dr. Sabbs opened Joey's chart. Looking up, he said, "Joey, along with the growth in your neck, we also found something in your nasal passage."

"What do you mean?"

"You have a growth or polyp in the paranasal sinus. Have you had any difficulty breathing?"

"Come to think of it, yes, I have. I guess it happened so slowly, I didn't pay much attention."

"We're planning on removing that growth at the same time as your neck surgery. After the packing is removed, you'll notice a significant improvement in breathing."

Her eyes widening, Lynn asked, "Do you think the cancer has spread there too?"

Shifting his attention to Lynn, Dr. Sabbs answered, "Since cancers affecting the paranasal sinuses are rare, I don't think so. These type of cancers occur mostly among the Bantu of South Africa."

Joey's head snapped in a double take. "The Bantu of South Africa? The facts you come up with amaze me. Why do they get cancer of the paranasal sinuses and not the rest of us?"

"Because they have a record of using homemade carcinogenic snuff. You don't use snuff, do you, Joey?"

Shaking his head, Joey replied, "No, sir, I don't."

Getting a chuckle out of his question to Joey, Dr. Sabbs continued, "I'm glad to hear that. That kind of stuff isn't good for you. Now, let's get back to what is going to be happening to you. I've scheduled you for seven o'clock surgery tomorrow morning."

"How long will he be in surgery?" asked Lynn.

"The surgery itself shouldn't take longer than three hours. He'll be in the recovery room for a few hours and then back in his room." Turning toward Joey, Dr. Sabbs said, "One more thing—we're going to pack your sinuses with a lot of gauze. So you can expect to be uncomfortable for several days until we pull the packing out."

"You mean I won't be able to breathe through my nose?"

"At least not until Monday. We'll evaluate it then and see how you are doing and if the packing can come out."

"Oh, great—dragon breath. I can envision the nights now, only breathing through my mouth."

Standing up and patting Joey's shoulder, Dr. Sabbs said, "Remember to brush your teeth and tongue before you get company, and you should be tolerable. I'll see you in the morning."

Squeezing Joey's hand, Lynn said, "You're going to be all right."

"Of course I am, hon. This is just a little detour in our lives."

Heading toward the door, Lynn continued, "I'll be right back."

Lynn found Dr. Sabbs at the nurses' station. "Dr. Sabbs, may I talk with you?"

"Of course."

"What should I do to help Joey?"

Pointing at two empty chairs, Dr. Sabbs said, "Let's sit down over here.... Lynn, you and Joey seem to have a good relationship."

"Yes, we do."

Leaning on the armrest of the chair, Dr. Sabbs continued, "A serious illness like Joey's can strain a relationship. Now I don't anticipate Joey to be bedridden, but it's not out of the question. More than once, I've seen with younger couples and older couples that the well spouse wants out of the relationship because their partner isn't able to live up to their expectations. Lynn, that kind of mindset is devastating to both people. To the well person, it plagues them with guilty feelings the rest of their life. For the ill person, because a loved one walked out on them in their hour of need, their chance of survival is reduced significantly."

Lynn snapped her head back to an upright position. Her eyes narrowing, she said, "Dr. Sabbs, I have no intention of leaving Joey."

"The relationship you two have is very special. Although everyone is susceptible to this, if a couple remembers their commitment to each other when a tragedy strikes, together they will make it through the hard times. Then, when the hard times are over, their relationship is even sweeter than before. Although Joey knows you love him, go back and tell him you love him and tell him you'll be there for him no matter what."

Hugging Dr. Sabbs, Lynn said, "Joey was right. You're a very special man. Thank you. I'll be sure to do that."

Surprised at the hug, Dr. Sabbs lifted his lips into a faint smile. "Although I may have painted a worst-case scenario, I don't think you have a lot to worry about. Joey is a fighter and will be back on his feet in no time."

Walking back to join Joey, Lynn heard a booming voice coming from his room. "Well, I do declare! Young man, it seems like we can't keep you out of this place. Perhaps we should reserve a room for you."

STEVEN J. DEKANICH

As Lynn entered the room, Joey said to her, "Hon, I have someone I want you to meet. Mrs. Schwartz, this is my wife, Lynn. Lynn, this is Mrs. Schwartz. She's the best charge nurse that I've ever met."

"Flattery will get you everywhere," Mrs. Schwartz said. Turning to Lynn, she extended her hand. "Lynn, it's a pleasure to meet you. It looks like Joey did something right for a change."

"Be kind! I'm a frail patient."

"Be kind?" blurted Mrs. Schwartz. Then to Lynn, she said, "You should've seen some of the things this young man did to my student nurses. I always had to keep an eye on him!"

Lynn shot a quizzical glance at Joey, to which Joey quickly responded, "Mrs. Schwartz, please explain to Lynn what you're talking about before you get me in trouble."

"Honey, I don't have to explain anything because I have to make my rounds now. If you want to try to talk yourself out of this, be my guest." Mrs. Schwartz smiled at Lynn, winked, and walked out the door.

Looking intently at Joey, Lynn asked, "What did she mean?"

"I'm not sure.... Oh, it might be the time when—"

Just then the door opened, and in walked Joey's mother and sister. "How are you feeling?" asked Cheryl Lynn.

"Like I've done this before."

And it was like before. By the end of the night, the waiting room was packed with Joey's friends and relatives. The only difference was the addition of three visitors—Lynn, and Mr. and Mrs. Dolder. Mrs. Schwartz, appearing in the doorway, reminded everyone that visiting hours were over.

Lynn, Cheryl Lynn, Mrs. Slunisky, and Aunt Helen were the last to leave. Tears welling in her eyes, Lynn said, "I'll be here at six tomorrow morning."

"So will we," said Cheryl Lynn.

As he walked his visitors to the elevator, Joey saw Mrs. Schwartz at the nurses' station. Taking Lynn's arm, Joey said, "Come with me."

Joey stopped in front of the desk where Mrs. Schwartz was sitting. "Mrs. Schwartz," he asked, "would you mind telling Lynn what I did where you needed to keep an eye on me?"

Putting down the chart she was reading, Mrs. Schwartz smiled and said to Lynn, "Well, one night he popped a stitch in his neck and bled all over himself. Then he walked over here and asked one of my students for a bandage. When she saw the front of him covered with blood, she just about passed out. That poor girl wasn't right for days after that."

"Did she ever graduate?" asked Joey.

"Yes, she did. She works here in ER. I guess after the experience with you, she felt she could handle any emergency. So, Lynn, that is one of the memorable experiences we had with your husband."

"You should have seen some of the things they did to me."

"And you deserved every one of them."

"Nobody deserves to wear a hospital gown."

With a mischievous grin, Mrs. Schwartz said, "I've reserved an extra short one for you in the morning with no ties."

Looking at Joey, Lynn said, "Ooh, I can hardly wait to see that on you."

Joey's face reddened. "Who's side are you on?"

Chuckling out loud, Mrs. Schwartz cackled, "Honey, with one of those short gowns, it doesn't matter what side you're on!"

Everyone was still laughing as they reached the elevator. As the elevator doors opened, Lynn threw her arms around Joey. Feeling the tears on her cheek, Joey said, "Don't worry. I'm going to be all right."

Looking up at Joey through a glaze of tears, she said, "I love you, and I'll always be by your side no matter what." With tears still coming down her face, Lynn gave Joey another hug and got on the elevator with the others.

The elevator doors closed, and Joey could still see the anguished looks on all their faces. Shaking his head and thinking of the pain and suffering he was causing the ones he loved, Joey erupted in anger. Losing control, Joey punched the framework around the elevator. Suddenly, the anger was displaced by another sensation—pain.

Holding his hand, he heard Mrs. Schwartz ask, "Did that make you feel better?"

As he continued to wince with pain, all Joey could say was, "That was stupid."

Mrs. Schwartz peered at the two small dents in the framework. "It was also destructive. Did you break your knuckles?"

Holding up his hand, Joey said, "No. I guess I was lucky."

"You're right on both counts. That was stupid, and you were lucky. What is wrong with you?"

"Seeing the looks on their faces and knowing I was the cause of their pain … I … I guess it was more than I could handle. You know, Mrs. Schwartz, Dr. Sabbs talked to me about this, and I thought I had a handle on it. But after seeing their faces"—he shook his head—"I don't know."

Mrs. Schwartz put her arm around his shoulder. "Joey, you're only human and subject to human emotions, and there is nothing wrong with that. The emotion of anger can be a friend if it is controlled."

"Yeah, but how do you control it?"

"Honey, if I had the exact answer to that, I'd be a whole lot better paid than what I am. The fact is, Joey, all of us get angry, and we need to find a way to vent anger without hurting anyone else or ourselves."

His hand throbbing, Joey shook his head in agreement. "And how should a person vent anger or frustration?"

"In my many years of working with people, I've found that each person reacts differently from situation to situation and mood to mood. If they still have their mental faculties about them, they can cope with things better."

"But what about the times when everything seems to be closing in on you and you can't see anyway out? How do you keep your mental faculties then?"

"What you just described is similar to backing a wild animal into a corner. The animal cannot reason, so its instinct is to react to the situation with violence. Joey, because we can think and reason, God made us higher than animals. Unfortunately, many choose not to use this God-given gift, and when they don't, the situation usually gets worse."

Smiling and holding up his aching hand, Joey said, "I see what you mean."

"Joey, emotions are neither right nor wrong—they just are. It is what we do with them that will ultimately determine our destiny. If we choose to react to things mindlessly with hate or frustration in our hearts, we are doomed to a life of turmoil and stress. But, if we choose to respond to things by thinking them through and asking for God's help, any insurmountable problem can be solved because we are in tune with our Maker who gives us inner peace no matter what happens."

"But what about people who you hurt through no fault of your own? Like me with cancer."

"You just said it. It is no fault of your own, so why should you feel guilty? Self-pity usually results in anger."

Joey looked at her and didn't say a word.

"Your family is worried about you because they love you, and that's a natural reaction. I know you love them, so you need to make a conscious effort to keep your emotions in check and use them constructively, not destructively. It's a mental game that all of us play on a day-by-day basis. Those who maintain their cool win—those who don't lose. Like I said before, animals react through instinct. We don't have inborn instincts that rule over us. We have our minds. We are made or unmade by the thoughts we think. God gave us the freedom to choose what we want to create, whether it's heaven or hell. Simple as that."

Shaking his head, Joey said, "You sound just like Dr. Sabbs."

"Perhaps a little of him has rubbed off on me over the years. Now, getting back to you and your lovely wife, she really loves you."

"Yes, she does, and I really love her."

Squeezing Joey's shoulder, Mrs. Schwartz emphasized, "Then prove your love by keeping your negative emotions in check and use them to help you instead of hurt you. With a person like Lynn by your side, you shouldn't have any problems recovering. And, if she isn't a reason to recover, I don't know what is. Now, young man, would you like a snack before retiring?"

As they walked down the hall to the nurses' station, Joey put his right arm around Mrs. Schwartz's shoulders and hugged her. "I'd love a snack. And one other thing."

"What's that?"

"I want to thank you for being here. It's a good feeling to know there is a well-qualified and caring person around when you need one."

"Thank you, Joey. We all try to be like that."

Joey was prepped and already dressed in the infernal gown when Lynn walked through the door with Mrs. Dolder. A smile on his face, Joey said, "Good morning."

Returning the smile, Lynn replied, "Good morning. Did you sleep well?" Seeing the covers pulled up around his shoulders, she leaned over the bed, kissed him, and whispered in his ear, "You have your hospital gown on, don't you?"

His face reddening, Joey scowled, "Yes, I do."

"Is he going to model it for us?" asked Cheryl Lynn as she, Mrs. Slunisky, and Aunt Helen walked through the door.

Everyone seemed to be in a cheerful mood. The seriousness of the moment didn't strike home until the door opened and the orderlies came in to take Joey down to the operating room. The room was quiet as the orderlies helped Joey onto the gurney. Looking around at everyone, Joey said, "Don't look so forlorn. Like Dr. Sabbs said, this isn't going to be anything like some of the operations I've had in the past. I'll be back up here in no time."

Lynn walked over to him and took his hand. "I'll be right here waiting."

"Maybe I'll even show you my hospital gown," he said with a grin.

Shaking her head, Lynn hit him in the shoulder. "You're crazy, you know that?"

"Yeah, it's fun."

They followed Joey to the elevator and wished him well. As the elevator doors closed, Mrs. Slunisky said, "Now comes the worst part—waiting."

As the minutes ticked by and turned into hours, the wait became unbearable. Lynn tried to think of all the good times they had since they were married, but invariably the thoughts of Joey being sliced open made her insides churn. Her elbows resting on the arms of the chair and her hands clasped in front of her, Lynn stared at the floor and thought, "Is he going to be all right? We made a promise to grow old together. Will God grant that to us? It's been four hours, and we haven't heard anything.

Lynn felt a hand on her shoulder and heard Mrs. Slunisky ask, "Are you all right?"

Shaking her head, Lynn replied, "It's been four hours." Tears streamed down her face as she continued, "This waiting is unbearable. I just wish I knew what was happening."

Squeezing Lynn's shoulder, Mrs. Slunisky said, "Let's go to the nurses' station and see if they've heard anything."

As they walked out into the hallway, they saw Dr. Sabbs stepping off the elevator. The look on his face told them he had been through quite an ordeal. Before he had a chance to say anything, Lynn asked, "Is Joey all right?"

The expression on his face softening, Dr. Sabbs said, "Yes, he's going to be fine." Hearing Dr. Sabbs' voice, the others came out of the waiting room.

"What took so long?" asked Lynn.

Waiting a few seconds for the others to come within earshot, Dr. Sabbs continued, "We had a situation with hemorrhaging but got it under control. The lump in his throat was malignant."

"Oh, my God!" gasped Lynn.

"It was confined to a small area, and I believe we got it all."

"What about the growth in his nose?" asked Cheryl Lynn.

"As expected, it was a benign polyp. His nose is packed, so he'll experience some discomfort for a few days."

The thought of her husband hemorrhaging still in her mind, Lynn again inquired, "Will he be all right?"

"Yes, he will be. Now one thing I want to mention. He'll have a large bandage around his neck with drainage tubes coming out of it, which makes the operation look worse than what it was, so don't be alarmed. He may experience discomfort, and the nurses will give him something for pain if needed. It shouldn't be anything that he can't handle. If you need to get in touch with me for any reason and you can't reach me here or at my office, Mrs. Slunisky has my home phone number."

"Dr. Sabbs, thank you for all you've done."

"Oh, by the way, Lynn, before we put him under, he told me to mention to you that he would model his hospital gown for you."

Like rain quenching a forest fire, Joey's comment seemed to dispel the doom everyone was feeling.

The only discomfort Joey had was in his nose. It felt like the world's supply of gauze was stuffed up his sinuses. Since it was impossible for him to breathe through his nose, he had nightmares dreaming he was suffocating and woke up with his mouth parched.

On Monday morning, Dr. Sabbs was examining Joey and said, "I'll bet you'd like to get rid of this packing in your nose."

In a muffled voice, Joey replied, "Myes, thir, I mwould."

While Nancy was setting up a tray of tools, Dr. Sabbs said to Joey, "You certainly have a lovely wife."

"Thand dyou. I thind tso too."

"That young lady was really concerned about you. I know that I don't have to tell you this, but I'm going to. Make sure you let her know how much you appreciate her for being at your side. Joey, at times when people go through a traumatic experience, they think they're the only ones affected, when in actuality the whole family is affected and everyone needs to pull together to get through it. I know you aren't like that, but I just thought I'd say it as a reminder."

"I nknow. Dyou want to keb me straight."

"That's right. Now, let's get that gauze out of your nose."

The swelling in Joey's nose prevented him from breathing normally, but at least he could breathe again. When Lynn walked in,

Joey had a smile on his face, and in a voice that didn't sound like it had a terminal nasal condition, he said, "Hi, hon!"

"Joey, you got your packing out!"

"Yes, I did. Sound different, don't I?"

"I think you always sound wonderful."

"Thanks! Dr. Sabbs said I'll be disconnected from the suction machine tomorrow. It shouldn't be long before I can go home."

"It's going to be good to have you home. Staying over at Mom and Dad's doesn't feel the same. I like having you beside me at night."

"Hon, the feeling is mutual. Speaking about a home, why don't we start looking for a house instead of renting?"

Lynn's eyes widened. "Are you serious?"

"Sure. Lying here, I had a lot of time to think. You know, although we have a nice place, we're not building any equity."

"How can we make the down payment?"

"My mom started buying U.S. savings bonds for me when I was little to use for my education. Since I got the scholarship and was working, I didn't use them. We should be able to put down a good chunk of money on a home."

Still not believing her ears, Lynn said, "This is a surprise. I wasn't expecting a life-changing experience when I walked in, but you sure gave me one. If you think we can afford it, let's do it."

"Hon, as long as we decide what we want in a house and location, if it's meant to be, the way will show itself."

"Is that you or those positive-thinking books speaking?"

Smiling, Joey replied, "I hope it's becoming one and the same." ✦

Chapter 29

It's finally happened!

Although Joey and Lynn enjoyed house-hunting, it had some frustrating moments. Almost every Realtor they talked with wanted to show them a home that was well out of their price range. One of the Realtors showed them a beautiful 2,000-square-foot Cape Cod-style home in the harbor area. On the way back to their apartment, Joey said, "That home is beautiful, but we can't afford something like that yet. Why are these Realtors showing us homes that are between ten and fifteen thousand more than the range we told them?"

Thinking about the huge kitchen with all the cupboard space, Lynn said, "Well, that one was really nice. The kitchen was incredible!"

"Yeah, the whole thing was really nice. But, hon, if we got something like that, we would be asking for trouble because all we would be doing is worrying where we were going to get the money for the next house payment. I don't want to get us into that situation. Don't you agree?"

With a sigh of disappointment, Lynn said, "I know you're right, but this house seemed to feel right."

"We'll find something that will be right for us. You'll see."

The only Realtor who was sympathetic to Joey and Lynn's needs was the one who found them their apartment—Mrs. Thomas. Late one evening, she called and asked, "Hello, Joey. Have you and Lynn found a home yet?"

With frustration in his voice, Joey answered, "No, Mrs. Thomas. We looked at several this week, but they just weren't right."

Mrs. Thomas hesitated a moment and then said, "Joey, I know you and Lynn specified that you wanted something in the thirty-thousand range, but for a few extra thousand, I think I may have found something that will be ideal for the two of you."

"Mrs. Thomas, of all the Realtors we've talked to, you've been the most receptive to our needs, and I thought you understood the importance of us staying within our budget."

"Joey, this is a new home in the Sleepy Hollow subdivision located in Plymouth Township. The builder is asking thirty-four thousand for it, but I think he'll take thirty- two."

"Mrs. Thomas, I don't—"

"Before you say no, please let me take a few minutes of your time to show you the property. It's a beautiful split-foyer with stone facing on the lower levels and white wood siding on the upper level. The house sits on close to two acres with a fishing lake bordering your property in the backyard."

"Did you say there was a lake in the backyard?"

"Yes, I did, Joey, and it's stocked with bass, catfish and bluegill."

"Mrs. Thomas, we'll be happy to look at the home."

The next evening, Mrs. Thomas took Joey and Lynn to see the property. Although it was half the size of the Cape Cod home that Lynn liked, this house had exactly what they were looking for with the bonus of a large yard and a fishing lake! Driving back several times to look at the house, Joey and Lynn fell in love with it. They stood together in the front yard, trying to figure out how they could make the down payment.

"One nice thing is that we would qualify for that special tax credit for first-time home buyers," Lynn said.

Joey sighed. "Yeah, I know, but we still need to figure out how to get the extra money for the down payment." He looked around at the unfinished yard. "Perhaps we could do some things around here ourselves, like finishing the yard."

"That's a good idea. Let's talk to Mrs. Thomas about it!"

The builder was willing to work with Joey and Lynn on cutting some of the costs, but they were still short. Sitting at their kitchen table, Joey and Lynn tried to figure out what else could be done to get the house within their reach.

Like a light coming on in Lynn's head, she excitedly said, "Joey, I know a possible source."

"What?"

"Before we got married, my father said if he could ever help out with anything to not be afraid to talk with him."

"Do you think he would loan us the money we need?"

"It wouldn't hurt to ask."

Mr. Dolder was more than willing to give Lynn and Joey the no-interest loan for the down payment, and within a month, their friends were helping them move into their new home at 1202 Van Winkle Drive.

When their family found out Joey and Lynn were doing their own landscaping, everyone wanted to pitch in and help. The Saturday

STEVEN J. DEKANICH

morning after they moved in, Joey and Lynn were getting dressed when they heard a knock on the front door. Joey looked at the clock and saw that it was seven-thirty. With a smile coming to his face, he asked Lynn, "What time did everyone say they would be here?"

"Between eight and nine, I think."

Joey trotted down the steps to the front door. "I'll bet everyone is already here."

Opening the door, Joey saw ten smiling faces staring at him. "You ready to get started, sport?" asked Anthony.

With everyone pitching in, the major task of landscaping was completed by eight o'clock that evening. Looking at their newly seeded and strawed two-acre lawn, Joey and Lynn realized without the help of their relatives, the yard project would have seemed insurmountable for the two of them.

Joey and Anthony each grabbed a tall glass of iced tea and then walked through the yard to the lake. Looking at the still water with bluegills playing in the shallows, Anthony said, "Joey, you have a nice place here."

"Thanks. We really like it."

"I have one question for you, though."

"What's that?"

"Have you given up on going to Oak Ridge?"

"As a matter of fact, one of the guys I work with made the comment that the company really has me now that I bought a house," Joey said with a smile. "The truth is, Anthony, the dream of going to Oak Ridge is just as strong in me today as it was the first time I heard about it. The only reason we started looking for a home was that we wanted to build up some equity instead of pouring our money away on rent. Do you think I'm crazy for still hoping to go down there?"

Putting a blistered hand on Joey's shoulder, Anthony said, "Any time a person has a dream they can hold onto and truly believe in, they're not crazy. In my opinion, a person with a true passion for something is very fortunate because they are on the cutting edge of life."

Although Joey enjoyed his job, he kept his dream alive. Oak Ridge was the first thing on his mind in the morning and the last thing on his mind at night. However, until the opportunity presented itself, he made up his mind to be the best engineer he could be. Because of his attitude, he was asked to serve on a start-up team for the world's largest ferro silicon furnace (furnace #23) and molten metal mixing station.

Along with Joey enjoying the challenges of his new job, he and Lynn were also enjoying their new house. The neighbors were great, and the location was perfect. Joey and Lynn spent hours sitting by the lake talking to each other or with some of the neighbors. Since they were spending so much time by the water, Joey thought it would be nice to build a fire and roast hot dogs and potatoes. This soon became a weekend tradition. On Saturday evening, Joey would start the fire, and Lynn would prepare the food. Soon the neighbors across the lake would load up other picnic supplies in their canoe, paddle across the lake to Joey and Lynn's side, and join them for the evening. After supper, they would sit around the campfire and listen to the croaking of the bullfrogs and enjoy the cool evening. These were very special times and something that they would always cherish. Life seemed almost ideal, although Joey mentioned the only way that it could get any better was to get an offer from Oak Ridge. Little did he know that a much more significant event was about to happen in his life.

STEVEN J. DEKANICH

In early May 1976, Joey and Lynn had some friends over for supper. After putting everything on the table, Lynn called Joey and their friends Dick and Cindy to come and eat. While Joey and Dick were talking about the various things going on at the plant, Dick overheard Lynn telling Cindy that she didn't know what was wrong with her because it seemed like every morning she was getting sick.

His eyebrows rising, Dick excitedly asked, "Did you say you're getting sick every morning?"

"Yes, I did," Lynn answered. "Why?"

A big smile coming to his face, Dick said, "I may be totally off-base here—"

"YOU ARE!" said Cindy.

Ignoring his wife's warning, Dick continued, "Lynn, having three children of our own and remembering what Cindy felt like, I'd venture to say you're going to have a baby!" Looking at Joey and lifting his water glass in the form of a toast, Dick said, "Let me be the first to congratulate you!"

Shaking her head, Cindy said, "Dick, we don't know if—"

"If I'm right, you make my favorite meals for me for a month."

"And if you're wrong?"

"I'll take you out every evening for a month."

Dick didn't gloat too much when Cindy had to cook his favorite meals! That's right—Joey and Lynn were going to be new parents! Finding out that Lynn was due in mid to late December, they excitedly began preparing the third bedroom for the new arrival. Hoping for a boy, Joey painted the room blue. He wanted to buy a lot of toy footballs and guns, but Lynn talked him into waiting until the baby was born. It seemed every time they talked with their friends or relatives, the baby was always the main topic. Joey kept saying that he was going to nickname the baby *JJ* for Joey Junior. It was a very exciting time for them, and then one evening in early August, Joey came home from work, bursting through the garage entrance door and shouting, "Lynn! Where are you?"

Startled by the frantic tone, Lynn hurried down the hallway and cried out, "Joey, what's wrong?"

Bounding up the foyer steps, Joey met Lynn in the hallway. Smiling from ear to ear, he said, "It's finally happened!"

"What? What's finally happened?"

With his wide smile getting even wider, Joey stood staring at Lynn.

Lynn hit him in the shoulder and demanded, "Will you tell me what's going on?"

Joey waiting a few more seconds before answering, "I have an opportunity to interview in Oak Ridge!"

Hugging him, Lynn said, "Joey, that's wonderful! How did this all come about? When do you go down?"

Pulling Lynn to arm's length, Joey looked into her blue eyes. "Actually, you and I and …"—he paused to look at Lynn's stomach— "JJ are going together over the Labor Day weekend. Ken Thoms set everything up. I have my interview first thing Tuesday morning following the long weekend."

Hugging Joey, Lynn said, "That sounds really great. It looks like you're not only going to be a father, your dream is finally going to come true."

His eyes traveling around the house, Joey said, "Yes, it is, but I think I'm going to miss this place."

"Maybe we can find a place like this in Oak Ridge, but to tell you the truth, wherever you are, that's where I'll be happy."

"Thanks, hon. I was wondering how you would feel about moving." ✦

STEVEN J. DEKANICH

Chapter 30

I want to be a part of it.

When Joey got off work on Friday, Lynn had their clothes packed and ready to load into the trunk of the car. After packing the car, she and Joey went next door to give their neighbors the key to their house. Their neighbor, Larry, answered the door and said, "Well, soon-to-be Southerners, y'all come on in."

Joey smiled and said, "Thanks, Larry. Here's the key to the front door. We're not expecting any deliveries, so it should be pretty quiet."

"That's fine, but we'll pick up your mail."

"Thanks, pal."

In his best Southern drawl, Joey said to Lynn, "Well, honey, y'ant to head on South? It's fixin' to git dork."

Raising his eyebrows, Larry said, "I'm from Virginia, and that sounded pretty good. I still think the Southern way of speaking should be the adopted way to speak for the whole country. Oh, before you go, Maggie is making a little something for you to take on your journey."

Soon Maggie came out of the kitchen with a large picnic basket. A warm smile coming to her face, Lynn said, "Maggie, you didn't have to do this."

"Don't mention it, Lynn. It's not much, but I think it will be a lot more nutritious than the stuff you get in restaurants." She started to hand the basket to Lynn, but thinking better of that, she handed it to Joey instead. "This thing is pretty heavy, and since you're not the one having the baby, I think you should carry it."

Joey took the bulging basket. His eyes widening and his muscles tensing at its weight, he wondered how a petite woman like Maggie was able to carry it so easily. Opening the side lid, Joey saw what appeared to be a feast for a king. His eyes lighting up, he said, "Thanks, Maggie. We really appreciate this."

"Son, for great neighbors like you, it's the least we can do. Y'all be careful, ya hear?"

Hugging Larry and Maggie, Joey and Lynn said goodbye and walked across the yard to their car. After putting the straining basket in the back seat, Joey held the door open for Lynn. Once they were settled in their seats, Lynn said, "That was really nice of Larry and Maggie."

Breathing in the heavenly aroma, Joey replied, "Yes, it was, and I'll make you a bet that we don't go more than five miles before we tear into the fried chicken!"

About ten o'clock that night, Joey and Lynn decided to stop at a hotel. Having passed Cincinnati, they found a Holiday Inn in nearby Florence, Kentucky. When Joey went inside to get a room, the desk clerk told him, "You must be living right because we just had a cancellation. If you would have arrived a few minutes earlier, I would have told you we were booked for the night."

"Thanks," Joey said as the clerk handed him the room key. "We made reservations at the Holiday Inn in Winchester, Kentucky, for tomorrow night because we wanted to stop and see Fort Boone's

STEVEN J. DEKANICH

Borough, but it never occurred to me to make reservations for the trip down."

"A bit of advice ... any time you're traveling, always make sure that you book your hotel ahead of time. Otherwise, it could be a very frustrating experience for you, especially on a holiday weekend."

Once they were inside the room, Joey and Lynn spread the contents of the picnic basket on one of the double beds. Even after eating several pieces of chicken along the way, they still had what appeared to be enough pieces to make up two more chickens, a large bag of potato chips, potato salad, canned pickles with a note taped to the side ("If you need ice cream, you'll have to go out and get it"), an apple pie, seven apples, a big bunch of seedless grapes, a six pack of cola, paper plates, forks, spoons, knives, and napkins.

Shaking his head at the incredible display of food, Joey said, "Can you believe this? I bet they spent twenty dollars on all this, not to mention all the time it took to cook everything. I wonder why they did it."

"I think they care for us as much as we care for them."

"Yeah, it looks like it. Let's eat!"

Saturday morning found Joey and Lynn heading south on I-75 toward their next destination of Winchester, Kentucky. After checking into their hotel, they headed to Fort Boone's Borough. Joey was fascinated with the sights and sounds of the fort. Looking at the small cabins that made up the fort, Joey said, "These things sure don't look like houses on TV, do they?"

"No, they don't. Times were a whole lot harder back then."

As he watched a lady dressed in colonial garb dip candles, Joey asked, "Would you want to go back to this time?"

The expression on Lynn's face suggested that Joey had lost his mind. "With all the modern conveniences of today, are you kidding? Besides, almost all of them died young."

"Maybe it's TV that's giving me these thoughts, but it seems like the people back then were a whole lot happier than they are now."

"Joey, like you said before, happiness is a state of heart and a state of mind. You should know yourself from all the books you've read that we all choose if we want to be happy and at peace with ourselves or if we want to be miserable. I'll bet there were both kinds of people way back in Boone's time too."

Joey and Lynn spent most of the day at the fort and cooking out in the park area. After that, they were more than ready to head back to their room and relax for the rest of the evening. After going to church on Sunday morning, they were anxious to get to Tennessee to see if it was as beautiful as the pictures showed it to be. As they drove further south, the landscape gradually changed from a very rugged appearance to lush rolling hills. As they arrived at the Tennessee border, they suddenly started traveling up and up and up! Concerned by the sound of the straining motor, Joey asked, "Doesn't this hill ever level out?"

Studying the map, Lynn said, "It isn't a hill, Joey. It's Jellico Mountain." Lynn was awestruck as she looked into the valley far below. "Joey, this is breathtaking! Look down there!"

His knuckles white against the steering wheel, Joey stared wide-eyed at the steep and curvy section dead ahead. "That's okay. I'll take your word for it."

Finally they reached the summit. The lush vegetation on both sides of the interstate, combined with the rolling terrain of endless trees, made it seem as if they were traveling through an enchanted forest. Making the descent down the other side was almost as nerve-racking to Joey as the climb was. Once again, he thought, "Doesn't this mountain ever end?"

But it did, and soon Joey and Lynn were pulling into the city that changed the future of the world. Although it was very normal-looking, Joey couldn't help but think about all the hustle and bustle going on during World War II. Pulling onto Illinois Avenue, they headed for their hotel. "This place just feels good, doesn't it?" Joey said. "Lynn, I can't tell you how many times I've dreamed of this moment, and now it's finally happening. We're going to be part of one of the most progressive cities—or is this classified as a town? Whatever, we're going to be a part of it all. I can feel it!"

Joey and Lynn spent Sunday and most of Monday exploring the Oak Ridge area. By early Monday evening, Joey suggested they go back to the hotel. Wanting to make a good impression, he thought it was important that he get a good night's sleep. However, Joey slept very little that night. The excitement and anticipation of the interview kept running through his mind. Finally he was in Oak Ridge, and he was going to realize his dream!

Hopping out of bed well before his wake-up call, Joey took a shower and got ready.

"You're really excited, aren't you?" Lynn said with a smile.

"You know I am. It seems like it has been an eternity getting here, but we finally made it."

"What time do you think you'll be back?"

"I'm not sure. My interview is scheduled for ten o'clock with a man named Joe Ball. I think he's the head of maintenance."

"What do you mean by maintenance? When I was in high school, that was the janitor's job."

Joey gave Lynn his best patronizing look. "Very funny. I think what they mean here is where they fabricate things for the plant."

"Oooh, so that's what it is."

"What do you have planned for today?"

"Since you'll have the car, I think I'll just sit by the pool."

Glancing at his watch, Joey said, "Well, I think I'd better go."

"Joey, it's only eight-thirty. Yesterday, when we went looking for the plant, it only took fifteen minutes to get there."

"Yeah, I guess you're right. An hour and a half is probably too much time."

Joey could only hold out for fifteen minutes before he was out the door and driving to his interview at the Oak Ridge Gaseous Diffusion Plant. Following the desk clerk's directions, Joey turned left out the hotel onto Illinois Avenue, drove past an outdoor theater, and came to the Oak Ridge Turnpike intersection. Turning left on the turnpike, he headed west. Amazed by the lush green scenery, Joey thought it was like driving through a park. In route to the plant, Joey remembered the literature saying the plant covered six hundred twenty-five acres. Hoping he had the correct entrance, he looked at his directions for the third time and said to himself, "They told me the main entrance is called Portal Two. I'm pretty sure this is it."

Turning into the entrance, Joey parked his car in the visitors' parking lot and walked to the guardhouse. Seeing the armed guards, he thought, "Security must really be tight around here." When one of the guards asked Joey if he could help him, Joey told the guard his name and whom he was supposed to be meeting. The guard scanned the visitors' list before spotting Joey's name. "Ah, yes, here you are. Now if you'll let me see your driver's license, we'll get you in touch with someone from our personnel department before your meeting with Mr. Ball."

About ten minutes later, Karen Tullman from personnel came to meet Joey and escorted him to the administration building. As they entered Karen's office, she asked "Would you like a cup of coffee?"

"I'd love one—with sugar and double cream, please."

Returning with two cups, Karen handed one to Joey. The two of them sat across from each other, with Karen's desk between them.

STEVEN J. DEKANICH

"So, tell me, Joey," she asked. "Did you get a chance to see much of Oak Ridge?"

"Some. My wife and I walked around the shopping center and drove around a bit, but we didn't really know of any particular place to go."

"We have so many wonderful sites around here. You must see some of them before you leave. I'll get you some information of different attractions, but first let me call Mr. Ball." After conversing with Mr. Ball's secretary, Karen hung the phone up and looked at Joey. "I'm so sorry to tell you this, but Mr. Ball is tied up with an emergency and won't be able to meet with you this morning."

Feeling as if all of the wind had rushed from his sails, Joey asked, "When will I be able to meet with him?"

"He won't be available until three o'clock. Is that too late for you?"

"My time is his time. I'll be back at three."

Karen escorted Joey back to Portal Two and apologized again before they parted company. Shaking her hand, Joey said, "Things happen. There's no need to apologize. I'll see you at three."

Disappointed but undaunted, Joey returned to the hotel. Finding Lynn sitting at the pool, Joey tried not to show his disappointment as he walked toward her. Lynn took off her sunglasses and smiled. "Well, hello, handsome. I didn't expect you back this soon."

Plopping down in a chair next to Lynn's, Joey said, "There was an emergency, and Mr. Ball can't meet with me until three o'clock today."

Looking at her watch, Lynn said, "It's a little past eleven. Do you want to do anything until it's time to go back?"

"We could go over and see the museum for a while."

Walking into the museum was like walking into a time machine with visions of the past. A large area of the museum was dedicated to the history of Oak Ridge. In 1942, the *Secret City* was built in the hills of East Tennessee and was a major site of the Manhattan Project. With high hopes of bringing an end to the war, the goal of this top-secret project was to produce the world's first atomic weapons. When Joey read that distinguished physicists such as Enrico Fermi and Robert Oppenheimer served on the project, his heart jumped. His eyes wide with excitement, he thought, "Could you imagine having been part of all this? To actually have worked with these men instead of just studying about their works and to know that you had a part in ending the war and saving thousands of American lives? You couldn't put a price tag on that!"

Totally engrossed in the history of Oak Ridge, Joey glanced at his watch and was surprised to see it was one-thirty. Turning to Lynn, he said, "Why don't we get something to eat? It's almost time for me to get back to the plant."

The journey back to the gaseous diffusion plant seemed to take longer than it did in the morning. Troubled by how the day was going, Joey parked his car. Walking up to the portal, Joey saw Karen standing inside with a smile on her face. Opening the door for Joey, she said, "Welcome back. Mr. Ball called, and he is running a few minutes late, but he will be here. So let's wait for him in my office."

"Sounds good to me," Joey said.

After they had reseated themselves in her office, Karen pulled out several brochures. "While we're waiting, let's go over some of the area attractions. Oak Ridge has an incredible amount to offer people. If a person gets bored in this town, it's their own fault. You'll find art, music, ballet, and theater have dominant roles in Oak Ridge. As a matter of fact, The Oak Ridge Playhouse, which is professionally directed, is almost as old as the city itself."

Sitting back in his chair, Joey said, "Actually, I've never developed a true appreciation for the arts, but I think it's time that I started expanding my horizons."

A smile forming on her lips, Karen asked, "What are some of your hobbies?"

"I've spent quite a bit of time with the Big Brothers program in Ashtabula. I also enjoy hunting, fishing, hiking, woodworking, and karate."

"Excellent! We have a Big Brothers Big Sisters program here, and there are several karate schools in Oak Ridge. In regards to the outdoor activities, there are three TVA lakes close by—Norris, Watts Bar, and Melton Hill. These lakes have close to seventeen thousand miles of shoreline and seventy-eight thousand acres of water." Answering Joey's question before he had a chance to ask it. "And the fishing is great, especially the trout fishing below Norris Dam. We also have a multitude of other species for the avid fisherman, and the hunting is excellent for deer, bear, boar, and small game."

"Did you say boar?"

"Yes, I don't know why anyone would want to risk their life going after something so ugly and dangerous, but a lot of sportsmen do. One place that I would recommend going this evening is Melton Hill Dam. It's close, and I think you would enjoy the picnic and observation area. The directions are on top of this stack of brochures that I have for you."

Taking the brochures, Joey was about to thank Karen when Mr. Ball walked into the room. "Hello, Karen. I apologize for being late, but it couldn't be helped."

"That's fine. We just rearranged things and talked about the area first instead of after the interview. Mr. Ball, this is Joey Slunisky."

Extending his hand, Mr. Ball said, "Joey, it's a pleasure to meet you."

"It's my pleasure indeed, sir," Joey said as they shook hands. "Thank you for taking time out of your busy schedule to meet with me."

Getting up from her chair, Karen said, "I'll leave you two gentlemen alone to talk."

After Karen left the room, Mr. Ball sat down in a chair next to Joey and quickly reviewed his resume. "Tell me, Joey," he asked, "why do you want to come to Oak Ridge?"

Sitting forward in his chair, Joey spoke in a voice so enthusiastic that it filled the room. "Oak Ridge has everything to offer that I've ever wanted to be involved with. Leading-edge technologies, materials development and application, and failure analysis to mention a few."

"The areas that I have openings in would be involved in studying and finding solutions for welding problems. I will also need to dedicate some engineers to work on the Clinch River Breeder Reactor Project, making sure the proper materials are being used where they should be used."

Joey's heart began pounding so loudly that he thought Mr. Ball could hear it. "Mr. Ball, this sounds great!"

With a faint smile, Mr. Ball said, "Reading your resume and your letter of introduction, I thought you would be interested."

"Yes, sir, I am."

"There's one thing I must tell you. Although you have the qualifications that we're looking for, there are several others we're considering, including a few people in-house."

The interview lasted for more than an hour and seemed to be very productive. Shaking Joey's hand, Mr. Ball said, "Joey, I've really enjoyed talking with you. We'll get back with you shortly to let you know our decision."

Driving back to the hotel, Joey thought, "Can you imagine working on the Breeder Reactor Project? That would be so great!" With his

STEVEN J. DEKANICH

spirits lifted, the journey back to the hotel seemed to take no time at all. Joey hurried to the pool, but when he did not see Lynn there, he jogged back to their room. He knocked on the door and waited a few seconds. Opening the door, Lynn was relieved to see the smile on Joey's face. Giving him a hug, she said, "It looks like the interview went well."

"It sure did. I'll tell you what. Why don't we get some fried chicken or something? We can have a picnic at Melton Hill Dam, and I'll tell you all about it!"

Driving on Route 95 to Melton Hill Dam, Joey and Lynn were awestruck by the scenery. The lush green summer foliage, blending in perfectly with the rugged grays and browns of the tree trunks, gave an illusion that there wasn't a single tree in the forest. It was all one entity to be enjoyed by anyone who could perceive it as such. Crossing the bridge spanning the Clinch River, they immediately turned left onto the road to the dam. The area was immaculate. The newly paved roads and expertly trimmed grass made them think they were driving into a country club, not a public use area. Shaking his head in amazement, Joey said, "Can you believe this? A person wouldn't mind paying taxes if he could see results like this."

Finding a picnic table close to the water, Joey and Lynn thought it was an ideal spot to have their final supper in Oak Ridge. Taking a deep breath, Lynn looked out across the water and said, "It's so peaceful here." Pointing her finger at the sky, she exclaimed, "Look at that!"

Silhouetted against a powder-blue sky was a flock of fifteen Canadian geese coming in for a landing. Flying in a perfect V formation, the majestic birds seemed to know they were being watched as they set their wings and made their descent to the water. Like a well-drilled flying team concluding an excellent performance, each bird touched down in the water and glided effortlessly to a stop.

Mesmerized by the sight, Joey said, "That was really something. This place is perfect for us. The work, the sights … everything."

Taking Joey's hand, Lynn said, "Yes, it is. I know we'll be living here soon. Call it woman's intuition."

Wednesday morning found Joey and Lynn heading north for Ashtabula. After an unaccustomed period of silence between them, Lynn asked Joey, "What are you thinking?"

After remaining quiet for a few seconds, Joey looked at Lynn and said, "I was just thinking what it would've been like to have been a part of the beginning of Oak Ridge. To have had an opportunity to have made a contribution like that to the world."

"An opportunity to have made a bomb?"

"It was more than that. It was a unified effort of people working together in perfect harmony because they all had the same goal in mind, which was to save our country and many other countries from almost guaranteed atrocities."

"Couldn't we have warned them what we were going to do?"

"Hon, we did, but to no avail."

"Perhaps if we would have tried harder to communicate with them, all those lives wouldn't have been lost."

"What about American lives? The Japanese were a very tenacious enemy, and they were excellent warriors totally dedicated to their country. They didn't give up after the first bomb was dropped. It took another one to stop the war. Sure, it was a drastic measure, but I don't think anything else would have stopped the war as soon as the atomic bomb did."

STEVEN J. DEKANICH

"When you put it that way, it sounds like we didn't have any alternative."

"We didn't, but killing people is not what I was thinking. What I was thinking of was having the opportunity to work with the great minds of the world—to see how they reason things out and act upon them. Hon, these were some of the top scientists of all-time, and they worked in Oak Ridge! The war days may be gone, but that city is still a center of scientific excellence, and I want to be a part of it." ✦

Chapter 31

What else is going to happen tonight?

Two weeks went by, and no response. Joey's stomach was tied in knots wondering what was taking so long. Mustering up enough nerve, he called Mr. Ball. Unfortunately, Mr. Ball wasn't in the office, which made the situation seem even worse. Joey left his name and said he would call back. After trying for several days, Joey finally connected. Joey waited for what seemed like an eternity for Mr. Ball to come to the phone. When he finally heard Mr. Ball's voice, he hesitated a few seconds before saying, "Hello, Mr. Ball. This is Joey Slunisky."

"Hello, Joey. How are you today?"

"Fine, sir. I was calling to see if any decisions have been made in regards to the openings that were available."

After a few seconds of silence, Joey heard mumbling, and then Mr. Ball asked, "Do you mean to tell me you haven't heard from personnel yet?"

"No, sir, I haven't."

"Joey, I'm sorry. You were a very strong contender, but we chose people from in-house to fill the positions. I apologize that you haven't heard anything from us in writing. I'll make sure that you do."

Joey thought to himself, "Why would I want a rejection letter?" but didn't say anything.

"Joey, although it didn't work out this time, I want you to know that I'll definitely keep you in mind for future openings."

"Thank you, sir. That's all I could ask for."

Hanging up the phone, Joey felt a sickening numbness overcome his body. Almost coiling up into a fetal position in his chair, he thought, "I really thought I had a great chance at that job. What happened?" Staring blankly at the wall, he was oblivious to everything around him. Feeling as if he had taken a brutal punch to the gut that knocked the wind out of him, he stumbled out of his chair, muttering, "I just don't understand."

Not only did he have to face the rejection, he also had to tell his friends and relatives that he didn't get the job. What was he going to say? Shaking his head, he thought, "It's easy to get praise for something you've done. But what about when you bomb out? God, I feel like a loser." Not wanting to face Lynn, he called her with an excuse that he had to work late.

When Joey did come home, Lynn immediately sensed something was wrong, "Hon, what's the matter?"

Hanging his head, he didn't say anything for several seconds. With a defeated and distraught look on his face, and with tears welling in his eyes, he shook his head and said, "I didn't get the job in Oak Ridge."

Shocked, Lynn whispered, "Oh, hon, I'm so sorry."

Joey walked past her into the kitchen and plopped down into a chair. He stared at the refrigerator and mumbled, "I want a job there so badly. Why can't I get there? What's it going to take?"

Rubbing Joey's shoulders, Lynn said, "You'll find a way. Remember what I said when we were in Oak Ridge? I know we'll be living there because I can feel it."

"Yeah, in another life maybe."

The news devastated Joey. Well-meaning friends told him he should accept the fact that he wasn't going to Oak Ridge and get on with his life. For a while, he believed his friends and lost his dream. Pouring himself into his work, karate, and volunteer work with Big Brothers, he soon suppressed his disappointment and almost got back to his old self.

On December 3, Joey was working weekend duty. This meant he was on call at the plant twenty-four hours a day from four o'clock Friday evening until eight o'clock Monday morning. Seeing everything was quiet with the furnace operation, Joey decided that he and Lynn could accept an invitation to a fish fry at the home of their friends, Ted and Kate. About seven o'clock that evening, the plant shift foreman called their friends' home and asked for Joey. Picking up the phone, Joey said, "Hello."

"Hello, Joey, this is Colons. We've got problems on number twenty-three furnace."

"What seems to be wrong?"

"It may be a leak on one of the contact plates. I think you need to come and check things out."

"All right. I'll be right there."

Apologizing to his hosts, Joey said he and Lynn would have to leave because he was needed at the plant.

Ted, who was one of Joey's fellow engineers, said, "Just because you have to leave, there's no reason Lynn has to go home, is there?"

　　　　　　　　　　　　　　　STEVEN J. DEKANICH

"No, I guess not."

"Good. Kate and I will take her home after the party. That will save you from having to backtrack."

"Thanks, Ted. Hopefully I'll be back here before everyone goes home."

That turned out to be wishful thinking on Joey's part. It took him several hours to resolve the problems at the plant. Exhausted, he finally made it out of there at two-thirty in the morning. Driving home through a blinding snowstorm, he thought, "What else is going to happen tonight?"

Sliding into his snowbound driveway, Joey got out and quickly opened the garage door. Protecting himself from the raging wind, he thought, "One of these days, I'm going to get a garage door opener so I won't have to get out of the car in weather like this." Knowing he would be getting up in a few hours and heading back to the plant, Joey immediately got ready for bed. Laying down next to Lynn, he whispered, "Hi, hon. How was the party?"

In a voice masked with sleep, she said, "It was fun. I was sorry you had to leave."

"Me too. How do you feel?"

"I'm all right. I thought I was having contractions, but they stopped."

"That's nice … YOU WHAT?"

"It's okay. The baby isn't due for a couple weeks. Get some sleep."

Easier said than done. Every time Joey dozed off, Lynn squirmed and moaned. Soon the squirming and moans came closer and closer together. Finally he asked, "Are you having the baby?"

"How should I know? I've never had a baby before."

Flicking on the light, Joey said, "We're not taking any chances. Call the doctor and let him know how you're feeling. I'll go out and shovel the driveway."

Throwing on his clothes, Joey ran down the stairs and into the garage. Opening the garage door, he was met with a blast of frigid air and a three-foot drift of snow. "Oh, great! Why now?" Grabbing a shovel, Joey began shoveling snow like a madman, and before long, the driveway was clear.

Closing the garage door, Joey ran up the stairs and called out, "Lynn, what did the doctor say?"

Trying to remain calm, she answered, "He said it would be a good idea to get to the hospital as soon as possible."

Adrenalin pumping through his veins, Joey felt his pulse and breathing quicken as he asked, "He did?"

"Yes. This may be it."

"Oh, God! Let's get you into the car."

While Joey nervously helped Lynn down the stairs, she asked, "Don't you think I should put a coat on first?"

"Huh? Oh, yeah. That's a good idea."

After helping Lynn into the car, he threw her luggage into the trunk and opened the garage door. Joey's eyes widened when he saw the snow had drifted back into the driveway. "I don't have time to shovel now," he thought. "I'm going to use the car to plow out a path."

Like a dragster leaving the starting line, Joey shot out of the garage. The car made it halfway down the drive until the hum of the tires losing traction told him that was as far as he was going. Pulling back toward the garage, he repeated the process several times until he made it to the road. Joey was about to drive out of the subdivision when Lynn asked, "Aren't you going to close the garage door?"

"Do we have time?"

"I'd say we do."

"Whatever you say." Joey jumped out of the car, made his way to the garage, grabbed the door, and slammed it shut. Getting back into the car, Joey drove out of the subdivision and onto the ridge road. The road was a solid sheet of ice! "It wasn't like this when I came home," he thought to himself. Suddenly, a tremendous blast of wind caught the car and forced it close to the ditch. "Oh, my God," thought Joey. "That ditch is almost five feet deep. It'll tip us over if we go in it." Joey felt as if everything was going in slow motion as the car uncontrollably slid toward the ditch. Somehow, miraculously, the car stopped precariously at the edge of the ditch. A sigh of relief came from both sets of lips as Joey and Lynn stared at each other.

"Whoa, that was close!" said Joey. He slowly moved the car away from the ditch and drove in the center of the road. Coming to an intersection, he said to himself, "If I turn right and go down the hill, I can get to the hospital in ten minutes. But with this weather, I may not be able to make it up the other side. I'd better turn left and take Route 11."

Turning left, Joey was almost to Route 11 when he saw a red flashing signal. He blurted out, "Oh, no, a train!" Looking at Lynn, he could see she was in a great deal of pain. "Are you all right?"

"I think we need to hurry."

An almost crazed look on his face, Joey stared at the slow-moving freight train methodically inching its way through the blizzard. "Come on!" he mumbled to himself. Suddenly, as if intentionally taunting him, the train came to a stop directly in front of them. "Oh, great! Why is this happening now?" Turning to Lynn, he asked, "How are you feeling?"

Wincing with pain, Lynn didn't answer.

What to do? Run the full length of the train and get the engineer to move it? Go back and face the hill? As if having pity on the desperate couple, the train began inching forward ever so slowly. After what seemed like an eternity, the caboose was finally in sight. Surprised to see a car at the crossing at this early hour and in this weather, an inquiring dimly lit face stared at them from the caboose as it slowly rolled by. As soon as the caboose had cleared the way, Joey crossed the tracks. Finally they made it to the hospital! A trip that normally took fifteen minutes took them an hour, but now Lynn was in good hands. Joey was allowed to stay with her for a few moments. Holding her hand, he said, "Some night, huh?"

"Yes, it is."

"For a while there, I thought I was going to have to deliver the baby."

"I think you would have done—" Lynn winced with pain.

A nurse standing nearby took Joey by the arm. "Sir, I think it's time for you to leave!"

"But—"

"No buts. Wait in the waiting room."

Joey kissed Lynn and did what he was told. Fatigued from the intensity of the problems at the plant and the ordeal of getting to the hospital, Joey sat down in the warm, peaceful waiting room, and before he knew it, he was fast asleep.

Awakened by a jolt on his shoulder, Joey opened his eyes and saw a very irritated nurse. Glaring at him, she said, "I can't believe you're sleeping. In case you're interested, you have a baby girl."

His eyes widening, Joey jumped up from his chair and asked, "How's my wife?"

Her expression softening a bit, the nurse answered, "Both mother and daughter are doing well."

"Can I see them?"

"Of course. First you must get dressed in a hospital gown."

"A what?"

"It's a gown that will go over your clothes. You'll also need to wear a mask."

"Anything you say."

STEVEN J. DEKANICH

Walking into the room, the nurse handed the newborn to Joey. Although he wanted a boy, when he held this new miracle of life in his hands, those thoughts immediately disappeared. Tears came to Joey's eyes as he held this unique creation. His heart began to swell, and a calming warmness seemed to be supporting both him and the child. Thinking her to be as fragile as a snowflake, Joey awkwardly cradled his daughter in his arms. From that moment, a unique and special bond was formed between them. They would consider themselves to be not only father and daughter but best friends.

Through teary eyes, Joey shifted his gaze from the baby to his wife. "Can you believe this? We're parents!"

"Congratulations, Daddy!" Lynn said with a smile.

"How about that? This is incredible. Hon, you did great."

"I think we both did."

Joey stayed as long as the nurses would allow him. After being kicked out, the exuberant new father went home and phoned Mr. Tarwater, the weekend duty manager. He told him the news and asked if he could get someone to relieve him.

"Joey, don't worry about a thing," Mr. Tarwater said. "Plan on staying with your family this weekend. We'll handle everything."

"Mr. Tarwater, thank you!"

"Any time, Joey. Congratulations!"

The next person he called was his mother. However, Anthony was the one who answered. "Hello."

"Hello, Uncle Anthony."

"What?"

"That's right!"

"Congratulations!"

In the background, Joey heard several muffled voices. "What's going on? What happened?"

Moving the phone away from his mouth, Anthony answered, "Lynn had the baby!"

The muffled voices becoming quite clear. "What did she have?"

"I don't know." Speaking into the phone again, Anthony asked, "What did she have?"

Trying to savor the moment and maintain the suspense a little longer, Joey dragged it out. "This morning, at eleven forty-four, we had a beautiful, bright-eyed, six-pound, seven-ounce baby girl!"

"That's great! How is Lynn?"

"Mother and daughter are doing great. Who's over there?"

"Just your mom and sister. They're making enough noise for ten people, and your mom keeps trying to get the phone out of my hand. Here she is."

"Hello, Joey. What did Lynn have?"

"We have a baby girl! Mom, you should see her. Her eyes are so alert, it's like she could see." Tears welled in his eyes, and his voice cracked a bit. "This is one of the most incredible things that has ever happened to me."

A knowing smile came to Mrs. Slunisky's face. "New life is a wonderful thing. It's the most precious gift there is. You, my dear son, are in store for a wealth of fond memories."

Joey called Lynn's parents next. Hearing Mrs. Dolder's voice, Joey said, "Hi, Mom."

"Oh, my God! Lynn had the baby, didn't she?"

Stunned that Mrs. Dolder knew the news before he said anything, Joey was speechless for a few seconds. "Yes, she did," he finally answered. "We have a beautiful baby girl. How did you know?"

"Call it mother's intuition. Is Lynn all right?"

"Yes, both mother and daughter are doing great. Mom, you should see her, she's the most precious thing I've ever seen. She reminds me of a little cherub."

STEVEN J. DEKANICH

"We'll be there in a few hours."

"You mean you're coming here today? I thought there was a big dance tonight at the Manechore Club. Since Dad is president, shouldn't you be there?"

"You know what the club can do. This is our first grandchild, and we will be there."

"I was hoping you'd say that. My mom and sister are also coming. If I'm not home when you get here, I'll leave a map to the hospital taped on the front door."

"Dad isn't here right now, but as soon as he gets back, we'll be coming. My first grandchild! I was hoping Lynn would have a girl, and now my wish came true. Joey, you don't know how happy you've made me."

Joey hung up the phone, happy that the rest of the family was just as excited as he was about the baby's arrival. He walked out of the kitchen and down the hall to the nursery. Lynn had done a great job decorating the room. There were pictures of happy clowns, stuffed animals, a crib with brightly colored decals affixed to the sides, a changing table stocked with diapers, and an oversized rocking chair. Looking at the rocking chair, Joey could imagine his wife slowly rocking their newborn baby and seeing the little one drift off to sleep, content in knowing she was in loving arms. Tears streaming down his cheeks, Joey fell to his knees.

"Thank you, dear Lord, for all that you have done for me. You have so richly blessed me with a beautiful wife and child. I am truly the happiest man alive."

Joey and Lynn were walking out of Lynn's room when Mr. and Mrs. Dolder greeted them in the hallway. Hugging Lynn, Mrs. Dolder said, "She is so beautiful, and her eyes are so alert."

Shaking Joey's hand, Mr. Dolder said with a smile, "Yeah, I can see she really takes after the Dolder side."

Joey cocked his head. "How so?"

Slapping Joey's back, Mr. Dolder replied, "No teeth and no hair!"

Joey, Lynn, and Lynn's parents were still standing at the nursery window looking at the new arrival when Mrs. Slunisky, Cheryl Lynn, Anthony, and Aunt Helen arrived. Seeing them coming down the hall, Joey called out, "Greetings!" Pointing at each one individually, Joey continued, "Come and see your new granddaughter, niece, and great-niece."

Seeing the large gathering of people, the nurse moved Joey and Lynn's baby closer to the window. Smiling, Cheryl Lynn said, "You were right. Look how clear her eyes are. You don't usually see that in newborns. What are you going to name her?"

"We had several names picked out and agreed on one. Her name is Annette Marie."

"Annette Marie. That's a pretty name."

Joey took off work on Wednesday afternoon to bring his new family home. Wanting to make sure the house was warm when he brought them home, Joey had turned the heat up. "I hope nothing happens to this furnace during this cold snap," he thought. "Ever since Annette Marie was born, the temperature has been dropping. The wind chill factor today is twenty-five below." Holding his hand up to a wall, he said out loud, "You can actually feel the cold coming through the wall. Furnace, don't fail me now."

STEVEN J. DEKANICH

Seeing her husband walk into the room, Lynn said, "Good morning, handsome. It looks like you have something on your mind."

"As a matter of fact, I do. Driving over here, I was thinking I've always viewed hospitals as institutions of pain and suffering. But in this case, the hospital has become an institution of joy and happiness."

Because of the weather, it was agreed that Joey and his family would not be going to Pennsylvania for Christmas. Instead, their families would come to them. On Thursday, December 23, Joey returned home from work and walked through the door with a smile on his face. Seeing him trotting up the foyer steps, Lynn said, "Hello. You certainly look more cheerful than you did this morning."

Hugging Lynn, Joey said, "I guess I was a little depressed this morning."

"Why?"

"Well, I was thinking that this is going to be the first time since I was born that I won't be home for Christmas."

"You're not thinking of us going back for Christmas, are you?"

"With this cold snap still holding on? There's no way I'd risk taking a newborn on a long trip. By the way, where is she?"

"I put her down a few minutes ago."

"How was she today?"

"I'll tell you all about what she did after you tell me what happened today to change your attitude."

"Like I said, after I left this morning, I felt down. But, I started thinking this is going to be a whole new experience for us, so why not enjoy it? I'm still going to be with the two most important people in my life, and so why should I be down?"

"You're right. Why shouldn't we enjoy it?"

"Guess what else happened."

"What?"

"I saw Ken Thoms this morning, and he asked me if we planned on staying in Ashtabula for Christmas. When I said yes, he invited us to join him, his family, and some of their friends at his house on Christmas Eve."

Because of the bad weather, Lynn hadn't left the house since she returned from the hospital. Realizing she had a touch of cabin fever, she exclaimed, "That sounds wonderful!"

"I have some other news for you."

Throwing her arms around Joey's neck, she said, "We're going to Oak Ridge?"

Since receiving the rejection, Joey blanked Oak Ridge from his mind. He was startled by Lynn's statement and didn't answer for several seconds. "N ... no, not that. When I told Ken we would probably be there, he also said that he assumed we would want to go to Midnight Mass. When I told him we wanted to but would probably wait until Christmas Day to go to church, he said he and Glenda would be more than happy to watch Annette Marie while we were in church."

"Do you think we should?"

"Why not? They've raised three of their own and seemed to have done a pretty good job at it. I think it'll do us and them good."

The next day, Lynn felt good dressing up for an occasion. Putting the finishing touches of makeup on, Lynn saw Joey watching her out of the corner of her eye. Looking at him, she asked, "Whatcha doing?"

"Admiring you. Did you know you're more beautiful today than the day we got married?"

"Oh, really?"

"Yes, really. You're not only beautiful on the outside, you've got a heart that's full of love, and it dumbfounds me as to why God has blessed me with someone like you."

Getting up from her chair, she walked to Joey and gently put her arms around his neck. She slowly pulled his face to hers and whispered, "I'm the one who has been blessed. Thank you for a wonderful life. Joey, I've never been happier than I am right now."

Their eyes seemed to look into each other's heart, and each could feel the sincerity and depth of love between them. As their lips met, a faint cry drifted from Annette Marie's room. A smile coming to Lynn's lips, she said, "Well, Daddy, it looks like the third member of our family is up. Shall we get her ready for her first big night out?"

"I'll tell you what. I'll change her, and you can get her things ready."

"Deal!"

After changing her diaper, Joey looked at Lynn and asked, "How much stuff are you taking? We're only going to be gone a few hours."

A condescending expression forming on her face, Lynn said, "Believe me, she needs all of these things."

"I didn't have that much stuff when I went on maneuvers with the rangers in the Civil Air Patrol."

"You would have if you had a baby with you."

Ken Thoms came out to greet Joey and Lynn as soon as they pulled into the driveway. A smile spreading from ear to ear, he greeted them, "Merry Christmas! We've been waiting for you and especially the little one."

Shaking Ken's hand, Joey said, "Merry Christmas! Thanks again for inviting us."

"It's our pleasure. I'm sure you have a lot of paraphernalia to bring in, so why don't you let me take Annette Marie in out of the cold and you two can bring in all your stuff?"

Carefully handing her precious bundle to Ken, Lynn waited until he was close to the house before she jabbed Joey. "See! He knows how much stuff a person needs when they travel with a baby."

Rubbing his ribs, Joey shrugged his shoulders. "I should've known that you knew what you were talking about. Sorry about that."

By the time they walked into the house, Annette Marie was out of her snowsuit and being cuddled by Kate Caldwell. "Oh, Lynn," Kate said. "You have such a beautiful baby."

Handing Joey a large glass of eggnog, Ken said, "Have you ever noticed when something is beautiful or is working right, women take credit for it, but when something goes wrong, it's the man's fault?"

A thin smile coming to his lips, Joey replied, "You have a point there."

Annette Marie was the center of attention for the next several hours, and Joey and Lynn couldn't have been prouder. When it was time to leave for church, knowing her daughter was going to be in good hands made Lynn feel less apprehensive about leaving for a few hours. Driving to Mother of Sorrows Church, Joey asked Lynn, "They really like Annette Marie, don't they?"

"Yes, they do, and I know that she will be well cared for."

Arriving at the church, Joey and Lynn had difficulty finding a parking space. "Look at this," remarked Joey. "It's a little past eleven, and the lot is almost full."

"I guess St. Anthony's Church isn't the only church where Midnight Mass is popular."

And what a Mass it was! The organ and the heavenly sounds of the choir drifted throughout the church and ignited the hearts of each parishioner. The electricity that Joey and Lynn felt at St. Anthony's was recreated in another church, and Joey realized it isn't a building that makes you one with God—it's what's in your heart.

The first rays of light penetrating the cold dark gray sky heralded the promise of a new day—a day for family and friends, a day for love and caring, and a day for setting aside grievances. The rays transforming the cold black nothingness into a crisp blue sky, and sparkling snow greeted the early risers on Christmas morning. Because of an early feeding, two of the early risers happened to be Joey and Lynn. Putting Annette Marie down, they decided to stay up and enjoy the sunrise and each other's company. Pouring their second cups of coffee, Joey said, "Just think. We would have probably slept through this glorious sunrise if we didn't have a little one to tend to."

Stifling a yawn, Lynn replied, "Yes, this is one time I'm glad she got us up. Speaking of getting up, when did you get up to put the turkey in the oven. It smells wonderful."

"I got up about an hour before Annette Marie, made the stuffing, and got the bird in the oven."

"You must be exhausted. Why don't you go back and sleep for a while? I'll take care of getting the rest of the things prepared."

"That's okay. I'm really not sleepy. Let's do it together."

Working together made things go faster. At eight-thirty, Joey was preparing the lettuce salad when his head perked up. Seeing the expression on his face, Lynn asked, "What's wrong?"

"Do you hear sleigh bells?"

Listening for a moment, Lynn said, "Yes, I do. Where are they coming from?"

Joey looked at the clock. "What time did the family say they'd be here?"

"Between ten and eleven. Why?"

After wiping his hands and trotting down the steps to the front door, Joey answered, "Because they're already here."

Opening the door, Joey was met with a cheerful sight. Aunt Helen was rhythmically shaking a long string of sleigh bells, and the group began singing, "Dashing through the snow, in a one-horse open sleigh …"

"This is incredible," Joey said, not quite believing his eyes. "We've never had carolers come to our front door before. Come on in out of the cold."

What a memorable day it was. Not only did everyone come early, but they brought all the fixings for a champagne breakfast. That was just the start of a day that ended with full stomachs and wonderful memories.

With everyone sitting around the supper table and several tableclothed card tables, Anthony raised his glass for a toast. "Joey and Lynn,"—then looking at the sleeping child in Lynn's arms— "and Annette Marie, we want to thank you for a delightful day and a magnificent meal. We have really enjoyed this. May God bless us with love, peace, and happiness every day of our lives."

After drinking to the toast, Joey put his glass down and said, "Anthony, that was very kind of you. Now, believe it or not, I have a song that I want to share with you all."

A quizzical look on her face, Lynn asked, "When did you write a song?"

"When you were in the hospital with Annette Marie. I had a lot of time to think, and it just seemed to come out. Now if you'll excuse me, I'll go grab my guitar."

Returning in a few seconds with an old flat-top guitar, Joey strummed a C chord and said, "The title is 'Ten Little Fingers and Ten Little Toes.' Hope you like it."

Ten little fingers and ten little toes,
Rosy red cheeks and a cute little nose.
Eyes so bright they light the sky.
A heart so free it seems to fly.
A smile so warm it melts the heart.
Laughter and giggles aren't far apart.
You've changed our lives. That fact is true.
We love you, love you, yes, we do!
Ten little fingers and ten little toes,
Rosy red cheeks and a cute little nose.
Eyes so bright they light the sky.
A heart so free it seems to fly.
It didn't matter—girl or boy.
You're God's gift, a wondrous joy!
We'll watch you grow, and then one day
We will hear you also say ...
Ten little fingers and ten little toes,
Rosy red cheeks and a cute little nose.
Eyes so bright they light the sky.
A heart so free it seems to fly. ✦

Chapter 32

I thought you gave up on that dream.

For many, Tuesday, January 4, 1977, was supposed to be the first day back to work for the new year. Looking out at the blinding snow and bitter cold with the wind chill factor dropping to forty below, quite a few of these people quickly forgot their new year's resolutions, the first vacation day was taken, sleepy heads hit pillows, and sweet oblivion overtook the great dreams of grandeur that were to be accomplished for the new year.

However, Joey was not one of those people. He couldn't get over the comment that Lynn made about them going to Oak Ridge. The more he thought about it, the more the desire burned within him. He decided that he would talk to Ken Thoms and ask if he could check on the possibility of other openings. Normally the bitter cold and blustery winds made it seem like an eternity walking from the change house to the furnace department, but his mind racing with possibilities, Joey felt his body heated with the fire of a dream, and try as it would, the cold never penetrated. Before he knew it, he was checking the operating status of the furnaces and molten metal mixing operation. After making sure everything was functioning

STEVEN J. DEKANICH

properly, Joey picked up the phone and called Ken Thoms. "Good morning, Ken. Happy New Year."

"And a happy New Year to you, Joey. What can I do for you?"

"I was wondering if you'd have a few minutes to talk sometime today."

"Let me check…. Yes. I'll be free at three this afternoon."

"Great. I'll see you then."

At three o'clock sharp, Joey knocked on Ken's door. Looking up from his desk, Ken smiled and said, "Come in and have a seat. It looks like the holidays have treated you well."

"A little too well, I'm afraid. I've gained so much weight, even my fat clothes are too small."

"Join the crowd. Every year it gets easier to put the weight on, but harder to take it off. Now, what can I help you with?"

"I wanted to find out if there are any other openings at Oak Ridge."

Staring at Joey for several seconds, Ken said, "After the last rejection, I thought you gave up on that dream."

"For a while, I did. Then over the holidays, Lynn mentioned Oak Ridge, and I realized that although I suppressed the dream, it never died. Ken, I know my desire to go there will probably affect my advancement potential here, but wanting to work in Oak Ridge has become a passion for me, and I'm willing to risk it."

Ken smiled and nodded his head. "I was wondering how long it would take you to get your dream back or if you would ever get it back."

"What do you mean?"

"Joey, there are millions of people who have a dream, but because it takes so much time and effort to attain that dream, they compromise and settle for less. Because they stop going after their dream, they often find themselves doing a job they don't want but feel they have no choice. You're one of the fortunate ones."

"How so?"

"Because you refuse to let a setback get in your way."

"But I did let it get in my way for several months because I was so disappointed when I didn't get the job and because people were telling me to forget about my dream and accept reality."

"You were going through a healing process from the rejection, but I think you realized that it is you who decides if your dreams will become a reality and not your friends. I was hoping it wouldn't be too long before you came to your senses and got your dream back."

"Why didn't you tell me this when I got the rejection from Oak Ridge?"

"Because it was something you had to realize yourself. When it became your decision, it was real for you and it would be acted upon."

"You don't think I'm wrong to keep trying to go there?"

"Knowing what your feelings are, I'd be a fool to try and keep you here. We'll be losing one of our best employees, but I'll do everything I can to get you interviews."

"Ken, thank you."

The following Monday, Joey was working on molten metal mixing calculations when his phone rang. "Hello."

"Joey, I have some good and bad news."

Recognizing Ken's voice, Joey felt his heart begin to beat faster as he said, "Tell me the good news first."

"I have an interview set up for you with the Nuclear Division of Union Carbide."

"And the bad news?"

"Your interview is in Paducah, Kentucky."

"Paducah, Kentucky?"

"Yes. Although there weren't openings in Oak Ridge, I found out the Technical Division in Paducah was looking for a metallurgist. You'll be meeting with a fellow named Dale Bluely next Wednesday."

"Thanks a lot."

"It's my job to keep employees happy, even if they want to leave this paradise."

The following Tuesday, Joey was flying from Youngstown Airport to Paducah in a small commuter plane. Not listening to the weather report, Joey was unaware of an approaching snowstorm with high winds. About halfway to Paducah, the storm hit with a vengeance. The winds violently rocked the small plane, and suddenly, without warning, the plane dropped five hundred feet. His stomach in his throat, Joey had no idea what was happening.

Calm and seemingly unconcerned, the pilot's voice came over the intercom. "Folks, there isn't any need to worry, but it looks like we're in for a rough ride. Please make sure your seat belts are fastened."

The remainder of the trip seemed like an eternity to Joey. Like sitting on an invisible roller coaster track, the plane would lurch in one direction and catapult itself in another. Joey's skin became clammy and pale, and his breathing became quick and shallow as he thought, "The things that I put myself through just to get to Oak Ridge. If this plane doesn't land soon—"

He squeezed the air sickness bag in his right hand, closed his eyes, and tried to bury the back of his head into the seat as the plane dropped several hundred feet. Repeatedly swallowing, Joey tried to get his mind off the sickening waves of nausea and onto the interview of the next day. No luck. All he could do was clear his mind of everything, hold onto the armrests, and wait to see if he could keep himself together until the plane landed.

Finally, mercifully, the wheels touched down, and the plane rolled to a stop. His body feeling like putty, Joey slowly made his way to the terminal and found the nearest restroom. Looking in the mirror, Joey thought that his ashen face seemed like it didn't contain a drop of blood. Bracing himself in front of a sink, he splashed cold water on his face until he began to feel human again. The queasiness leaving his body, Joey called a taxi and, compared to the plane ride, had an uneventful trip to the hotel.

The next morning, Dale Bluely met Joey in the hotel lobby. Dale, a pleasant but poised man in his early forties, was the director of the Technical Division. Firmly grasping Joey's hand, Dale said, "Good morning, Joey, and welcome to Paducah. Did you have a good trip in?"

The green having left his face, Joey replied, "Yes, sir. It was a bit bumpy but pleasant."

"Excellent!" Dale said with a smile. "Why don't we head over to the plant? Here's a copy of your schedule for today. After we sit down for a few minutes, I'm going to turn you over to Steve Black. Steve is the department head of the Metallurgy Laboratory. He'll show you the lab and take you on a tour of our facility."

"Sounds good. Let's go."

Getting into the car, Dale said, "It may be dark by the time we get out of the plant, so let's take a quick drive through our humble town before going to the plant."

"Okay."

Driving through the city, Dale described some of the particulars. "Paducah has a population around thirty-five thousand. You'll find the climate, with today being an exception, is very moderate. Our average mean temperature is close to sixty degrees. There are three state parks within fifty miles, and if you like outdoor activities, the

Land Between the Lakes can offer just about anything your heart would desire. Do you have any children?"

"Yes, sir. A newborn baby girl."

"A new father, huh?"

"Yes, sir. Annette was born on the fourth of December, and she already has me wrapped around her little finger."

"I know what you mean. I have several of my own and, except for a few times, wouldn't have traded them for anything. You won't have to worry for a while, but the Paducah schools are fully accredited, and if you're interested in parochial education, the parochial schools go through senior high. Paducah has a junior college, and Murray State University is within an hour's drive from here. You'll also find the arts are very much alive here."

"With everything you've been telling me, it sounds a lot like Oak Ridge."

Nodding his head, Dale continued, "Yes, to a point. But we think we live in a prettier part of the country."

After the brief tour of Paducah, the duo went to Dale's office. Sitting behind his desk, Dale said, "Let me give you a brief overview of what we do. The two gaseous diffusion plants that we operate, the one here and the other in Oak Ridge, produce uranium enriched in the fissile U-235 isotope for use in nuclear power-generating facilities not only in this country but abroad. Our plant was completed in 1954, and it differs from Oak Ridge in that it serves as a base for the initial enrichment of uranium. Our product is used to feed the Oak Ridge plant and another gaseous diffusion plant in Portsmouth, Ohio."

"I didn't know there was a diffusion plant in Ohio."

"Yes, there is, but it is not under our operation. These plants are a key source of enriched uranium used to fuel nuclear electric-generating stations, naval propulsion, and research and isotope production."

After an informative meeting with Dale, Joey was introduced to Steve Black. Touring Steve's lab, Joey was impressed with much of the laboratory equipment. Slowly nodding his head, Joey said, "This is quite a place."

"We think so," Steve replied. "Although the labs in Oak Ridge are better equipped, we do very well with what we have. We're able to perform quality failure analysis investigations and material characterization studies."

His ears perking up, Joey asked, "Did you say failure analysis?"

"Yes, I did."

"That was one of the things I enjoyed the most when I worked at Sharon Steel."

"Really? That's good. You'll find the equipment failures we encounter here deal not only with steel but with a multitude of other materials. It makes the work here very interesting, trying to find out why something failed and making recommendations to keep it from happening again...."

The sun was setting as Dale and Joey walked to Dale's car. Shutting his door, Dale asked, "What did you think of our facility?"

"It's great!" Joey responded enthusiastically. "The type of work that you do is exactly what I'm interested in."

"I'm glad to hear that. I think the work that we do, especially in Steve's area, is very interesting and important to the plant's operation." Pulling into the hotel parking lot, Dale continued, "I'm assuming you don't have plans for this evening."

"No, not really."

"Why don't you have dinner at my place? I'll pick you up about six-thirty."

"That sounds good."

Steve and his wife also came to Dale's home and joined them for dinner. After an enjoyable meal and a pleasant evening, Dale drove Joey back to the hotel. Pulling into the parking lot, Dale extended his hand and said, "Joey, it's been a pleasure meeting you. Although I'm looking at some people in-house, I want to say you're a very strong contender for the position. You'll know within the week what our decision is."

Shaking Dale's hand, Joey said, "Thank you for giving me this opportunity. I hope I'll be working for you in the near future."

The next morning before he left the hotel, Joey popped two motion sickness pills. Feeling a bit groggy when he got on the plane, Joey fell asleep as soon as he was seated and didn't wake up until the small plane bumped down at the Youngstown Airport. Seeing the expression on her husband's face, Lynn thought he was drunk. "Are you all right?"

Slowly closing and reopening his eyes, Joey put his arms around Lynn's neck and said, "Sure I am. Those motion sickness pills work, but they sure can put you to sleep."

As they walked back to their car, Lynn said, "After talking with you last night, it sounded like the interview went well."

"I think so. Dale said I would know within the week."

Two weeks went by, and Joey didn't hear anything. Thinking the pattern was similar to when he interviewed in Oak Ridge, Joey was reluctant to call. Finally, on Monday, January 31, Joey's office phone rang. "Hello."

"Hello. I'd like to speak to Joey Slunisky please."

"This is he."

"Joey, this is Dale Bluely."

Joey's eyes widened, and his heart jumped into his throat. "Hello, Dale."

"Joey, I apologize for not getting back to you sooner, but this was a very tough decision, and I want to tell you that you were a very strong contender."

Hearing similar words before, Joey closed his eyes. Suppressing an urge to sigh, he said, "But I was not chosen for the position."

"That's correct, and I'm sorry. But on a more upbeat note, with your qualifications and desire to work in failure analysis and materials characterization, I took the liberty of contacting the Technical Services Division at the Oak Ridge Gaseous Diffusion Plant and passed on your resume and my recommendation for interviewing you."

A feeling of hope surging in him, Joey opened his eyes. "Dale, thank you for doing what you did."

"I'm sorry it didn't work out for you here, but perhaps it will in Oak Ridge. Good luck." ✦

Chapter 33

This is the dream job that I've been waiting for.

Joey shared the information with Ken that Dale had sent his resume to the Oak Ridge Gaseous Diffusion Plant, and they agreed that Ken wouldn't pursue other avenues on Joey's behalf until they heard something from Oak Ridge. The month of February dragged on with no word from Oak Ridge. Although Joey kept trying to tell himself not to get his hopes up, there was something deep inside telling him he would have another opportunity. Even when he was playfully ribbed by well-meaning friends, and some not so well-meaning, that he'd better get used to running furnaces for the rest of his life, he didn't give up hope.

Monday, March 28, was bitterly cold and gusty. The thermometer outside the kitchen window registered minus ten. Joey, who hadn't been feeling well for the last several days, dreaded the thought of going out in the weather. As he was grimacing at the thermometer, Lynn walked up behind him and hugged him around the waist. "The weather's bad, and you're feeling terrible, so why don't you stay home from work today and come back to bed?"

Joey inclined his head toward Lynn's shoulder. Inhaling and exhaling a deep breath, he said, "Believe me, I'd love to, but we've got some people coming in today who want to make an experimental alloy. This is the closest thing to experimental science that I'll get while I'm here, and I don't want to miss it."

"Okay, but if you start running a fever, promise me you'll come home."

Once he got out into the weather, he regretted his decision not to stay home in bed, but he had made a commitment that he would be there and have his people assist in any way they could to ensure the experiment would be successful. By mid-afternoon, the alloy was made and cast. While he was waiting for the chemical analysis reports, Joey decided to go inside the #23 furnace control room and grab a cup of coffee. While he was pouring the thick dark liquid, he heard one of the operators call out, "Joey, phone call for you."

"What's happened now?" thought Joey as he picked up the phone. "Hello."

"Joey! It's about time I tracked you down. I was getting ready to personally come out and find you. Where have you been?"

"Actually, we made a special run today, and I spent most of the morning and afternoon out on the floor." Suddenly realizing that Ken wasn't making a social call, Joey blurted out, "Did you hear something?"

Wanting to increase the anticipation, Ken didn't say anything for several seconds. Finally he said, "Yes, I did."

Almost spilling his coffee cup into a control panel keyboard, Joey set the dripping cup on a desktop nearby. The phone cradled in his shoulder, he quickly grabbed a paper towel and wiped his hands as he enthusiastically demanded, "What did you hear?"

"They want to talk with you on the twenty-first of April."

"This is incredible! Ken, thank you!"

STEVEN J. DEKANICH

"I didn't have anything to do with this. You did it all yourself. Joey, I've got a feeling this may be it."

Hanging up the phone, Joey looked up at the ceiling. "Thank you, Lord," he silently prayed, "for giving me another chance!"

A nearby control room furnace operator furrowed his brow. "Joey, are you all right?"

Looking like a cat that just swallowed a bird, Joey flashed a big smile. "Believe me, I couldn't be better!"

As the day progressed, the weather worsened, and when Joey finally left the plant at seven o'clock, a full-blown blizzard had set in. Wanting to see the expression on Lynn's face, Joey didn't tell her about the interview. As he inched his way through the blinding snow, all he could imagine was the look on her face. Pulling into the snow-filled driveway, Joey got halfway to the garage when the car bogged down. Not wanting to take the time to get the snowbound vehicle free, Joey stopped the engine and forced the door open through the drifted snow. Trudging through the thigh-high snow, Joey thought, "I wonder if they have weather like this in East Tennessee." Since the snow had drifted halfway up the garage door, Joey decided to go around to the front door. Not wanting to search for his keys, Joey rang the doorbell. A few seconds later, Lynn opened the door, and Joey quickly jumped inside. Taking his snow-covered coat off, Joey shivered and said, "Man, it's cold out there."

Lynn hugged her husband in relief. "Joey! I'm so glad you're home. I've been listening to the news, and you can't believe how many accidents there've been in the last few hours. I was really worried about you. I called your office, and they said you left an hour ago."

Pulling off his dripping boots, Joey said, "The roads are really bad. I can't remember the weather ever being like this."

"The weatherman was saying the last time it snowed like this, they got tanks from the armory to clear the roads." Putting her arms around Joey's neck, Lynn looked into his eyes. "God, I'm glad you're home. Are you okay?"

"Hon, I couldn't be better. Let's sit down in the kitchen, I have some interesting news to tell you."

Frowning, Lynn followed Joey into the kitchen and sat down. "What's going on?" she asked.

"Remember what you asked me just before Christmas?"

"What?" Then she got excited. "Joey! You heard something?"

"Yep. Ken called today and said they've scheduled an interview with me for April 21."

A big smile spreading across her face, Lynn grasped Joey's hand. "I knew you would hear something! Joey, I'm so happy for you."

"Yeah. I pray the third time is a charm. Ken said he thought this might be it."

"Call it woman's intuition or whatever, but I agree."

Although numerous operating problems at the plant kept Joey running day and night, the time still dragged. The weatherman called for rain mixed with snow on Wednesday morning, April 20, and true to his word, that's exactly what Joey woke up to. Knowing he would be interviewing in Oak Ridge the following day, Joey wasn't about to let anything dampen his spirits. As he got ready for work, he heard Annette Marie begin to cry in her crib and, a few seconds later, Lynn's soothing voice as she picked her up. As he finished up in the bathroom, Lynn knocked on the door and said, "Someone wants to say good morning to you."

With a smile coming to his face, Joey quickly opened the door and saw the best sight in the world—his family. He stood there for several seconds before Lynn asked, "What are you thinking?"

A warm feeling coming over him, Joey answered, "I just realized something. Regardless of how this interview turns out, the one dream that really matters in my life has come true."

"What's that?"

"You and Annette Marie."

Five o'clock that evening, Joey drove with Lynn and Annette Marie to the Youngstown Airport. Halfway there, Lynn asked Joey, "I know you said you didn't want any of the family to know about your interview, but did you tell anyone at work?"

"No, I didn't. This is one time that I wanted as few people as possible knowing about this. It seemed like every time I told people I was interviewing down there, something fell through and I didn't get the job. You didn't tell anyone, did you?"

"You asked me not to, so I didn't. Oh, by the way, did you take your airsickness pill?"

"No! I'm glad you mentioned it. After that last experience, I don't want to take any chances."

The flight to the Knoxville Airport was thankfully uneventful and pleasant. After getting his luggage, Joey hailed a cab and asked the driver to take him to Oak Ridge. After being assured by the driver that it was a routine trip for him every day, Joey got in and prepared for the forty-five minute trip. As they pulled onto Alcoa Highway, Joey said to the driver, "The weather seems very pleasant here. Is this normal this time of year?"

"It sure is. Where are you from?"

"Ashtabula, Ohio."

"Oh, okay. I'm originally from Cleveland, so I know what you're used to this time of year."

"How long have you lived here?"

"I moved here seven years ago. Climate-wise, I don't know of a better place to live than East Tennessee. You have all four seasons, but definitely not the kind of winters you're used to. I'd say not much is blooming in Ashtabula right now."

"That's right. Although everything is melting, there's still a lot of snow up there. I didn't think winter would ever be over. The last time I saw grass was October. It started snowing the third week in October, and it seemed like it hasn't stopped. It was getting so deep in places, the plows couldn't push anymore snow against the banks. It was scary at times driving down the road and seeing walls of snow piled up on either side of you."

"Well, you won't have to worry about that down here. As a matter of fact, when it gets daylight tomorrow, you're going to see a lot of things in bloom."

At seven o'clock the next morning, Joey was scheduled to meet with the Special Services department head, Mary Jones, in the hotel lobby. Arriving in the lobby at six forty-five, Joey decided to glance at some of the housing information brochures until Mary came. Promptly at seven, she walked through the door, and since Joey was the only person in the lobby, she extended her hand and said, "You must be Joey Slunisky. I'm Mary Jones."

"It's a pleasure to meet you," Joey said, shaking her hand.

"I'll tell you what. Before we go to the plant, let's go to Shoney's and get some breakfast."

"Sounds like an excellent idea."

Walking out to the parking lot, Mary headed for a red 240Z. His eyes widening, Joey carefully stroked the 240Z like it was a sleeping jungle cat. "This is quite a vehicle."

"It's a lot of fun to drive. Do you like sportscars?"

"I've never owned one, but yes, I do. I have a couple of friends in the racing circuit and had a few opportunities to take their cars around the track. Talk about feeling alive! Those were some incredible experiences!"

"Did you race them?"

STEVEN J. DEKANICH

Laughing, Joey answered, "No, I think they thought it'd be best for everyone if I was on the track alone."

"I see," said Mary as she turned the ignition key. Like it was alive, the 240Z growled in protest for being awakened and slowly stalked its way out of the parking lot and sprinted down Illinois Avenue. It only took a few minutes to get to Shoney's.

While waiting for their breakfast, Mary said, "Tell me about yourself and why you want to come here."

Taking a quick sip of coffee, Joey said, "I feel very fortunate for having participated in a student metallurgist program while attending college. It gave me an opportunity to see many different aspects of metallurgy and materials ranging from production to research and development. Although the production part is very challenging, after working in that area for several years, I realize now that I have a passion for working in a laboratory."

Mary smiled. "That's a very interesting choice of words. I've never heard a baby boomer say they have a passion for their work."

"Honestly, some of the happiest times in my life were when I was working in the Met Lab performing a failure analysis study."

"Why did you choose to come to Oak Ridge?"

"Mary, when I first saw the pictures of the Oak Ridge area, I fell in love with it and promised myself that someday I would work here. To have an opportunity to work with leading-edge technologies, as are available here, would be a dream come true."

"With the position that we currently have open, I think you'll find a lot of things you're looking for."

Taking the same route to the gaseous diffusion plant as last September, Joey noticed a marked change in the landscape. Instead of the lush late summer greens, the yards and forest seemed to be alive with color. Not letting his eyes leave the breathtaking landscape, Joey said, "I don't think I've ever seen a more colorful place than Oak Ridge in the springtime."

"It's beautiful, isn't it?" said Mary. "We have domestic and wild dogwoods scattered throughout the city and through the woods. Also, there are the azaleas. Driving through Oak Ridge and Knoxville, you'll see just about every color imaginable. In fact, to celebrate spring, we have an annual event called the Dogwood Arts Festival."

"What happens during the festival?"

"A multitude of things ranging from entertainment to crafts. I think the best part is the dogwood trails. These are special routes through some of the well-established neighborhoods in Knoxville. Believe me, every one of the estates with the manicured lawns, colorful dogwoods, and exquisitely designed flowerbeds would rival anything you see in *Better Homes and Gardens*."

"Since she's a flower fanatic, it sounds like something my mother would really enjoy."

Pulling into the main entrance, Joey remembered the guard portal and his interview with Mr. Ball. As they got out of the car, Mary said, "There should be a clearance waiting for you here so we can get you into the plant. After we talk for a few minutes in my office, I'm going to turn you over to one of my section heads, Richard Forman. Richard manages the materials evaluation section and has an opening in his metallography area in the Metallurgical Services Laboratory. He will be interviewing you."

The clearance was waiting for Joey, and after a few formalities that included showing his driver's license and swearing that he was a U.S. citizen, they proceeded to Mary's office. Walking to her office,

Joey couldn't help noticing the neatly trimmed grass with vibrantly colored fluorescent pink, red, and white azaleas bordering the buildings. Admiring a pink and white dogwood bursting with color, Joey said, "I can't get over the difference that several hundred miles makes on a climate. In Ashtabula, we're going through the snow mixed with mud stage. This is great."

"Yes. We typically get an early spring," Mary told him. "Many of the avid gardeners begin working the soil and planting seeds as early as Washington's Birthday."

After the two were comfortably seated in her office, Mary said, "With your interest in Oak Ridge, I'm sure you know quite a bit about this place, but let me briefly touch on a few things. This plant was the first gaseous diffusion plant built for the production of fissionable uranium. After a massive construction effort, the plant began operation in 1945 and has truly played a historic role in the production of uranium for use as fuel in nuclear reactors for power generation and naval propulsion. The actual process is classified, and you'll learn about it later. The gaseous diffusion plants are among the largest industrial facilities in the world. Because of their enormity and the vast amount of equipment needed to operate, there are two things you can be sure will happen."

"What's that?"

"Failures and the need for better materials utilization."

"Failures? You mean where uranium is released into the environment?"

"A release may happen on a rare occasion, but you'll find we have safeguards to prevent occurrences. I'm talking about general equipment failures."

A man's voice interjected, "Like the kind that may keep a compressor from operating?"

Mary appeared startled by the sound of Richard's voice, but her pleasant expression quickly returned. She turned her head to address the man standing in the doorway of her office. "Yes, Richard, like the kind that could keep a compressor from operating. Joey Slunisky, meet Richard Forman."

Getting up from his chair, Joey shook hands with his prospective new boss. "Pleased to meet you."

Firmly gripping Joey's hand, Richard replied, "Good to meet you." Looking at Mary, Richard continued, "Sorry for interrupting."

Mary raised her eyebrows and replied, "What else is new? I was just getting into some of the different failure types that we have, but since you're here, I'll let you take Joey over to your office and tell him more about the kind of work we do around here. Like I said before, I'll be tied up until three, so plan on having Joey back to my office around then, and I'll take him back to the hotel."

"Will do." Looking at Joey, Richard motioned toward the door. "C'mon, we've got a lot to talk about."

As they walked toward D Lab, Richard's laid-back nature put Joey completely at ease and prompted him to ask a question. "What did Mary mean when she asked you 'what else is new' when you apologized for interrupting her?"

A devilish smile crossed Richard's face. "Oh, I guess you might say I enjoy giving her a hard time, but she's always been a good sport about it."

"She seems like she's really on the ball."

"She is. Truthfully, I've got more respect for her than a lot of other managers out here. She's not afraid of supporting her people."

"That's good."

"Don't tell her I said that because it may ruin my reputation with her."

"Got it."

They walked through the west entrance of D Lab. Richard's office, Room 24, was the first door on the right. Before he opened the door, Richard asked Joey, "Would you like a cup of coffee?"

"Yes, I would."

"We've got a pot set up back in the stress lab. Since you're an uncleared visitor, we need to walk back there together."

Walking down the hall with Richard, Joey noticed signs on the wall that said, "Caution! Uncleared visitors present. Protect classified information!" Looking at Richard, he asked, "Were these signs put up because of me?"

"As a matter of fact, they were. Before you will be able to start work here, you'll need what is called a 'Q' clearance. That clearance will give you access, on a need-to-know basis, to secret information."

Joey raised his eyebrows. "Interesting. I had no idea that a clearance would be required for this work."

Opening the door to the stress lab, Richard said, "You're in an installation whose operation is vital to national security."

"Real James Bond stuff, huh?"

"You might say that."

While Richard was getting the coffee, Joey looked around the lab and saw hundreds of pieces of electronic recording equipment. Marveling at the mass array of electronic gadgetry, Joey asked, "Is this one of your labs?"

"Yes, it is," Richard answered as he handed the cup. "Along with metallography, I manage the stress analysis lab and the mechanical testing lab."

"This is quite a collection of instrumentation."

"We think so. I'd introduce you to the technicians, but they're out on a job. Are you familiar with stress analysis?"

"No, not really."

"Briefly what we do here is study the internal stresses of different components to see if the stress is great enough to cause the part to fail. It's like taking an ice cube out of a freezer and dropping it into a glass of warm water. There are a lot of stresses built up in the ice cube because of the warm water and cold ice. Consequently, the ice cube will either crack or shatter. Our job here is to analyze the different materials in the process to see if there are stresses great enough to cause a part to fail. You'll be working closely with this group on the different failure analysis projects."

Returning to Richard's office, Joey said, "This place is even more incredible than I imagined."

Motioning Joey to have a seat, Richard agreed. "Believe me, Joey, this place is a metallurgist's or material scientist's dream. You'll be involved with just about every kind of material imaginable ranging from ferrous and nonferrous alloys to composites and plastics to adhesives and parting agents."

Quietly shaking his head in awe, Joey hung onto every word.

"Primarily, the job I'm looking to fill requires working with plant personnel to ensure the right materials are being used," Richard continued. "Another area will be working with the metallographers in metallographic sample preparation and evaluation and making sure we are getting the best use out of our research metallographs, and to take a lead role in failure analysis studies. In failure analysis studies, it will be your job to find out why something blew up, broke down, or fell apart and make recommendations to keep it from happening again."

"Richard, this sounds like a dream come true," Joey said.

At three o'clock, Richard and Joey headed back to Mary's office. Joey couldn't help reiterating a statement that he made several times during his interview and tour through the metallography lab. "This all sounds incredibly interesting."

"I think you'll enjoy it. One thing I've been meaning to ask you. On your resume, you said you enjoyed hunting and fishing."

"Yes, sir, I do."

"Good. You'll find the hunting and fishing in East Tennessee is great if not better than any place in the nation."

"I take it you enjoy them too?"

"Yes, I do. In fact, several of the guys from metallography, the stress lab, and the mechanical testing lab hunt and fish."

The right chemistry for forging a good working relationship and friendship began almost immediately after their being introduced. Joey felt as if he had known Richard all his life and hoped the job would be his. Just as they reached Mary's office, Joey said, "This place is sounding better with each passing minute. Richard, thank you for taking the time to interview me and show me around the lab."

"It's been my pleasure," Richard said, shaking Joey's hand.

Hearing them outside her door, Mary rose from her desk. "Well, it sounds like we had a successful interview."

"I'd say we have a strong contender here," said Richard.

"Good. Hopefully things will work out, and you'll become part of our team. Let's swing by to meet our division director, Dr. Levi. After that, I'll take you back to the hotel."

"Sounds good."

Pulling in front of the hotel lobby, Mary stopped the 240Z. Extending her hand, she said, "Joey, it's been a pleasure. Although we will be interviewing a few people in-house, I think we may have a good match with you. We'll let you know in a few weeks."

Shaking her hand, Joey said, "Mary, thank you for your time and consideration. This position is more than I hoped it would be, and I can assure you if I am chosen, I'll exceed your expectations. You won't regret hiring me."

When he got back to his room, Joey couldn't wait to call Lynn. Dialing their phone number and then hearing the sound of her sweet voice say hello, Joey said, "Hi, hon. This was an incredible interview."

"Tell me about it."

"The way they talked, it seemed as if I already have the job."

"Is it something you're interested in?"

"Yes and more. Hon, this is the dream job that I've been waiting for!" ✦

Chapter 34

Oak Ridge is offering you a job!

In a deep sleep, Joey was having a vivid dream. Finishing an intense game of volleyball, Joey searched the shoreline for his family. Seeing them building a sandcastle at the water's edge, he draped a thick white terry cloth beach towel over his tanned shoulders and jogged over to them. A gentle ocean breeze soothed his glistening, overheated body, and by the time he reached Lynn and Annette Marie, he felt refreshed. Kneeling down beside them, Joey scooped Annette Marie up in his arms. Holding her close to him, he felt the sweet smell and softness of her baby hair against his cheek. His attention switching from his daughter, Joey saw how the warm glow of the setting sun highlighted Lynn's already radiant complexion. Filled with a warm feeling of peace and contentment, he longingly looked into Lynn's eyes and said, "This is quite a place, isn't it?"

Breathing in the fresh ocean air, Lynn sighed. "Yes, it is. Hearing the waves gliding into shore, seeing the seagulls and sandpipers, Joey, this place is almost as nice as Oak Ridge—"

Lynn's voice was gradually displaced by a frantic ringing that grew louder and louder. Still in a fog, Joey looked at the bedroom clock. "It's three-thirty in the morning! What now?" he muttered as he jumped out of bed and ran to answer the phone in the kitchen. "Hello."

"Joey?"

Hearing the overwrought voice of his youngest shift supervisor, Joey answered, "Yes, Charlie. You wouldn't believe the dream that you just destroyed. What's going on?"

"We've got some real problems here."

"Charlie, it's three-thirty in the morning. I told you this was your shift, and it's up to you to make the decisions."

"I know, but we've had a couple of people get hurt pretty badly."

The irritation leaving his voice, Joey asked, "What happened?"

Taking a deep breath before answering, Charlie began, "About a half hour ago, Jim Young was working at the molten metal mixing station when one of the addition chutes got clogged. He was trying to free the clog with a hex bar when the bar slipped and Jim fell off the ladder. Joey, I think he broke his arm."

"You said there was a couple of people who got hurt. What else happened?"

Charlie had never experienced anything like this before, and his voice cracked as he continued, "Around the same time Jim got hurt, the other accident happened. It was really a freak accident. The furnace was already plugged, and the mud gun was recharged for the next tap. I'm not exactly sure what happened. For some reason, it looked like a lot of pressure built up inside the gun. Johnny Craig was walking in front of the gun when it blew a big chunk of clay out of the nozzle. Joey, it hit Johnny right in the face and knocked him out cold."

"Oh, God, no. Where are they now?"

"We've got an ambulance coming to take them to the hospital."

"Have you or the plant foreman called their families to let them know?"

STEVEN J. DEKANICH

"Yes. Thank God Cookie was working tonight, and he pretty well took charge of things. The families have been notified and are on their way to the hospital."

"Okay, Charlie. I'm going to the hospital and will probably be there for the next several hours until I find out how Jim and Johnny are. What I want you to do while everything is still fresh in your mind is write down as many of the details of each accident as you possibly can and get statements from other people who may have witnessed the accidents."

"Will do."

With a hollow feeling in the pit of his stomach, Joey hung up the phone. He walked quickly past Annette Marie's room and into the master bedroom. Switching on the nightlight, he frantically began searching for his work clothes. Awakened by the activity, and grogginess thickening her voice, Lynn asked, "Joey? What are you doing?"

"We just had a couple of bad accidents at the plant. I'm going to the hospital to be with the families and find out what the status is."

"What happened?"

"The way it sounds, we had one guy break his arm and another get hit in the face with hot clay from the mud gun."

Getting out of bed and walking Joey down to the garage, Lynn hugged her husband and said, "Call me and let me know what's happening."

"Will do."

Arriving at the hospital in record time, Joey ran through the emergency room doors and headed to the reception desk. "Can you please tell me the status of Jim Young and Johnny Craig?" he asked.

Putting down her paperwork, the pleasant-looking ER receptionist asked, "May I ask what relationship you have with the patients?"

"I'm their manager."

"I see. Mr. Young's arm was badly strained, and he and his family just left. Mr. Craig is currently in surgery." Pointing to a disheveled and anxious-looking young lady in her early twenties, she said, "His wife is sitting over there."

"Thank you."

Reluctantly, Joey walked the distance between them and said, "Mrs. Craig?"

"Yes."

"I'm Joey Slunisky. May I sit down?"

The puzzled look on her face indicated that she did not recognize Joey. Suddenly, his name registered, and she replied, "You're Johnny's department head, aren't you?"

"Yes, Mrs. Craig, I am."

She motioned to the seat beside her. "Please sit down."

"Have you heard anything?"

"No, I haven't. When I got here, Johnny was being prepped for surgery. As I was signing the release forms, the doctor came out." Putting her hands over her face, she could barely continue. "He … he said Johnny may be blind after this. All of our family lives in Virginia…. I don't know what to do." Unable to control herself any longer, she began to sob.

Joey put his arm around the distraught woman and pulled her close to him. "I am so sorry this happened. Johnny's a fighter. He's going to be all right. You'll see."

The minutes dragged on into hours, and the waiting became unbearable for both of them. Trying to make conversation, Joey said, "Johnny told me that you two met in a very unique way."

Memories of the past brought a smile to the young lady's face. "Yes, the way we met was different, to say the least. Johnny's family had just moved to our small town, and our church was sponsoring a white water rafting trip. Johnny and I were in two different rafts. His raft was ahead of the raft I was in, and it got hung up on some rocks just before a mean stretch of rapids. My raft started into the rapids when all of a sudden we hit something, and the next thing I knew, I was in the water caught in the swift current. I don't know how, but as I was being swept by his raft, Johnny reached out and grabbed my arm and pulled me into the raft with his group. That was the start of a wonderful relationship."

"It sounds like you and Johnny are very happy together. That's something that seems to be rare these days."

"Johnny and I both work at making our marriage special."

"Mrs. Craig."

She turned around in her chair to face the doctor who operated on Johnny. Her heart in her throat, she barely managed to ask, "How is he?"

"Your husband is a very fortunate man. The fact that he was wearing his safety glasses saved his eyes."

Putting her hand to her mouth, Mrs. Craig whispered, "Oh, thank God!"

"The impact of the hot clay broke his glasses and actually forced them into the eyebrows, and we had to stitch that area. There also was a considerable amount of clay imbedded into his skin. We were able to get some of it out, but he will need to see a plastic surgeon to get the balance taken care of. When you see him, he's going to look like he was on the losing end of a mugging, but he's young and will recover in no time. He should be out of the recovery room in the next hour or so. You can see him then."

With tears coming to her eyes, Mrs. Craig breathed a sigh of relief. "Thank you for all you have done," she told the doctor.

After the doctor left, both Johnny and Mrs. Craig looked as though a heavy weight had been removed from their chests. The reassurance that Johnny was going to be all right brought smiles to their faces. Taking the woman's hand, Joey said, "Mrs. Craig—"

"Please, call me Donna."

"Donna, I'm thankful that everything turned out all right. I must get back to the plant, but I'll be back this evening to check on Johnny. In the meantime, if there is anything I can do, don't hesitate to call."

"Just by being here and showing your concern, you've done more than you know. Thank you."

The rest of the day was spent conducting formal accident investigations. By five-thirty that afternoon, Joey felt the lack of sleep and intensity of the day taking their toll on his body. All he wanted to do after checking on Johnny was go home and sleep on the couch. Temporarily lost in a quiet moment, Joey began to close his eyes when the ring of his phone startled him. "Hello."

"Joey! How are you feeling after this grueling day?" came Ken's voice on the line.

"Ken, this was a side of management that I never experienced before. I found out responsibilities extended far beyond just operating furnaces."

"I think you handled yourself very well during all of this, and I'm proud of you. However, there is one small detail that must be handled before you leave for the day."

Joey closed his eyes and sighed. "What's that?"

"It can't be handled over the phone. Could you come to my office?"

"Sure, I'll be right there."

When Joey walked into his office, Ken could see the stress of the day in his hollowed eyes. "Come in and take a load off your feet. This won't take long."

"I thought we covered everything."

"Have you met Ed Loy?"

"Who is he?"

"He's the personnel director at Oak Ridge."

"No, I can't say that I've ever met the man. Why?"

Ken smiled and looked into Joey's eyes. The rigors of the day had numbed Joey's brain, and he wondered why Ken had the mischievous look of a little boy who got caught at a prank but knew he wasn't in trouble. Suddenly, the word Oak Ridge registered, and Joey leaned forward in his chair. "Did you say Oak Ridge?"

"Yes, I did. Joey, Mr. Loy called to notify me that they were going to extend you an offer."

Not believing what he had just heard, Joey asked, "Would you mind repeating that?"

"Son, your dream has come true, Oak Ridge is offering you a job!"

Joey shook his head in disbelief, and a big grin came to his face. "This is incredible. After all these years of waiting and praying and pursuing this dream, in a matter of moments, it has become a reality."

Ken sat back in his chair and crossed his legs. "It wasn't a matter of moments. Joey, you've stood on the threshold of this dream for many years and never backed down. Most people wouldn't have done that. After a while of not achieving their goal, many would've rationalized to themselves that the dream they were chasing wasn't worth it or they were fine in doing what they were doing. Most of these people end up miserable for the rest of their working career. What is it that kept you going?"

Without a moment's hesitation, Joey replied, "From the first time I saw the pictures of Oak Ridge and read what they had to offer, I knew I wanted to be there and I knew I would be there some day. It's a feeling that's hard to describe. It's almost like … well, in any sport when you have that feeling regardless of how big or experienced your opponent is, you know you're going to win … and then you do. That's how it felt. Now I'll admit, there were times when I really became discouraged."

Smiling and clasping his right knee with both hands, Ken said, "Yes, how well I remember. The way I perceive it, Joey, is that your dream and desire is deeply rooted, and even though it may have died on the surface, it was only a matter of time before it sprang to life again with stronger roots of conviction. Son, we're going to hate losing you, but I'm happy for you, and I admire your passion in hanging onto your dream. ✦

Chapter 35

The realization of a dream.

Joey received a formal letter offering him a position as a metallurgical engineer in the Metallurgical Services Laboratory with a starting salary of $1,500 per month. After accepting the offer, Joey was asked to fill out a security clearance form that was more complex and lengthier than any income tax form he had ever seen. Sitting at the dining room table, Joey labored for several hours and still wasn't finished. Putting the form aside, Joey sighed loudly. "This is incredible!"

"What's that?" asked Lynn, entering from the kitchen.

"They literally want to know everything about me from the day I was born all the way up to the current time."

"Well, with the kind of place you're going to, I think it makes sense they would want to have everyone checked out." Lynn picked up the form and scanned it. "Wow! They even want to know things about my family."

"Yep. I'll definitely need your help when I get to that section."

Several days after sending in his clearance, Joey answered his office phone and heard a familiar voice. "Hello, Joey. This is Karen Tullman. How are you today?"

"Karen! I haven't spoken with you since interviewing with Mr. Ball. I'm doing great! How are you?"

"Just fine. Joey, the reason I'm calling is we've scheduled a house-hunting trip for you from Thursday, May 19, through Sunday, May 22. Are these dates compatible with your schedule?"

"Karen, even if they weren't, I would make them compatible."

"Excellent! I will mail you an itinerary that will include the names and times of the Realtors that you will be meeting with."

Leaving Annette Marie with Lynn's parents, Joey and Lynn drove to the Youngstown airport. After a long period of silence, Lynn touched Joey's arm. "You look like you're a thousand miles away. What's on your mind?"

Turning his attention from the road to look into her gray-blue eyes, Joey answered, "I guess you might say that I'm walking down memory lane in my mind. Hon, so much has happened since we started going together. I'm thinking about college, about Ashtabula, and about the cancer."

After several seconds of silence, Lynn said, "Go on."

Taking her hand, he continued in a low voice, "You've always been there for me … not only in good times, but also in bad. Whenever I was down, I knew I could count on you to lift me back up." Squeezing her hand, Joey whispered, "I'm a very lucky guy, Lynn, and I thank God that you chose to spend your life with me."

Tears welling in her eyes, she leaned over and kissed Joey on the cheek. "I feel the same way about you." Moving closer to Joey, Lynn put her head on his shoulder and said, "I thought you were thinking about Oak Ridge."

"I was, but something made me realize that without you and Annette Marie sharing this with me, going to Oak Ridge really wouldn't mean as much."

STEVEN J. DEKANICH

Her head still on his shoulder, Lynn sighed. "Joey Slunisky, I love you more than you'll ever know."

The flight to Knoxville was smooth, and it seemed as if they were landing in no time at all. Joey and Lynn retrieved their luggage from baggage claim and were on their way to pick up their rental car when they heard, "Hey, buddy! I see you got the job!"

Joey squinted at a tall lean cabbie and exclaimed, "You're the driver from Cleveland who took me into Oak Ridge a couple of months ago!"

"Yep! Need a lift into Oak Ridge?"

"Sorry. They supplied us with a rental car. But thanks for asking."

"No problem. Let me be the first to welcome you to East Tennessee … God's country."

The itinerary for Thursday and Friday was grueling and somewhat irritating. Joey and Lynn looked at more than twenty homes, mostly off Lovell Road and the West Knoxville area. When they returned to the hotel at eight o'clock Friday night, Lynn fell backwards on the bed. "This is really work, and I haven't seen anything that I actually liked."

"I thought there were a couple that struck your fancy."

"You and I both know they were out of our price range. I wonder why they keep showing us homes in Knoxville instead of Oak Ridge."

Plopping down on the bed next to Lynn, Joey said, "I don't know. I guess a lot of the people who work at the plants live in Knoxville. C'mon, let's get cleaned up and get something to eat. Tomorrow will be better. You'll see."

At nine o'clock on Saturday morning, Madeleine Peale met Joey and Lynn in the hotel lobby. Smiling at the young couple, Mrs. Peale asked, "Have you two had breakfast?"

"Yes, ma'am," Joey replied, "we have."

"Okay. Before we go looking, let's sit down here, and I'll show you pictures of the homes that I have to offer and their locations on an area map."

Impressed with her thoroughness, Joey said, "Mrs. Peale, I can't tell you what a relief it is to talk with someone as organized as you. It seems as if we were on a wild goose chase for the last two days."

Feeling more at ease with Mrs. Peale than any of the other Realtors, Joey and Lynn enjoyed looking at the homes but didn't see anything they really liked. The sun was beginning to set when Mrs. Peale said, "There's a new subdivision opening up just outside of Oak Ridge with a home that I think you'll both like. The builder is asking about five thousand more than what you're willing to pay, but I think we can work something out."

From the back seat of Mrs. Peale's car, Joey caught her eye in the rearview mirror. "Mrs. Peale, we talked about prices this morning, and we told you how we felt about going over our budget."

A twinkle coming into her eyes, she said, "Joey, just let me show you the house before you say anything else."

The new home was a white split-foyer with red brick facing and a paved driveway. Joey's eyes widened, and his attempt at looking disinterested failed. Walking in the front door, Joey and Lynn were captivated by the new home smell. The house was almost identical to their home in Ashtabula with one exception—it was almost twice the size! Walking out on the back deck, Joey asked, "How big is the lot?"

"Almost an acre and a half."

Nodding his head, Joey said, "Very nice, very nice indeed. Would it be possible to come back here tomorrow?"

Smiling, Mrs. Peale replied, "Of course. Now please, let me treat you both to dinner."

That night in the hotel room, Joey sat on the bed with Lynn. "I think we found our home," he said.

"I think so too."

"Let's drive back out there and look at it. I left the side garage door unlocked."

The next morning, when Mrs. Peale met them in the lobby, Joey said, "Instead of looking at other houses, let's go back and look at the home in the Lake Hills subdivision."

Mrs. Peale raised her eyebrows and nodded her head. "Okay."

They spent over two hours walking through the house and looking at the property. "Mrs. Peale, I think you were correct in your assumption," Joey said. "Everything feels right, and we'd like to make an offer for this home."

Mrs. Peale smiled. "Okay. Let's go back to my office and draw up a contract. Since this is one of the first houses to go up in the subdivision, I think you're making a wise decision."

Shaking her hand, Joey said, "Mrs. Peale, instead of house, I think the correct term is home."

That evening, Joey and Lynn drove back to their new home. Pulling into the driveway, they saw a man and a woman planting shrubbery at the house across the street. As they got out of their car, the couple walked toward them. The man smiled and extended his hand. "Hello. My name is David Queen, and this is my wife, Jerry."

Shaking David's hand, Joey replied, "Pleased to meet you, I'm Joey Slunisky, and this is my wife, Lynn."

"Are you planning on buying this home?"

"Yes. As a matter of fact, we made an offer today."

"Good! It looks like we might be neighbors."

A natural chemistry for a strong friendship began to develop between the two couples, and by the time they finished talking, the sun was kissing the horizon and sending streaks of crimson through the clouds.

One week and two counteroffers later, Joey received a call from Mrs. Peale. "Good morning, Joey. I have good news for you. The builder accepted your offer!"

With a big smile coming to his face, Joey responded in excitement, "Mrs. Peale, that's great! I was hoping we'd have a place to move into by the time we relocated to Oak Ridge on July 11."

"I will overnight the contract to you for your review and signature."

Hanging up the phone, Joey immediately picked it back up and called Lynn. "Hi, hon. What are you doing?"

"I just put Annette Marie down for a nap. Why do you sound so excited?"

"The builder accepted our offer!"

"Really? After his response to the last counteroffer, I didn't think he would've settled for this offer."

"But he did, and that's all that matters! Now, my dear, we need to get busy and spruce up our home so it sells before we leave. Ken said if we can't sell it by the time we move, the company will buy it from us, but we'll be able to make more if we sell it ourselves. I'm planning on taking three or four days of vacation so we can get everything done."

Joey and Lynn got busy putting fresh coats of paint in every room and putting the finishing touches on their yard that they had always wanted to do but never seemed to find the time. After planting the last flower in the new flowerbed in the front yard, Lynn stood up and wiped the hair from her face. "Did I tell you what your sister said to me when they visited us last Sunday?"

STEVEN J. DEKANICH

Picking up the garden tools, Joey shook his head. "No. What did she say?"

"She said it was too bad that we didn't do this work while we were living here so that we could have enjoyed the fruits of our labor."

"She's right, you know. We've been wanting to do this work for quite some time now, but have never set it that high on a priority list."

Giving him a sideways glance, Lynn said, "You may not have set it that high, but I did."

"Let me rephrase my last sentence. I guess you might say it was high priority, but the urgency level wasn't there."

On Friday, June 24, Ken Thoms had a going-away party for Joey and Lynn. Oh, what a party it was! The fellowship, reminiscing, and excellent food combined to make it an incredible evening. Until the party, Joey and Lynn didn't realize how much these people meant to them, and they knew they would remain friends forever.

The following Monday, Joey's department surprised him with another going-away party. Joey was sitting in the #23 furnace control room reviewing the operating log when Jimmy Rutherford walked in. "Joey, we need you downstairs right away."

Perking up, Joey asked, "What's going on?"

"I'll fill you in as we go."

Thinking some emergency was underway, Joey jumped from his chair and quickly followed Jimmy to the operating floor. When they reached the base of the stairs, Joey demanded again, "What's going on?"

Pointing to the lunchroom, Jimmy smiled and said, "You'll see."

Frowning, Joey walked in the direction Jimmy was pointing and opened the lunch room door. When he saw the sight on the other side, the only thing he could think to say was, "I don't believe this."

The lunchroom tables were lined with large serving pans of trout caught by Red Holly, salads, and deserts. Looking around the room, Joey saw the smiling faces of fifty men. Suddenly he felt Jimmy's hand on his shoulder. "There were a lot of guys who couldn't make your party last Friday, so we decided to have one for you ourselves."

Shaking his head, Joey said, "You guys didn't have to do this."

"We know that, but we wanted to."

Getting a little teary-eyed, Joey said, "I don't think I've ever worked with a better group of men than you. You've always been there for me."

Red put his foot on a bench and leaned his elbow on his knee. "That's because you've always been there for us. We've always known where you stood and that we could count on you to back us. We're all going to miss you, Joey."

Taking a deep breath and slowly letting it out, Joey looked at the men whom he spent more than eight hours a day with for the last several years. Unable to speak for several seconds, Joey finally managed to say, "Thank you…. I'm usually not at a loss for words—"

"Great! Let's eat!" shouted a voice from the back of the room.

"Yes!" said Joey, grateful that someone had broken the silence. "I can't believe all the trout." Walking to the table, he continued, "We have baked trout, broiled trout, and breaded trout. Red, how long did it take you to catch all of these fish?"

Handing Joey a plate, Red replied, "Let's not go into that right now. You've got a lot of hungry guys waiting for you to start the food line."

STEVEN J. DEKANICH

After gorging themselves on trout, salad, and desserts, the men presented Joey with a new spin-cast fishing outfit. While Joey was admiring the graphite rod, Red said, "The trout fishing in the Smokies and at the base of Norris Dam is great. Catch a few for us."

The go-away parties for Joey and Lynn were not yet complete. On Sunday, July 3, Lynn's family had a party for them. That was followed by another party hosted by Joey's family on Monday, the Fourth of July. All of the goodbyes, embraces, smiles, and tears behind them, Joey, Lynn, and Annette Marie were on their way to Oak Ridge! Lynn's parents decided to accompany them and help get things situated. Crossing the Kentucky state line just south of Cincinnati, Lynn looked at Joey and said, "Only one more state to travel across, and we'll be in Tennessee."

Squeezing Lynn's hand, Joey replied, "Yep. Our new home … and the realization of a dream!" ✦

Chapter 36

Creative adaptations.

It was almost five o'clock when Joey shouted, "Welcome to Tennessee! Let's stop at the welcome center."

The welcome center was a virtual cornucopia of information. Picking up flyers on the Great Smoky Mountain National Park, Joey said to Lynn, "Look at this brochure. It looks like a great place to take your mom and dad."

Lynn held Joey's arm as she read the brochure. "Yes, it does," she agreed. "Maybe we can go next weekend after we get settled."

Mr. Dolder walked up behind them, feigning a Southern drawl highlighted by a real German accent. "Y'all ready to head south?"

Smiling, Joey said, "Instead of south, we're going to be heading straight up. Wait until you see the mountain that we're going to be climbing." Looking around the welcome center, Joey asked, "Where's Mom and Annette Marie?"

"Mom wanted to take in some of the scenery, so they went outside," Lynn answered.

"Let's get loaded up and see if the van will make it up Jellico Mountain one more time."

When they were all situated back in the van, Mr. Dolder asked, "How much further?"

Putting the van in reverse, and slowly backing out, Joey said, "It should be another hour before we get to the hotel. After we get settled in, we'll take you to our new home."

A smile lighting up her face, Lynn said, "I can hardly wait to see it again. Since tomorrow is supposed to be your first day at work, are you sure you won't get into any trouble staying home to help us get moved in?"

"Because my clearance hasn't come in, Richard said I could actually take Monday and Tuesday to get moved in."

"So what will you be doing until your clearance comes in?

"I'll be staying in a room called the bullpen, which is outside of the gate. While I'm waiting for the clearance, they'll have me checking and verifying unclassified materials specifications. Also, I'll be putting together and teaching a class on basic metallurgy."

Although they got very little sleep, the excitement of moving into their new home energized Lynn and Joey. As Joey turned into the driveway, Lynn said, "Can you believe this is happening? Your dream has come true."

"That's all that I thought about last night," Joey said as he put the van in park. "I was almost afraid to close my eyes for fear I would wake up and realize it was only a dream."

Opening the door and bouncing his foot on the new asphalt, Mr. Dolder said, "This looks pretty real to me."

Lynn looked up at the sky and took a deep breath of the warm, moist early morning air. "What is that wonderful aroma?"

Pointing at a huge tree covered with pink blossoms, Mr. Dolder said, "It's that mimosa at the end of your lot. I haven't seen one of those trees in ages."

Her eyes widening, Lynn said, "It's beautiful! I don't remember seeing this tree when we first came down."

"I don't think it was in bloom," said Joey.

"Let's walk over there and check it out."

Getting closer to the tree, Mr. Dolder exclaimed, "Look! The tree is full of hummingbirds."

Everyone was so mesmerized by the brightly colored aggressive little creatures that time slipped away without anyone realizing it. The roar of the moving van turning onto Lake Hills Drive brought everyone back to reality. Lynn said, "They're here, and we haven't even unlocked any of the doors."

Joey and Lynn jogged up to the house ahead of the truck. Taking the keys from her purse, Lynn opened the front door. Joey put his hand on her shoulder before she took a step. "I believe something needs to be done before going in."

"What's that?"

Whisking her up in his arms, Joey said, "My lady, I'm going to carry you across the threshold of our new home."

Tightening her arms around his neck, Lynn pulled Joey's face close to hers and passionately kissed him on the lips.

After bringing in the major pieces of furniture, the movers systematically marked off the boxes for each room, stacked them in an orderly fashion, and, by one o'clock, were gone. The serious expression on Joey's face told Lynn it was time for lunch. Nudging

STEVEN J. DEKANICH

her mother, Lynn said, "You know how Dad gets grouchy when he gets hungry?"

"Yes."

"Joey does the same thing. Look at him."

Nodding her head, Mrs. Dolder said, "I see what you mean. I think we better feed both of them."

Walking behind her husband, Lynn slipped her arms around his waist and squeezed. The touch of her arms around him immediately brought a smile to Joey's face. Whispering in his ear, Lynn said, "Mom and I are going to pick up something to eat. Any preference?"

His mouth beginning to water, Joey said, "Actually I've been thinking some Kentucky Fried Chicken would really taste good."

"Then that's what it will be. We'll be back in a few minutes."

Wednesday morning, the heavenly aroma of thick sliced bacon frying in a skillet permeated the shower stall. A smile coming to his face, Joey breathed deeply and basked in the anticipation of a hearty breakfast. Quickly finishing his shower and getting dressed, Joey hurried down the hallway. Before turning into the kitchen, he saw his mother-in-law sitting on their oversized rocking chair holding a sleeping Annette Marie. Walking over to them, he whispered, "Good morning."

Smiling and pushing her glasses up the bridge of her nose, Mrs. Dolder said, "Good morning. This little one got up for an early feeding. I told Lynn that I would try to put her back to sleep while she made your breakfast."

Admiring the cherub face of his little girl, Joey said, "Looks like you did a good job in putting her to sleep." Gently touching Annette

Marie's nose with his index finger, Joey smiled, turned, and went into the kitchen.

"Wow! This looks like a breakfast fit for a king!"

"For your very first day, I thought you'd need something substantial."

Mr. Dolder walked up the steps from the basement and followed Joey into the kitchen. "Mind if I join you?"

"Not at all," said Lynn. "There's plenty for all of us."

Spreading a thick pat of butter on his toast, Mr. Dolder said, "I just want you to know how proud we are of you. Not many would have stuck to their dream like you did."

"Thanks, Pop. That means a lot."

"I don't know if I ever told you about the opportunity I had to use my glass-blowing skills with a small company in Pittsburgh."

"No, sir, you didn't."

Taking a sip of black coffee, Mr. Dolder said, "There was an old man who came to this country from Austria and started the glass company. He was familiar with my glasswork and approached me several times. He said he wanted me to take over the company when he retired."

"Why didn't you ever do it?"

"Family pressure. My mother and father thought I should stay in Sharon and work at Sharon Steel like the rest of the family."

"I still don't understand."

"Back then, we had it ingrained in us that you didn't go against your parents' wishes." Shaking his head and staring at his plate, Mr. Dolder sighed deeply. He slowly raised his head until his eyes met Joey's. "To this day, I regret not going."

"Wow, I had no idea."

"That's why I'm proud of you because you didn't give up on your dream. Whenever you have a dream that in your heart you know is right, don't ever let anyone or anything steal it. Go after it until your dying breath."

Mr. Dolder's words were still in Joey's head as he turned into the parking space. "I had no idea that Pop had that opportunity," he thought. "This morning was a good reminder to stay focused on whatever I'm going after."

Walking up the sidewalk, Joey saw Richard standing outside the guard station holding an armload of papers. "Good morning, sir," Joey said. "How's it going?"

"Morning. How did the move go?"

"Pretty well. Actually, Lynn and her mom and dad are still unpacking stuff."

Richard laughed out loud. "Believe me, you'll still be unpacking for weeks to come."

"That sounds about right."

"I have an eight-thirty meeting, but wanted to get you situated before going to it. Follow me."

Trotting up a set of steps away from the guard station, the duo came to an empty classroom. "So this is the bullpen?"

"Yep. As you can see, you're the only one here … at least for a little while." Richard handed the stack of papers to Joey. "To pass the time of day, I brought you a few specifications to review and approve."

Joey's arm dropped with the weight of the papers. With wide eyes and a grin coming to his face, he said, "Only a few? When do you need them?"

"I won't need them until Friday. You'll need the ASTM reference manuals to check everything out. Several people from the lab said they would bring the manuals to you later this morning. In the meantime, glance at the specs and the approval forms and get familiar with them. We'll go over any questions this afternoon."

About ten o'clock, Joey heard a group of people coming up the steps from the guard station. Joey stood up when the four technicians walked in. With smiles on their faces, each was carrying an armload of different ASTM manuals. Returning their smiles, Joey said, "Hello. I'll bet you're the people Richard said would be coming to visit."

Putting his books on the table, the lead technician said, "You're right. My name is John Moody, and this is Barbara Stevens, Walter Scott, and Jane Bridgeman."

Joey shook their hands. "It's a pleasure to meet you. I'm Joey Slunisky."

"Another person will be joining us shortly. He's a metallurgist too … and a damn good one. Actually, it was his idea for you to review the unclassified specifications. It's good that he has this work for you. Otherwise, it would make for long hours spending the day in here."

"How long do you think it will take to get my clearance?"

"I think they're taking anywhere between four to six months."

"Wow, that's a long time."

During the month of July, several very adept engineers and scientists joined Joey in the bullpen. All unclassified assignments were usually completed within a few hours, which left the balance of the day for creative adaptations: reading technical journals, developing state-of-the-art rubber-band-firing guns that proved deadly on wayward flies, and intense games of chess.

Listing several references on the security application, Joey knew the investigation was progressing because of the feedback he received from the references. One day, Will Fueler's wife answered a knock on her front door. An FBI agent flashed his badge and said he would like to talk with Will. She told him he was in his workshop in the back of the house. While the agent was making his way to the workshop, she got on the intercom and shouted, "Will, what did you do? There's a guy from the FBI coming around the house to see you!"

Joey's clearance came through on Friday, August 13, and any indication of bad luck never showed itself. In fact, for the next year, Joey's life couldn't have been better. It's been said, to achieve harmony in life, a person needs something to do, someone to love, and something to hope for. This combination is like a three-legged stool; when all legs are of equal length, the stool is balanced and provides a sound structure.

Joey's work was fascinating. It gave him a good balance between the technical and managerial areas. Many times, when working on various materials projects, Joey became totally consumed with the task at hand and oblivious to time. The challenges and rewards of his dream job made him feel alive.

Joey had two people in his life who he loved very much—his wife and daughter. He also had strong feelings of commitment and allegiance to the people in his laboratory and several peers.

Joey had a seven-year goal to convert his routine plug and chug metallography laboratory into a state-of-the-art, internationally recognized metallurgical/metallography laboratory. Aggressively soliciting senior management's support, he was well ahead of schedule after the first year.

Joey's life was perfect, and every aspect seemed to provide stability. Little did he know that fate was about to kick the stool out from under him. ✦

Chapter 37

No, not again.

Joey was looking at a specimen on a research microscope when he heard John call out from another part of the lab, "Joey, Lynn is on line one."

Pushing back with his feet, Joey rode his chair to the edge of the lab desk where the phone sat. Picking up the phone and pushing line one, Joey said, "Hey, how ya doing?"

"Great! I've got some good news."

"What's that?"

"David and Jerry said they would watch Annette Marie if we wanted to go out tomorrow night for our anniversary."

"That sounds great. Where do you want to go?"

"Well, since you asked, why don't we go to Regas? I've heard a lot of people raving about their steaks."

A smile coming to his face, Joey nodded his head to the affirmative. "That sounds like a good idea."

"I'm glad you think so."

"Did you want me to call for reservations, or do you want to call?"

"Well, actually, I already called, and we're set for six-thirty tomorrow."

Regas more than lived up to its reputation for ambience and an excellent cuisine. A contented sigh easing from his lips, Joey put his fork and knife on the empty plate. He was about to say how much he enjoyed the steak when his eyes met Lynn's. Subdued lighting mixed with flickering candles gave Lynn a radiance that held Joey spellbound. Reaching out across the table and taking Lynn's hand, Joey said, "You'll never know how much you mean to me, and I thank God every day that you came into my life."

With tears welling in her eyes, Lynn responded, "I love you with all my heart."

Squeezing her hand, Joey said, "I wrote something for you that I hope will express my feelings." Reaching for the package that he carefully placed under his chair when they were seated, Joey handed it to Lynn.

Her eyes widening, she opened the package. It was one of their wedding pictures in a frame with a poem that Joey wrote superimposed on it. Through teary eyes, Lynn read:

ONE SPIRIT IS YOU
THE OTHER IS ME!
Loving wrapped in heaven's embrace
Two spirits meet, come face-to-face.
The warmth of love enveloped them both,
Truly two spirits meant for betroth.
A love so divine all heaven can see
One spirit is you, the other is me!
From heaven to earth, our spirits came
And blessed two people with your and my name.
We grew and we met, went out on a date

And came back to your house ever so late!
Flowers and smiles and even some tears
Have built a bond to last through the years.
We joined hand in hand as man and wife
And to me you are my essence of life.
We've always said our marriage is blessed.
You stay in my heart, my special guest.
From heaven to earth, two spirits came
And blessed two people with your and my name.
Let's look deep in our eyes, and sometimes we'll see
One spirit is you, the other is me!

With tears streaming down her face, Lynn held the picture with both of her hands as she read the poem over and over again. Looking up at Joey, she said, "This is so beautiful. How did you have it done?"

"One of the guys from the photography department has his own dark room in his home. I told him my idea, and he made a picture of the picture and superimposed the poem on it. Do you like it?"

Pulling a tissue from her purse and dabbing her eyes, Lynn answered, "Yes, I do.… I love you more with each passing day."

The next day, Joey tried concentrating on a report, but his mind constantly drifted back to the evening before. What a marvelous evening, and what a wonderful way to start a new year of their lives together. Lost in his thoughts, Joey propped his left arm up and allowed his neck and the side of his chin to rest in the palm of his hand. Unconsciously pressing a neck muscle between his thumb and index finger, Joey felt a lump. All thoughts erased from his brain, Joey sat up poker-straight in his chair and frantically began squeezing the area. Getting up from his desk, Joey hurried down the hallway to the men's room. As he looked in the mirror, the menacing growth seemed to glare back at him. Closing his eyes, Joey whispered to himself, "No, not again."

Lynn's eyes widened as she looked at Joey's neck. "My God, Joey, what are we going to do?"

"I don't know. I have an appointment to see Dr. Horowitz first thing in the morning. Lynn, while everything was okay, I didn't mind having Dr. Horowitz check me out. But now, I'm not so sure. I'm wondering if I should go back to Pennsylvania and see Dr. Sabbs … I don't know. Maybe I'll wait to see what happens tomorrow."

"Hi, Daddy," said Annette Marie. "Want to roll the ball with me?"

Seeing his little girl standing in the kitchen doorway holding a big orange ball brightened his whole spirit. Smiling, Joey said, "Sure, honey. We'll play for as long as you want."

Solemn-faced, Dr. Horowitz said, "Mr. Slunisky, I'm sorry to say that you will need surgery."

Joey felt Lynn's hand tighten in his. Clearing his throat, Joey said, "Do you think it's malignant?"

"With your history, it is a good possibility. That is why I scheduled you for an appointment with Dr. Biggs."

"Is he any good?"

"He's one of the best in the Southeast."

"Dr. Horowitz, if you don't mind, I'd like to talk with Dr. Sabbs before we proceed."

"Of course. I have no objection to you talking with him. Just do it as soon as you can."

The eleven o'clock news was just coming on when the ringing phone startled Joey. Running to the phone, Joey picked it up and said, "Hello."

"Hello, Joey. This is Dr. Sabbs."

"Dr. Sabbs! Thank you for calling me back."

"I got your message about the lump and your scheduled surgery. I talked with Dr. Horowitz about your case and also did a little checking on Dr. Biggs. Dr. Biggs has a stellar record, and I think you would be in good hands with him."

"That may be, but he's not you."

"I appreciate your confidence in me, but I don't think it's necessary that you come to Sharon to have surgery. Dr. Biggs is more than capable of performing the surgery."

"I guess you're right, but this time, I'm really scared. It was different before when it was only me. Now, I have a wife and daughter. What will happen to them if something happens to me? Why is this happening again? I thought all of this was over."

"Joey, I don't know why it's happening again. But you must stay focused on taking care of this and moving on with your life. This is another bout that you have to fight."

"Up to this point in my life, things have been so good. I don't know if I'm up to this."

STEVEN J. DEKANICH

"You've been up to it before and you can do it again. I don't know if you ever saw the plaque in my office from an old prizefighter by the name of James A. Corbett. Corbett wrote a poem that is very appropriate for your situation. It goes like this:

When your feet are so tired that you have to shuffle back to the center of the ring,

Fight one more round.

When your arms are so tired that you can hardly lift your hands to come on guard,

Fight one more round.

When your nose is bleeding and your eyes are black and you are so tired that you wish your opponent would crack you on the jaw and put you to sleep,

Fight one more round.

Remembering that the man who always fights one more round is never whipped.

"Joey, all you have to do is fight one more round."

"I'll try my best."

"Joey, don't try … do it!"

Recovering from the shocking news, Mrs. Slunisky and Aunt Helen flew to Oak Ridge to be with Joey and his family. Saturday was spent picnicking and hiking in the Cades Cove area of the Smoky Mountain National Park. All too soon, Sunday evening came, and it was time for Joey to go to the hospital to be admitted. Hearing the doorbell, Lynn trotted down the stairs to the front door and opened it. "Hi, Jerry."

"Hello."

"Come on in. We really appreciate you watching Annette Marie while we take Joey to the hospital."

Jerry smiled and said, "Don't mention it." Picking Annette Marie up and hugging her, Jerry continued, "She's like one of my own, so take your time and do what you need to do. When is Joey scheduled for surgery?"

"At seven o'clock tomorrow morning."

After Joey finished with the admittance formalities, a volunteer escorted him to his room. Walking by the nurses' station, Joey felt strange not seeing a familiar face. The volunteer opened the door to the room and allowed Joey and his relatives to enter. The volunteer walked to the food tray table next to Joey's bed and began to open the new patient package. Pulling out the insulated pitcher, she said, "I'll get you some ice water."

Looking around the room, Joey said, "Sure looks different than Sharon General Hospital, doesn't it?"

Slowly rubbing Joey's arm, Lynn said, "I'm sure everything will be all right."

Stone-faced, Joey looked at Lynn for several seconds. Forcing a smile, he said, "Yeah, I'm sure it will be."

Aunt Hellen pulled a package out of her huge purse. "Joey!" she yelled, tossing him the package. "I bought you some new pajamas. Go put them on."

Instinctively catching the package, Joey said, "Thanks. I'll be right out." Opening the door to the bathroom, Joey turned and said, "Sure wish they had a Bello's Pizza here."

Waiting for Joey to shut the door, Lynn softly said, "I'll be right back."

Opening the package, Joey carefully pulled all of the straight pins and cardboard inserts from the garment. "Look at that," Joey thought. "She had this thing monogrammed!" Pulling off his T-shirt, Joey saw his refection in the mirror. The lump in his neck formed a grotesque protrusion. Slowly running his fingers over the lump, Joey said to himself, "I wonder what's going to happen this time."

Startled by a knock on the door, Joey heard Aunt Helen say, "Are you all right in there?"

Looking at his watch, Joey realized he had been standing in front of the mirror for ten minutes. "I'll be right out," he called.

As he exited the bathroom, Aunt Helen said, "We thought you fell in."

A slight smile curling his lips, Joey said, "I guess I did for a while, but your voice pulled me out." Looking around the room, Joey asked, "Where's Lynn?"

"She said she'd be right back."

About twenty minutes later, Lynn returned carrying a huge pizza box. Smiling at Joey, she said, "I knew you'd want a pizza, so I ordered one from Big Ed's just before we left. It isn't Bello's, but it's the next best thing."

His eyes widening and a smile coming to his face, Joey sat on the edge of his bed. He motioned for Lynn to put the pizza on the food tray table and said, "Let's have some before it gets cold." Joey was working on his third piece of pizza when Dr. Horowitz and Dr. Biggs knocked on the door. Motioning for them to come in, Joey quickly swallowed the pizza, and said, "Dr. Horowitz, Dr. Biggs, this is my mother and Aunt Helen, and you've already met Lynn."

Both doctors said in unison, "Please to meet you."

Turning his attention to Joey, Dr. Biggs said, "Are you ready for tomorrow?"

Joey shrugged his shoulders. "As ready as I'll ever be."

"Barring any complications, the operation shouldn't take more than two hours."

"How will this compare with the operations that I've had in the past?"

"Any operation is serious, but this operation shouldn't be as traumatic as the radical neck surgeries that you've had. I foresee you being in the hospital for a couple of days and returning to work within a week."

"This doesn't sound so bad. I think I can fight one more round."

"Excuse me?"

"Oh … nothing. Just thinking out loud."

"Very well. Unless you have any more questions, I'll see you first thing in the morning."

After three hours, Joey was still in surgery. Finally, at eleven-fifteen, Dr. Biggs walked into the waiting room. Lynn sprang to her feet when she saw him. "How is Joey?"

"He's doing fine."

Getting up from her chair, Mrs. Slunisky asked, "Why did the surgery take so long?"

"Along with the visible tumor, we found a string of seven other tumors extending from his neck down into his lung cavity."

Cupping her mouth with her hands, Lynn said, "Oh, my God. Is he going to be all right?"

"I believe he will be, but he will need to stay in the hospital a few more days than we anticipated."

"Were the tumors malignant?"

"It will take a few days to get the biopsy results. He should be in the recovery room for several hours and then back in his room. I'll be in later on this evening to check on him."

Wednesday afternoon, Joey lay napping in bed when Lynn gently touched his hand. "Joey, are you awake?"

Slowly opening his eyes, he responded in a raspy voice, "Hi. How long have you been here?"

"We just got here."

Looking around the room, Joey saw his mother and Aunt Helen and weakly waved to them. Squeezing his hand, Lynn asked, "How do you feel?"

"My throat feels like a truck drove through it, and I have a burning sensation in the upper part of my chest. I guess they still have me on a bunch of pain medication."

"Yes, they do, but hopefully you'll be getting off of it soon. Dr. Biggs called and said he would be here early this afternoon with the biopsy results."

"What day is it?"

"Wednesday."

"Wow! I guess I've been out of it."

"Just a little. They had you on some pretty strong pain medication."

"Can I have a drink of water?"

"Sure. It looks like the ice has melted. Let me get you a fresh glass." Lynn poured the glass of water into the bathroom sink, returned to the tray table and poured a fresh glass of ice water. She slightly raised the back of the bed and carefully put the straw into Joey's mouth.

As he took a sip, Joey's body seemed to levitate off the bed. In a barely discernible voice, he said, "Man, it feels like I have a million razor blades in my throat."

"How's our patient today?" said Dr. Biggs as he walked into the room.

Trying to recover from the levitation experience, Joey shook his head no.

"He still seems to be in quite a bit of pain," Lynn said.

"We anticipated that he would be and had him heavily sedated until this morning. The pain should ease in a few days. However, if you feel you need something, I've left instructions at the nurses' station for administering pain medication." Checking the tubes protruding from Joey's neck, Biggs continued, "You're a very fortunate young man. Five of the eight tumors were malignant."

Whispering, Joey asked, "I had eight tumors?"

"Yes, and interestingly, the lump that you saw was benign. Had we not operated, the five malignant tumors would have spread into your lung cavity and would probably have been fatal."

"Wow."

Tears streaming down her face, Lynn looked at Joey and said, "Thank God that first lump showed up."

Nodding his head in agreement, Dr. Biggs said, "This particular cancer is much more aggressive than the type you had before. We'll need to put you on a monthly checkup cycle."

First to recover from this shocking statement, Aunt Helen asked, "Are you sure you got all of the cancer?"

"Yes, we're quite certain. However, the possibilities of recurrence are very real."

"What will all of this mean?" asked Lynn.

"It could mean additional surgeries or radiation treatments, or both."

Dr. Biggs' diagnosis was correct. For the next five-years, Joey went through a living hell with recurrent cancer. Because of the frequency of recurrence, Joey was referred to the oncology department of the University Hospital. He would strive to get back into shape, get focused on his family and work, and then the monster would rear its ugly head again and knock him flat on his back. Each time he got knocked down, it was harder to get back up. During these trying times, Lynn remained at his side. Her love, understanding, and support provided the foundation that Joey needed to pick himself up and start over again. Another factor also contributed to his recoveries. When Joey hit rock-bottom and self-pity plagued him, someone would always come along and administer the proverbial kick in the pants.

A surgical procedure left Joey without a voice for ten months. The doctors weren't sure if the vagus nerve leading to the vocal cords was severed or damaged. Going into the fifth month of barely being able to whisper, Joey was appointed as the principal investigator of a catastrophic development uranium enrichment machine failure. Performing the failure analysis, Joey presented the findings to a group of fifty engineers and scientists. Many controversial issues were raised, and audience discussion ensued. Because he could not project his voice, it was difficult for Joey to maintain the order and schedule of the meeting. Thoroughly frustrated with the meeting, Joey and his new manager, Ted, were driving back to Joey's lab. During the ten-minute drive, Joey kept mumbling, "Damn, why don't I have a voice? That meeting lasted twice as long as it should've."

Temporarily taking his eyes off the road, Ted said, "Actually I thought the meeting went well."

Almost hyperventilating to project the sound of his whisper, Joey asked, "What do you mean? It went terrible. I couldn't control it. Damn, why do I have to be like this?"

Pulling the car off the road and stopping on the berm, Ted slammed the car into park. He glared at Joey and said, "Look, the only person that is bothered by you not having a voice is you. Get over it!"

Surprised at Ted's outburst, Joey didn't say anything.

His voice softening, Ted continued, "Your presentation went better than you thought it did. It was based on solid technical findings and facts. If you noticed, the people starting the chatter were from the machine manufacturer's company. The majority agreed with you, and there was an understanding and acceptance by everyone that your report would be issued as you presented it. Or didn't you hear that? You are so hung up about the fact that you can't talk, you're missing the obvious things. You are an incredibly talented engineer and scientist. Don't let not having a voice screw that up. You still have your mind." ✦

Chapter 38

It's your decision.

Lynn's support and Ted's attitude adjustment got Joey back on track. After ten months, Joey's voice hadn't returned. Although friends and relatives prayed his voice would return, Joey was ready to accept the fact that he wouldn't have a normal voice for the rest of his life. By praying to God, reading positive-thinking books, and improving his focus and attitude, Joey was able to excel at work, and his responsibilities began to expand. He was asked to chair a materials development program for the Army and was scheduled to attend a meeting at the Pentagon. Checking in the hotel the night before the meeting, Joey was in for the surprise of his life.

Seeing him walk to the registration desk, the clerk smiled at Joey. "Good evening, sir. How may I help you?"

Returning the smile, Joey said, "Yes, you should have a …" Joey's smile became a huge grin. "My voice! My voice is back!"

Startled by the wide-eyed look on Joey's face, the desk clerk stepped back from the desk. "Sir, are you all right?"

Joey's words seemed to run together. "You don't understand. For over ten months, I haven't had a voice, and now I do! Oh my God, this is incredible!"

Getting the key from the young woman, Joey rushed to his room. Throwing his luggage on the bed, he reached for the phone to call Lynn. Suddenly, Joey stopped and slowly placed the phone back on its receiver. His heavy breathing broke the silence in the room. Tilting his head back until he looked up at the ceiling, Joey fell to his knees with tears streaming down his face and said, "Thank you, God!"

Sitting at the kitchen table, Joey watched Annette Marie cut her chicken into perfect squares. When she was almost finished, he said to Lynn, "Ya know, I'm really enjoying my work, but I feel like something is missing."

"What do you mean?"

"I don't know. I can't put my finger on it, but I feel like I could be doing more than what I'm doing."

Handing Joey a bowl of mashed potatoes, Lynn said, "I think your request has been answered."

"What do you mean?"

"Kim Davis from the Knoxville Cancer Center called this afternoon and asked if you would consider talking with their patients."

"Me, talking with their patients?"

"Yes, she said it was a support group or something like that. I told her you would call her tomorrow."

The next morning, Joey called Kim from his office. "Hello, Kim. This is Joey Slunisky returning your call."

"Joey! Thank you for calling me back! I would like to schedule a time to meet with you to talk about a program we're starting."

"What's the program about?"

STEVEN J. DEKANICH

"Our mission is to provide education and support to cancer patients and their families to help them cope and live with a diagnosis of cancer. We thought a person like you would be ideal to be a speaker and facilitator at our meetings. Would you be willing to help us?"

"Kim, I would be honored to help out."

The meeting room was packed to above capacity. Swallowing hard, Joey said, "Ya know, Kim, I've talked to larger crowds than this about technical issues and never got nervous … but right now, if I could leave, I think I would."

Smiling, Kim said, "It is a much larger crowd than we expected for a first meeting, but don't worry about it. Just be yourself and tell your story. Afterward, we'll have a question-and-answer session."

Taking a deep breath and slowly exhaling from his mouth, Joey said, "Okay. Let's do it."

Kim gave Joey a brief introduction and turned the podium over to him. "Thank you so much for coming here today," he said. "Before we get started, I'd like you to introduce yourself to the person next to you and give him or her a hug."

Waiting for the buzz to subside, Joey continued, "A common cause has brought us together. Although we're not blood relatives, we're family. Each of you has a story to tell, and many in this gathering have gone through a living hell. I urge all of you to reach out to other cancer victims and give them hope. I've found on my worst days, if I did something for someone else, it made me feel better.

For me, cancer first struck in 1969. Since then I've had eighteen recurrences of throat, thyroid, and parathyroid cancer. Radical neck and shoulder surgery left me with half a neck and only a small portion of my left shoulder muscles. The darkest moment of my life was looking into a mirror and seeing that a once vibrant teenager had been transformed into a ghoulish figure whose head flopped uselessly over his shoulders while his left arm hung lifelessly at his side. Over the years, the recurrences resulted in eighteen surgeries and five high-intensity radiation treatments. After the last operation, I lost my voice for ten months."

"How did you cope?" asked a pale young lady with a bandana on her head.

"Support and prayers from relatives, friends, and a great doctor helped me through the dark times and provided me the courage to keep from giving up."

"Did you ever want to give up?

"Oh, yes. More times than you can imagine, especially in the later years. But God blessed me with an earth angel. And that's the woman sitting right over there."

Lynn nervously smiled.

His eyes tearing up, Joey said, "When I first started dating Lynn, my physical deformities were very evident, but I was never uncomfortable around her because she saw me as I could be and not as I was. Through the years, with every recurrence, she has been by my side. Believe me, many times, I was not a pleasant person to be around.... I gave her many reasons to leave, but she didn't. Her love and support are my foundation, and anything I am, I owe to her. I pray that each of you has someone special come into your life.... I've probably rambled on for too long. Does anyone have a question?"

The young lady with the bandana raised her hand. "Since I've been going through chemotherapy, it seems like most of my friends and relatives have disappeared. It makes me feel so alone."

"What's your name?"

"Brenda."

"Brenda, when something tragic happens, a lot of people don't know what to say or do. Although they want to, the majority won't do anything. The longer they don't do anything, the worse they feel and become more withdrawn. Who is the closest friend you have that you haven't seen since you came down with cancer?"

"Allison."

"You may have to reach out to Allison to let her know that you still consider her a friend and would like to talk with her. Now, if Allison is not ready for that, you have a lot of friends in this room who you can turn to, including me."

A solemn-faced elderly woman put up her hand "My name is Mary.... I can't help but think that I got cancer because of something that I did."

"Mary, cancer is no respecter of persons. It strikes young and old and good and bad. I believe our God is a kind and loving God and doesn't use cancer as a way of punishing us. You are not responsible for your disease. But you're responsible for doing what it takes to get better. Mary, we can't control the things that happen to us, but we can control how we respond. That response, whether it's positive or negative, will determine if we experience a heaven or hell here on earth."

Suddenly an angry young man pushed himself out of his chair and knocked the chair to the floor. "What about me?"

"What about you?"

The young man slammed his fist into the table. "I was going to be the starting quarterback this fall, and now look at my neck!"

The left side of the young man's neck protruded over his shoulder. Joey's eyes widened as he saw himself in this young man. "What did the doctors say?"

His nostrils flaring, he answered, "They say I'll never be able to play football. Hell, they don't even know if I will be able to move my arm."

Keeping his eyes locked with the young man's, Joey walked around the table and walked up to him. Extending his hand, Joey asked, "What's your name?"

"Steve."

Joey shook his hand. "Steve, it's a pleasure to meet you. Let me ask you something. Do you believe you can overcome this?"

"I don't know, and I don't know if I even want to try."

"Why would you say something like that?"

"Cancer runs in my family, and every person who got it died."

"I see. So you automatically assume because you have cancer, you have to write your own death sentence."

"Look, man, you ain't God, and you don't know how long I'm going to live."

Joey leaned back against the table and folded his arms. "A long time ago, a very wise doctor told me these words that I'm about to share with you. These words made me see things from a different frame of mind and helped me get better. Hopefully they'll do the same for you. You're right. I'm not God, and I don't know how long you're going to live. But I do know this. If you survive and are destined to live a long life, your quality of life will be determined by what you do from this point on. It's your decision." ✦

STEVEN J. DEKANICH

The End

About the Author

Steve Dekanich is a writer, metallurgical and nuclear engineer, husband, father and grandpapa. Steve's writings span numerous areas from technical writings and international awards in the fields of metallurgical and nuclear engineering to being awarded *First Place in the Nation for Communications* by the U.S. Savings Bonds Division of the U.S. Government. Steve wrote a special poem that was used as a Hospitality House team theme for an American Cancer Society *Light the Night Walk*. A Dove Award winning artist made the poem into a ballad.

From an early age, Steve's life was wrought with illness and challenges ranging from scarlet fever, 19 recurrences of cancer, losing his first wife to cancer, open-heart surgery, the list goes on and on. Steve's faith in God and the intervention of several *Earth Angels* helped him to overcome the trials and move on with his life. He has been able to share his experiences with other people going through similar challenges and helped them through their ordeals.

Steve currently resides in Louisville, Tennessee with his wife Aloysia (Ali). ✦

STEVEN J. DEKANICH

Bibliography

Dekanich, Steve. "Ten Little Fingers & Ten Little Toes" and "One Spirit Is You, the Other Is Me." In *Coming Together*. Chapel Hill, NC: Professional Press, 1995.

Frankl, Viktor E. *Man's Search for Meaning*. Boston, MA: Beacon Press, 2006. Print.

Mandino, Og. The God Memorandum. In *The Greatest Miracle in the World*. New York, NY: Bantam. 1977.

Peale, Norman V. *The Power of Positive Thinking*. Englewood Cliffs, N.J: Prentice-Hall, 1956. Print.

Schwartz, David. *The Magic of Thinking Big*. New York, NY: Simon & Schuster Inc. 1987. Paperback.

Notes

STEVEN J. DEKANICH